MAPPING MURDER

Walking in Killers' Footsteps

Other books by David Canter

Psychology for Architects
The Psychology of Place
Environmental Interaction
Football in Its Place
Psychology in Action
Criminal Shadows

MAPPING MURDER
Walking in Killers' Footsteps

David Canter

For: Lily, Daniel, Hana (and Rosie)

This edition first published in Great Britain in 2005 by
Virgin Books
Thames Wharf Studios
Rainville Road
London W6 9HA

First published in hardback in 2003 by Virgin Books
First published in paperback in 2004 by Virgin Books

ISBN 0 7535 1096 0

Typeset by TW Typesetting, Plymouth, Devon

Printed and bound in Great Britain by
Mackays of Chatham PLC

CONTENTS

LIST OF MAPS   vii

 1. HUNTING KILLERS   1

CRIMINAL FOCUS
 2. THE DISTRACTIONS OF CELEBRITY   20
 3. THE SIGNIFICANCE OF PLACE   34
 4. CRIME IN ITS PLACE   45
 5. MEMOIR OF A KILLER   55
 6. THE SUSTAINING WEB   70
 7. DARKNESS VISIBLE   82

THE CIRCLE OF CRIME
 8. A FRAUGHT INVESTIGATION   96
 9. PROFILING THE DIARIST   109
10. MAPPING THE MURDERS   122
11. LAS VEGAS SURVIVORS   140

MARAUDING CRIMINALS
12. CRIMINAL GRAVITY   158
13. MENTAL MAPS OF CRIME   174
14. STEALING SEX   187
15. 'I'VE BEEN WAITING FOR YOU GUYS'   199
16. A PATH OF VIOLENCE AND TERROR   217
17. TRAVELLING OFFENDER   228

MOVING TARGETS
18. *VICTIMES DE PEDOPHILIE*   244
19. A DESTRUCTIVE GEOGRAPHY   255
20. FINDING A TRAVELLING KILLER   265
21. BODILY VIOLATIONS   282
22. INVISIBLE CRIMINALS   300

POSTSCRIPT 316
NOTES 322
SELECTED BIBLIOGRAPHY 331
ACKNOWLEDGEMENTS 335
INDEX 337

LIST OF MAPS

1. WASHINGTON SNIPERS' SHOOTINGS 4
2. BARRY GEORGE'S AREA OF ACTIVITY 44
3. WHERE FRED WEST'S VICTIMS DISAPPEARED 90
4. THE WHITECHAPEL MURDERS AND MIDDLESEX STREET 126
5. LAS VEGAS CRIMES WITH DRAGNET ANALYSIS 151
6. THE YORKSHIRE RIPPER'S CRIMES 166
7. CHOLERA IN SOHO, 1853 170
8. DUFFY AND MULCAHY'S RAPE LOCATIONS 177
9. THE MALAGA RAPIST'S SKETCH MAP 184
10. THE SOUTH AUCKLAND RAPES 200
11. MARC DUTROUX'S ABDUCTIONS AND ATTEMPTED
    ABDUCTIONS 258
12. ABDUCTIONS AND MURDER SITES OF ROBERT BLACK 274
13. SIMON WADLAND'S TELEPHONE CALLS WITH
    DRAGNET ANALYSIS 304
14. MARDI GRA BOMB LOCATIONS WITH DRAGNET
    ANALYSIS 307

then begins a journey in my head

Shakespeare *Sonnet 27*

A Note on Gender

Throughout the book offenders are assumed to be male and the victims are usually assumed to be women. This is because all the offenders I have considered here have been men and the great majority of their victims have been women. As I discussed in *Criminal Shadows* ten years ago – and has almost certainly been true since Cain and Abel – men commit the vast majority of violent offences. Men, of course, are also the victims of sexual assaults, and statistics show that young men, especially, are more likely to be the victims of violent crime than women. It is also the case that there are an increasing number of violent female offenders. However, the important matters raised by the existence of male victims of violence, and by female murderers and sexual abusers, are not dealt with in the present volume.

1. HUNTING KILLERS

Travelling in from Kentucky, Ronald Lantz pulled his truck into the McDonald's car park at the I-70 services, just north of Washington DC. It was a little after midnight so he was listening to his favourite radio show, 'The Truckin' Bozo'. Unexpectedly there was a newsflash. The police were urgently looking for a blue Chevrolet Caprice, licence plate NDA 21Z. Glancing out of his truck window, to his surprise he saw the car parked a few yards away.

Ron was looking at the source of the most terrifying series of shootings that America has seen in recent times. For 21 days, people in the states around Washington DC, and in the capital itself, had been avoiding leaving their homes. They had rushed from building to building, petrified at the possibility that they might be the next unlucky person to pass unwittingly into the snipers' line of fire. Ten had already been killed, and a further three seriously wounded, each with a single shot. The frighteningly accurate snipers had paralysed the heart of the nation, holding the world's media in thrall. Now Ron was sitting there, fully aware that he was just yards from the vehicle the police had at last traced as the one owned by the deadly killers. But the police had no idea they were looking for two killers: the Washington Sniper killings, as they were dubbed by the press,[1] were assumed to be the work of one man.

Ron did not get the hell out, as many of us might. He called 911 and followed the instructions he was given. He moved his lorry to block the exit, then sat tight and waited for the police to arrive. Joined by the service area patrolman, Larry Blank, who was trying to find out what all the fuss was on his police scanner, the two men sat there for more than two hours, with mobiles as life-lines, blocking the escape route as police silently moved their troops into place. Finally, at 3 a.m., with choppers overhead and searchlights blazing, the SWAT team moved in, smashing the car windows and screaming instructions at the car's occupants to surrender.

Woken from their sleep, bleary-eyed and bewildered, John Muhammad and John Lee Malvo offered no resistance. As one officer reported, 'They practically slept through the take-down.'

Although Chief Moose, the man leading the hunt, had known which car he was looking for a couple of days earlier, he was forced into calling a midnight press conference when the information leaked out. Less than an hour afterwards Ron had told him where the car was. The Washington Snipers, pursued for weeks by a military-style campaign, with road-blocks closing main routes and teams of surveillance helicopters searching from the air, were caught by the simple expedient of using the eyes of the public.

Turning to the public was close to being a last resort, and even the potential value of that had been hotly debated amongst the many investigating teams. Every conceivable possibility had been considered for finding who was responsible for the apparently random killings.

THE MAP OF MURDER

The two men woken in their blue Chevrolet were John Muhammad, a 41-year-old Gulf War veteran and winner of marksmanship awards, and 17-year-old John Lee Malvo, an illegal immigrant from Jamaica, whom Muhammad habitually introduced as his step-son. They had terrorised a 100-mile area in Maryland and Virginia, around Washington DC, shooting whoever came into their sights. They had begun by killing seven people in Montgomery County, before roaming along Interstates 50 and 95, wounding three and killing another three along the way.

The victims had all been killed from a distance, with a single rifle shot, the killers disappearing without a trace in the ensuing confusion. The unpredictability and apparent sense-lessness of the shootings caused immense fear and chaos. Parks were empty. Schools operated under 'code blue', which bans any outdoor activity. There was traffic gridlock.

It was the lack of any obvious rationale to the crimes, mixed with the deadly rifle accuracy and the size of the killing area around the American capital, that caused such conster-nation and media interest. At its height 1,400 journalists were living in tents outside the investigation headquarters at Rockville police station in Maryland, producing saturation television coverage. Some 24-hour cable channels had record viewing figures for the year.

To call these shootings serial killings was to put them, curiously, in the same category as those of the killers who prey on vulnerable underdogs, seeking out victims in the twilight zones of cities. Their victims usually have something in common, even if only their availability and weakness. The public panic and media fascination with the sniper was driven by the feeling that the shootings might be arbitrary. It quickly became clear that the victims shared nothing. They were not all immigrant men, as had been the case in Stockholm in 1992, when ten people were picked off with a laser-sighted rifle in a racist shooting spree. Those victims around Washington came from a wide mix of ethnic backgrounds. There were men and women amongst the dead, as there were young and old, school children and adults. Neither was there a clearly focused target, as there had been in the dreadful school shooting in Columbine in 1999, or the murder of 21 people by a security guard in a San Ysidro McDonald's in 1984. Those victims had been unfortunate in being in a place that had a special significance for the spree killers. But the place for the Washington Snipers was the whole area circumscribed by the Interstates and beltway around Washington.

The killings spread out from Silver Spring, close to the heart of the capital, all the way to Ashland, just north of Richmond, Virginia. This map of the dead and wounded cries out for interpretation. It is trying to tell us the personal narrative of the killers. Does it reveal a deadly vendetta against some abstract institution, as some insisted? Or is it a reflection of a sadistic urge to kill and kill again? Was it perhaps more of a deadly adventure acted out for excitement? Or could it have been a form of suicide, murdering others as a step towards their own tragic deaths?

The map of these killings, like the maps of any other violent crimes, captures a journey in space and time. Not just travels to find victims, but an inner journey the offender is taking: learning what excites him, the roles he can play, how to go beyond the limits. The personal voyage is both a creation for

1. WASHINGTON SNIPERS' SHOOTINGS

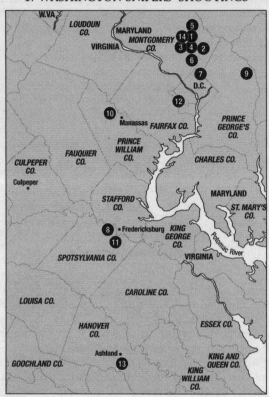

1. 2 October 2002. No injuries
   Windows shot out of Michael's Craft Store, Georgia Avenue, Aspen Hill

2. 2 October 2002. Murder
   James D. Martin, Shoppers Food Warehouse car park, Wheaton,
   Silver Spring

3. 3 October 2002. Murder
   James 'Sonny' Buchanan, Rockville Pike, Rockville, Maryland

4. 3 October. Murder
   Prem Kumar Walekar, Mobil petrol station, Aspen Hill Road, Maryland

5. 3 October. Murder
   Sarah Ramos, outside a post office, Rossmoor Boulevard, Silver Spring

6. 3 October. Murder
   Lori Ann Lewis-Rivera, Shell petrol station, Knowles Road, Kensington

7. 3 October. Murder
   Pascal Charlot, corner of Georgia Avenue and Kalmia Road, Washington DC

8. 4 October 2002. Wounding
   Unnamed woman in car park of shopping mall, Spotsylvania County

9. 7 October 2002. Wounding
   A thirteen-year-old schoolboy at Benjamin Tasker Middle School, Prince George County, Maryland

10. 9 October 2002. Murder
    Dean Harold Meyers at Sunoco petrol station, Sudley Road, Prince William County

11. 11 October 2002. Murder
    Kenneth Bridges at Exxon petrol station, Route 1 and Market Street, Spotsylvania County

12. 14 October 2002. Murder
    Linda Franklin, outside a store at Seven Corners Shopping Center, Fall's Church, Fairfax County, Virginia

13. 19 October 2002. Wounding
    Unnamed man at the Ponderosa Steakhouse, England Street, Ashland, Virginia

14. 22 October 2002. Murder
    Conrad Johnson, Grand Pre Road in Aspen Hill, Montgomery County, Maryland

---

the murderer and a journey of self-discovery. The map hints at the travels across this private landscape, if only we can fathom how to unravel those hints.

THE EXPERTS MOVE IN

We live in a world where 'expertise' is the substitute for considered discussion. When faced with a difficult problem, such as what the Washington Sniper killings were all about, content producers for newspapers, radio and television fill the vacuum in understanding by quoting anyone who claims some special expertise. There is the belief, held fondly by the public at large, although I suspect not by journalists –

who are filling column inches and broadcast time to tight deadlines – that anyone who claims special expertise has some profound basis for their opinion – one that is not available to the public at large. Yet as Marymount University's Professor of Forensic Psychology, Mary Lindahl, said with some ferocity after the glut of 'expert' opinions offered during the search for the Washington Sniper, 'The public could profile as well as the experts on TV . . . most were wrong.' Indeed some have suggested that the attempts to stop the tragic and unnecessary deaths of so many people around Washington may have been weakened by the outpourings of 'experts' of every ilk.

The range of opinions offered was staggering. Some thought it was the work of Al Qaeda operatives. Others considered it a homage to the 'Son of Sam' murders, to mark their 25-year anniversary. An even more exotic suggestion was that it was a re-enactment of a storyline in the television programme *Homicide*. Computer nerds, addicted to shoot-'em-up video games, were also blamed. And, inevitably, the Devil got in on the act. 'This has something to do with a satanic ritual,' said 'holistic adviser', Zorel. 'If you look at the map and connect the dots, it looks like a cross upside down, but people aren't realising it, not even the police.'

Beyond these vacuous speculations were those that came from people who claim to make a profession of giving advice to the police – that curious group of specialists who are graced with the label of 'profiler'. They agreed with unusual unanimity that the sniper was white, although the reason for this assertion was far from clear. 'When you break down the demographics of the Washington region, there is a statistical probability that the sniper is a white man,' Gregg McCrary, a retired FBI profiler, told the *Washington Post*. Was McCrary therefore saying that the sniper was a typical Washington resident? Brian Levin, Director of California State University's Center for the Study of Hate and Extremism, revealed something of his own prejudices when he said, 'It's a kind of a wallpaper white male, a disenfranchised, disrespected man who's getting back at society.' Chris Whitcomb, a former FBI agent, backed up his misguided speculation by claiming a numerical basis for his opinion when he informed NBC that, 'Statistically, it's going to be a white male.' But which sample or study Whitcomb was drawing on was never indicated. Even a casual search of the internet shows that black serial killers are not unusual. And who is to say that a sniper roaming the Interstates has to have similarities to the serial killers on the FBI casebooks?

One sniper came from Alabama, the other from Jamaica. Neither would pass for white under any lighting conditions. Other predictions were no more accurate. Dr Michael Welner from New York University declared the sniper to be 'single, 20s–30s'. This presumably drew on the typical characteristics of most murderers who attack strangers. Should this have been the reference group for such an unparalleled campaign? Muhammad was in his forties and had been twice married. Malvo was a teenager.

One person who is apparently always ready to offer up detailed 'profiles' of cases, Brent Turvey, told the *Washington Times* that the killer was so exact in the attacks that he was unlikely to contact police or give away any evidence that would help the investigation. But in the end, the snipers were located because they could not resist bragging about their involvement in an earlier Alabama robbery/shooting, providing the clues that eventually led to their arrest. So it was a good job the police ignored Turvey's confident advice.

Unfortunately many people mistakenly believed these various opinions to be derived from the detailed analysis of hundreds, if not thousands, of cases, building up common trends in true scientific fashion. It was therefore wrongly assumed that their obvious inaccuracy was a failure of science and of the statistics on which many scientific conclusions are based. 'Criminal profilers may be the logical outgrowths of a society that believes all of human reality can be quantified . . . a touching faith in the truth revealing ability of statistical analysis,' wrote the *Washington Post* dismissively.

These various 'profiles' are problematic not because of the weaknesses of science, but because of their own scientific weakness. Some claimed the suggestions had been based on statistics. But how could there be general trends, or statistics, for a set of killings so unusual? And even if there had been, statistics do not make science. Knowing how many women have thought about killing their partners, or how many men have been unfaithful – frequencies, percentages, statistics – may be a small step towards a scientific understanding of jealousy, but it is a very small step indeed. It does not explain how cheating husbands emerge, and nor does it predict which wives will follow through on their musings and kill.

THE SECRET OF GEOGRAPHICAL PROFILING

Science always has two components: explanation and prediction. Explanation alone drifts into arid philosophising. Prediction without understanding can be useful, but soon becomes mechanical and barren. Most of what we think of as the progress of technology, the development of civilisation, has come from the interplay between explanation and prediction. For profiling to become a science we need to expand our understanding of criminals and to test that against calculations of what they will do.

Understanding is not full-born in a mature state. It starts with speculation, often derived from observations. Many of the suggestions about the sniper are best considered as pre-scientific, rather than unscientific: they are early attempts with little information to sketch out basic theories. Unfortunately the media want hard and fast findings, and many people are prepared to present their conjectures as just that.

For guesses to develop into theories they need clear contact with some form of fact. These facts are derived from the rigorous observation at the heart of science. The more such observation leads us to objective facts, the more fertile will be the ground in which theories will develop into explanations.

In 1985 I was called on to help the police locate a serial killer and rapist.[2] I had to speculate in the absence of any accumulation of systematic knowledge about or understanding of such criminals; I had to do the best I could with the information and theories available. I found that the unexpected success of my contribution relied heavily on my study of where the crimes had occurred. The use of crime locations to understand the offender and propose where he might be living is today known as Geographical Profiling. Since that time I have followed up those initial, effective conjectures with many studies.[3] These studies have shown not only that my early ideas were reasonably sound but, even more importantly, that other scientists were productively following similar tracks. I put the reason for this success, at least in part, down to the fact that the most objective and observable aspect of any crime is *where* it happens.

One of the most interesting suggestions about the sniper offered by experts, therefore, was that he was living in Montgomery County. A 'red zone' area in the county was identified by 'profilers' as probably containing the sniper's home, and this was used by the investigation task force. This proposal was based on the map that pinpointed the locations of the shootings but, as it turned out, this suggestion was wrong as well. The snipers had been living for weeks in the car in which they were caught. At one point they had even been moved on by police, who thought they were just vagrants, when one of them was found sleeping in their car. But, as we shall see, the reason it was wrong was not a failure of statistics or mathematics. It was a failure to understand and explain the geographical distribution of the offences and to fathom the personal narrative they tell of the killer.

The secret of geographical profiling is to go beyond the dots on the map to understand the significance of the places the offender is choosing, and the meaning to him of the journey he is making. There is always a choice available to any offender of where to offend. That choice comes from within his criminal being, and understanding how that choice is made opens doors into the criminal's mind. Zorel may not have been right to see a satanic influence in the shape of the sniper's dots on the map, but she was pointing in the right direction when she proposed looking at what the pattern of locations meant.

The people shot dead around Washington by the snipers had nothing in common with each other. They were not being selected because of their particular characteristics. As with so many of the victims we shall be considering, we have to ask, 'Why are they falling prey?' The answer has to be not who they are, but where they are. Criminals always have some choice in where they commit their crimes. Many different processes will influence the decision they make about their crime location, but these processes all come together in the place where the crime occurs.

Places are never without significance. Our lives are scratched into the surface of the Earth's crust, scratches that tell our personal history as much as our social history. Sometimes the marks are left by human actions such as murders or other violent crimes. The marks left by these killers need to be interpreted; we need to look not just at what they are but why they are in that particular location. The locations themselves are part of the journeys the criminals are making. It is these journeys and the places that define them that we shall be exploring.

CRIMINAL JOURNEYS

The journey of the Washington snipers spread out over a wide swathe, touching three states. It started in an almost casual way on 2 October 2002. The first shots were fired at the window of a craft store in Aspen Hill; no one was hurt. But later the same day, a few miles away in Silver Spring, a man was shot dead in a car park. The determination behind the attacks became clear the next day. In a series of incidents distributed around Montgomery County, five people were each killed with a single shot when they were going about their daily activities: outside a post office, at a petrol station or in other public places. None of the shootings were more than five miles apart, except for the last that day, as the killers moved south to the edge of the District of Columbia on the very doorstep of Washington itself. From there the shootings spread ever further afield along the Interstate highways, with the furthest over 100 miles away in Virginia.

These men were not picking off victims days or weeks apart in the pattern typical of many serial killers. They had not lured people into their car to rape and kill then dispose of the bodies along their journey. Although a rifle was their chosen weapon their actions were very different from those of Charles Whitman, who took a 12-gauge shotgun up the 307-foot-high clock tower at the University of Texas in 1966, shooting at anyone who came into his sights, and killing sixteen people. Muhammad and Malvo's spree of killing involved careful, fatal precision, using the cover provided by the tree-lined suburbs of Washington.

We all have a particular style of dealing with the world, and serial criminals are no different. Their distinct characters are embedded in how, where and when they commit their crimes; but most particularly where. It is these consistencies of place that start us on our journey to understand and predict criminals' violent actions. Criminal journeys are more than just movements through time and space. Each step that makes up the overall picture betrays some intention: from the purposeful exploration of the opportunity to offend, taking some account of the risks involved (although this is often a remarkably limited assessment), to the actual task of committing the crime.

Offenders' journeys have two surprising features – pointers to their criminal nature – that have been found over and over again in studies of serial offenders. One is the way in which the home, or at least where criminals are based, acts as a focus for their actions. The other is the geographical scale over which they operate.[4]

The base of a criminal is usually his home but, as we shall see, this can take various forms, and may be the home in which he grew up rather than the house in which he is currently living. It acts as an anchor for his floating world, allowing him to sally out and return with confidence. It can become a haven or even a den into which he brings his victims. In some cases it is a moving location, even a vehicle, such as that used by Muhammad and Malvo.

The base, and the role it plays in the life of the criminal, helps shape the scale of his activities, from those who are very local – seeking opportunities for crime within walking distance of where they live – through those who travel much further afield, ten or twenty miles, and on into a third group for whom travelling is the essence of their criminal style and who may cover hundreds of miles.

When it is considered that criminals can, in a simple sense, choose anywhere to offend, it is remarkable that so many studies[5] that have sought to classify serial killers and rapists have found that the main differences between them are reflected in the size of the geographical range over which they operate. It is noteworthy, as we shall see, that the serial killer Fred West did not pick up any one of his victims more than a few miles from his base in Gloucester. Perhaps the most notorious serial killer of all time, Jack the Ripper, is known as the Whitechapel murderer because of the very limited area, a few minutes' walk in any direction, that contains the sites where he found and despatched his victims. By contrast, Marc Dutroux is characterised by having abducted young girls from the four corners of Belgium. John Duffy, known as the Railway Rapist and murderer, who brought me into this dark world of violence,[6] had a more subtle but no less distinct geographical pattern spreading out from the Kilburn area of North London; he eventually killed at the points of a triangle, each thirty miles away.

It is these maps of murder that are the most distinct footprints of these criminals. Just as the literal shoe print can tell us something about the height and build of the person who left it and, with a bit of extrapolation from shoe type, may hint at the lifestyle of the wearer, the metaphorical footprint on a map that captures the criminal's characteristic spatial pattern of offending reflects rather more of his make-up than is immediately apparent. It shows something of the psychological drama the criminal is living and relates directly to the way he deals with his victims.

This is a fascinating discovery, that serial killers and rapists are not random or arbitrary in their actions. They have a recognisable mode of acting on the world around them, which includes how they find their victims and what they do to them. A form is given to their journeys by this consistency. But what creates such a dependable pattern of activity? In essence it comes from each offender himself.

The opportunities for crime, where there are possible victims or ready access and escape, will of course shape the pattern of offence behaviour. If an offender's predilections are for a particular type of victim then he will be drawn to locations in which those sorts of people are available: examples that are looked at in later chapters include the prostitutes that Sutcliffe killed, the defenceless young women and girls that Thompson sought, and the vulnerable women on the street that became the focus of attention for Garrett Young. The snipers found the wide highways of Maryland and Virginia ideal hunting grounds. Their closeness to the capital gave their actions an added excitement and a media presence that they clearly enjoyed. They did not seek or want any contact with their victims, who were just ciphers, exciting targets to be shot at. The snipers told the police that the shootings were 'about more than violence', but were never able to elaborate on what that extra was. Their contact with the police who were hunting them only added to the adventure that seems to have started, as some thought, as almost a form of recreation.

It is interesting to think of those serial offenders who do not live within the area of their crimes as 'commuters',[7] an analogy with people travelling to work. This does not really do justice to these criminals because they are defined by an absence. It is unsatisfactory as a description because it implies that the offender's home has no relevance to the locations of the murders and rapes. The snipers who came from Alabama were 'commuters' in this limited sense. This suggests that the place where the offence happens is arbitrary and driven entirely by the opportunities of which the criminal is aware. But what we need to take on board is that some criminals choose to travel, some extensively, some less widely, and that the range of their journeys typifies them.

JOURNEYS AS STORIES

All stories are journeys. All journeys are stories. For John Muhammad and John Lee Malvo, setting out to kill as many people as they could, the narrative of their destructive adventure is etched on the freeways into and out of Washington where they lived out their roles as mindless murderers.

As we shall see in Chapter 5, the fiction Fred West invented was of a happy family life, in which he could ensnare young women and drag them down into the terrible recesses of his psyche. The journey he concocted had a narrative movement from the freedom of the streets into the confined abusive cell of his suicidal despair. The journeys of the murderers and rapists we are considering, as with any other journey, are also enactments of roles the travellers assign to themselves.

In Chapter 16 the open wilderness of Newfoundland is revealed as crucial in understanding how Garrett Young played out his violent life story, casting himself as the man who used women. The dirt tracks and deserted quays became a weapon in his campaign of vicious assault and rape.

We shall also see in Chapter 11 that behind the bright lights of Las Vegas Justin Porter's dense pattern of murder, rape and robbery tells a different story: a deadly adventure spiralling out of control.

The maps of these murderers and rapists tell us about the criminal journeys they took from the control and safety of their homes to the opportunities they found on the streets around where they lived and beyond, opportunities to indulge their depraved thrill of abducting, attacking and in some cases killing. They reveal their exploitation of the freedoms of the modern city to live out a vicious role in the malicious drama they build for themselves.

INNER NARRATIVES

The shadows cast on a map by the locations of a series of crimes can be interpreted to reveal the inner narrative structuring the offender's life. This unfolding personal story is especially relevant because the violence we are considering is not the sudden impulsive outburst of a pub brawl that spills over into murder, in which a slight movement one way or the other could have reversed the roles of victim and killer. Nor is it the manipulative actions of a man against a partner where an emotional explosion becomes a severe beating. The sexual assaults that draw our attention in the following pages are not those that emerge from relationships in which the man pushes far beyond acceptable bounds to rape because he thinks he can get away with this crime. That said, in the examples that follow, there are rather more parallels than many appreciate to the crime that is called, with a chilling irony, 'date rape'.

The murders and rapes that fill this book are premeditated. Often they are planned over a long period of time and usually they become a dominant part of the thoughts and actions of the violent men who commit them. Frequently the series of crimes they commit runs over many years. These actions are not some aberrant, impulsive reaction to a particular frustration or fear. They are what typify the men whose lives they shape. The unfolding patterns of their crimes, perhaps more than for the actions of most of us, can be seen as dramas. They are unfolding plots driven on by the inner struggles of the offenders.

In crime fiction criminals are usually the antagonists of the piece. They create the conflicts and challenges to be overcome by the hero, who detects the crime and brings the criminal to justice. It seems to me that it is not entirely speculative to recognise that in the inside-out world of vicious men they live their lives as the protagonists of their own dramas, as most of us do. They reach for their desires, however depraved or distorted we may consider them. They have objectives and ambitions that are satisfied or thwarted. The extent to which they are consciously aware of living out a drama will vary with the degree of insight they have into their condition. Many will just feel an imperative to act and a belief that either they will not be caught, or the consequences of being caught can be ignored. Others will have a more articulate idea that they have a right to satisfy their desires, or that their victims even deserve the depredations visited on them. Yet others may even see themselves on a mission that they have a right to pursue.

Almost invariably, the profoundly destructive acts of the men we are examining are embedded in narratives that we might consider banal, even commonplace, if it were not for the devastation they are part of. They involve angry reactions to slights and insults, unrequited lust, small-scale jealousies, or even just a search for excitement. Even though these men are not living out heroic, adventurous lives, they are casting themselves in superhuman roles.

Muhammad and Malvo were on the run from a small-time robbery in Alabama. Muhammad's only success in life had been as a marksman in the army, for which he won awards. Is it too far-fetched to think that he showed off his skills to his young friend and, egged on by how readily he had got away with the first murder, that he wanted the excitement of doing it again and again?

Before the snipers were caught I was invited to speculate about them for a newspaper. I wrote:

> if the police really are trying to establish contact with the
> sniper they have real difficulties. For as skilled as the
> sniper is in shooting, killing and escaping he has a
> serious problem in being able to contact the authorities.
> 'In the past several days you have attempted to

communicate with us . . .' said Mr Moose with no hint of the frustration the huge task force must have in the fact that a man that can send a bullet with such deadly accuracy cannot get an elementary message through with any clarity. [It later emerged that some telephone calls from the snipers were dismissed as hoaxes.] Coming after so many killings the contact with the police appears an after-thought in every sense of the word, following a lack of planning by the killer of where the shootings would take him, and a lack of preparation for how he might get any gain out of it or extricate himself in any way. [The request for money only emerged very late in the shootings.]

This shows confusion in the sniper's thoughts on anything except how to secretly shoot, kill and escape. The difficulties the police are having in communicating with him are part of the sniper's problems in dealing with others out of which his shooting spree has probably evolved.

The stolid figure of police officer Moose offering careful and cautious, often formulaic, statements to the world's media and through them, apparently, to the killer himself, contrasts with the image of the foxily cunning sniper scurrying through the woods, possibly thinking only of where he can find and execute his next victim without getting caught. Can a man (and given how usual it is that such havoc is caused by men, that it is a man is the safest bet in the whole confusing saga) whose actions defy any obvious rationale, really make sense of what Mr Moose is saying to him?

In the past, people who have killed a number of strangers without any obvious political or even obscure ideological basis have typically been very confused about themselves and their emotions. Their frustrations, jealousies or anger have spilled over into an act of violence that has then escalated, as with each successful, unsolved killing they become more practised in finding opportunities for furtive violence, but their emotional turmoil still ebbs and flows beyond their control. They focus on their own stealth and skill to give their emotions meaning, putting faith in their weaponry to let them out of the abyss they are sinking into.

Like all of us in states of heightened emotion, demanding habits that require just enough concentration to get us through provide a temporary release from the emotional pressure that would otherwise rip us apart. Like a businessman who goes jogging to recover from the deal he has just fumbled, so the sniper will find solace from thinking solely about where he will attack next and how he can evade capture. The feelings that drive him on are never absent for very long. Often the murderous sprees in which their killings culminate end in suicide either by their own hand or by the way they allow themselves to become the target for law enforcement. [When a small army was looking for them they were found asleep in a McDonald's car park.]

When they were arrested no reason for the shootings was given, but they spoke with pride about their prowess, telling police how they shot some victims in the head because it was particularly gory. They said, 'A perfect shot was to let you know something. You weren't dealing with a random shooter. We wanted you to know it was us.' They also talked about their military-style preparation before each shooting, survey-ing the location, in contact with each other over two-way radios. They took pride in the chaotic aftermaths, and told police how they would watch the television coverage after-wards, as well as explaining that they deliberately moved between different policing areas to sow confusion. On some occasions they would even go up to police at the scenes and ask what had happened.

Criminals' dramas take many different forms. The forms they take are there to be seen in the maps of their murders if we can learn how to read them.

CRIMINAL FOCUS

Seek for yourself, O man; search for your true self.

Saint Augustine, *The Confessions*

The proposition is therefore that the 'domocentric' locational experiences of lawabiding citizens are a reasonable starting point for building models of criminal movements.

Canter, D. and Larkin, P. (1993) 'The Environmental Range of Serial Rapists', *Journal of Environmental Psychology*, 13, pp. 63–69

. . . the act which sets the tragic process going must be primarily a violation of *moral* law, whether human or divine; in short that Aristotle's hamartia or 'flaw' must have an essential connection with sin or wrongdoing . . . The majority of tragic heroes do possess hybris, a proud, passionate, obsessed or soaring mind which brings about a morally intelligible downfall. Such hybris is the normal precipitating agent of catastrophe . . .

Northrop Frye (1957) *Anatomy of Criticism*, Princeton University Press, p. 210

2. THE DISTRACTIONS OF CELEBRITY

TIME, PERSON, PLACE

At 11.00 a.m. on Monday 26 April 1999 a man walked down a nondescript West London street and followed a woman in through her gate, just a few steps from her door. As she was reaching for her keys, he fired one shot to her head. She died instantly on her doorstep.[1]

Crime is always a coincidence. People and places come together in a dangerous juxtaposition to create the circumstances for the crime. Perhaps more than with any other human interaction, the element of chance is key: a few minutes, or a few yards, one way or the other, and the crime might not have happened. The dot on the map where the crime occurs encapsulates layers of meaning: the explosive mix of a criminal's and a victim's habits.

The significance of the place in which the deed is done is especially important for murder. Many implications follow from elemental aspects of the crime location.[2] Was it indoors or outdoors, a place easily open to the public or private and normally secure? What is the typical pattern of activities, throughout the day and week and year, associated with that location? Most important of all, what meanings did the place hold for the various people who made use of it? As we shall see, all these aspects of place held clues to the identity of the murderer in this case, but the distractions of celebrity masked their significance for a considerable length of time.

Such shootings are virtually unknown in London, unless they are part of criminal gangland 'executions'. No woman had been killed in the UK in that way ever before as far as anyone could establish. What made the murder even more unusual was the victim – and her celebrity was to distort the investigation in many different ways.

The victim was Jill Dando – an attractive, 37-year-old television presenter, well known and well liked. She presented travel programmes and was the idol of the *Daily Mail*. To complicate matters further, in the course of her work she regularly fronted the television programme *Crimewatch*, which draws on the public fascination with crime to help catch criminals. This led to instant speculation that her killing was orchestrated by the criminal underworld. Furthermore, she had been active in raising funds for Kosovan refugees, leading to suspicions that Serbian terrorists had killed her as a reprisal for the recent bombing of a television centre in Belgrade.

The murder of Jill Dando and the subsequent two-year-long investigation to apprehend her killer teaches us a lot about the problems police face in carrying out such an investigation, even with all the databases and other resources they have available. Despite the very systematic procedure that Senior Investigating Officer (SIO) Hamish Campbell put in place, the lesson from his investigation is that the search for a motive and national and international trawls for possible suspects, the time-honoured keys to police investigations, must now be complemented with colder calculations emerging from the study of criminal psychology.

STRATEGIES FOR DETECTION

Detectives take many different approaches to exploring the maps of murder, as with other crimes. Perhaps the time has come for these differences to be more consciously recognised, so that the most appropriate approach is chosen rather than the one with which any particular SIO is most comfortable. The analogies with other forms of hunter are instructive. Some detectives act as lepidopterists trying to catch and pin down an elusive butterfly, collecting a variety of winged insects so that they can pin them to a board for close examination. In the unsuccessful inquiry into the killing of Rachel Nickell on Wimbledon Common in 1993 over twenty suspects were arrested and closely examined. In other inquiries similarly large numbers of people may be brought in for intensive questioning before they are released without charge.

In other cases the detective operates more like a hunter following a trail across a map, each trace leading him on to the next, until eventually he tracks the criminal to his den. The detection and arrest of Garrett Young that we look at in Chapters 16 and 17 was a successful application of this approach.

Yet other investigations discover that the offender has an affinity to a particular location. Like an angler, the detective baits his line to see if he can draw in the culprit. The Mardi Gra bomber, considered in the final chapter, was caught directly in this way. Cashpoints in a limited area of London were set as traps and closely observed in the hope that he would use one of them. The hooking of the Washington Sniper was a more indirect form of fishing. The snipers popped up to contact the police who then quickly worked out who they were, although this happened against the background of quasi-military manoeuvres to find the killers.

Some investigation teams are gold-diggers, sluicing through mines of information to find the nuggets that will lead them to the culprit. The identification of Joseph Thompson in south Auckland after his years of rape was (as we shall see in Chapter 15) the result of just such an enormous process of filtering out the significant culprit from hundreds of possible suspects.

I would suggest that the most successful detectives are those who adjust their strategy to the style and patterns of movements of their prey. This can range from a broadband sweep to a narrow concentration on the most likely option. At one end of this range many possibilities are actively explored, with police mapping the criminal landscape and circling in. At the other end there is an intense focus on particular lines of inquiry, following a trail like a bloodhound sniffing out revealing scents. Many hunts for criminals move through this range as the search unfolds. The successful ones, though, seem to me to be those that choose a strategy that reflects the criminal's psychological and geographical journey. The success of the detective depends on how well he shapes his mental map and his hunting strategy to match that of his prey, the criminal.

THE INVESTIGATOR'S MENTAL MAP

Every murder investigation is different, but then so is every patient who comes to see a doctor. We do not expect doctors to work from scratch in trying to decide on what to do with a patient, and it might be expected that police officers also work from general principles to the particularities of the case they are studying. Yet there are many pressures on them that lead them to adopt a more ad hoc approach than would be the case with experts in other domains. They have to bury themselves in the details of the particular case. As Hamish Campbell put it, 'There is a need to get in to the detail. It is the factor which frequently undermines a criminal – the minutiae which even they cannot control or account for.' Senior investigating officers also always have one eye on the trial and whether any details they have missed will be used by the defence to undo their case. There is therefore a constant hunt to see where particular details may lead, sometimes at the risk of losing sight of the overall picture.

The search for clues, and routes to the culprit, are built upon their experiences and idiosyncratic mental maps of the sorts of murders that can occur. If you listen carefully to senior investigating officers giving an account of murders they have investigated you will hear that they tackle the investigation by asking, 'What have we got here?' They have a set of templates available to hold up to the murder they are looking at to see which one might fit. These are ideas such as gangland murders, 'domestics', prostitute killings, pub brawls, contract killings, sexual homicides and the like. Drawing on what they have heard about, or other murders they have investigated, they have a set of stereotypes that capture their idea of who, how and what surrounds the death. The strategy that is put in place to solve the murder draws on the recognition by the detective of what sort of murder he is dealing with. If he discovers that the victim was a prostitute this will immediately raise questions about who her clients were and what the possibilities are that one of them was the culprit. If the victim was found with traces of drugs and was known to have been part of a criminal network then culprits will be sought through the criminal underworld.

This 'map' that senior investigating officers have in their heads of the sorts of murders that are possible is what distinguishes them from inexperienced detectives. This, after all, is one important difference between an expert and a novice[3] in any domain. An expert has, at least implicitly, a catalogue of possibilities to draw upon. The novice must take each case as it comes, to work out for each dead body which directions to explore. While there is no guarantee that the experienced police officer really does have a more effective understanding of murder and how it occurs, at least he[4] will have more systematised possibilities to draw upon than a novice usually has.

The mental catalogue or map of possible murders that investigators work from has two crucial components. One is the nature of the victim; the other is the location associated with the killing. Together these two constituents provide a description of the situation that characterises the murder. Each different situation offers its own typical route to the killer. A pub brawl draws attention to the need to locate anyone who may have been in the pub around the times that were relevant. If the death is seen as the product of a domestic dispute then close relatives come into the frame. When detectives cannot determine for themselves the sort of murder they are dealing with, then they reach for the magical potion that gives all fictional thrillers their power – 'motive'.

There are many dangers inherent in harnessing the murder situation, and especially the slippery notion of motive, as a means of leading the way to the culprit. What if the pub brawl were between a husband and wife and as such better regarded as a 'domestic' murder? What if the prostitute found dead on the pavement was killed by a close associate? What if the woman found strangled in her bed was active in the criminal underworld? So police investigators are masters of speculation, constantly debating amongst themselves the possibilities of a murder not being what it first appears.

But although the place where the body was found carries great potential import in understanding the nature of the murder and of the killer, the significance of the location of the death is often only considered tangentially. As we see over and over in this book, it often provides the strongest guide to finding possible suspects. If the body is found in a different location from that in which the murder happened, that opens up other considerations, but these still return to the need to understand the relevance of the place of death. That location will have a meaning for the victim and will play a particular role in the offender's personal geography. It is the fusion of these two into a deadly mixture that creates the murder.

THE DISTRACTIONS OF CELEBRITY

The victim is the starting point for a murder inquiry, but how to follow the lead offered by a knowledge of the victim's identity is more problematic. Detectives become social psychologists, even sociologists, forming views about the personal interactions characteristic of a particular type of victim. How do the victim's lifestyle and patterns of contact with others offer the opportunity for murder? Does that lifestyle make them especially vulnerable or offer particular situations in which a killer might be present?

What detectives are doing here is drawing on their day-to-day understanding of the habits they consider typical of different types of people. They enrich that understanding with the details they uncover about the specific victim, looking for clues in associates and contacts.

Having listened to many police investigators describing the murder investigations they have carried out, I have not often formed the impression that they approach a murder inquiry with a great deal of sophistication about the conditions under which killings take place. With one or two very unusual exceptions, each murder is treated as a new challenge. There is a procedure to go through – securing the scene at which the body was found, obtaining forensic evidence, calling in the forensic scientists, seeking witnesses, making public appeals for information – but all of this is done with the aim of getting evidence, directly relevant practical indicators that will create a trail leading to the culprit. At some points the team of detectives will speculate on who might have done the killing, but if you were to listen in on such discussions you would not hear anything being suggested that is rooted in an informed understanding of the processes that give rise to murder. The conventional explanations that fill the newspapers, of revenge and jealousy, greed and anger, are drawn on as they might be by ordinary civilians around a beer in a local pub.

So although the police will, usually, be better informed than those outside the investigation, and closer to the actual facts of the case, there will be little in the way of abstractions as to forms and types of murder and the conditions under which they occur to inform their discussions. The mental map of murders they draw upon are not influenced by any objective charts that lay out the routes to murder, but are personal creations drawn from their own experience of previous cases, their endless discussions with other police officers, and what they have read in newspapers and books, as well as all the fictional accounts of crime to which they, like the rest of us, are exposed.

The mental map concocted from police know-how may lead investigators into a quagmire if it is applied to a murder unlike any that has been explored before, especially if detectives think the victim is unlike any they have come across before. Investigators saw Jill Dando as living a lifestyle apparently very different from that of most murder victims familiar to the average police officer. This created a real challenge for them to build up a comprehensible picture of her vulnerabilities and dangerous contacts. Of immediate concern was the fact that she was known by many more people than she knew. There are some advantages to a victim's celebrity, because detectives can quickly build up a picture of the victim's movements. They were able to build up a second-by-second account of Dando's activities on the fateful morning and knew what she was doing to within 120 seconds of the time of her death. Yet her celebrity produced problems as well. It became an obsession for the police team, and for commentators, searching for clues in her public persona to her untimely death.

MEDIA PRESSURE

One of the most significant consequences of her celebrity was the huge public interest in her death. All over the country people wanted to help the inquiry even if they had nothing to offer. Major national newspapers took on the solving of her murder as a campaigning topic. As Senior Investigating Officer Hamish Campbell, who was then a detective chief inspector, later told me: 'The media erupted. There was some comment in the paper every day for a year.' This put pressure on the inquiry by creating diversions through uninformed speculations about possible suspects that Campbell felt he had to take time to quash, so that the misinformation did not have a distorting effect on anyone who had yet to come forwards with information of relevance.

The media coverage encouraged vast numbers of people to come forwards with information, burying the investigating team in irrelevance and, as it turned out, masking crucial information for many months.

These days tabloid and indeed general public interest in a murder can be predicted with some accuracy.[5] The more of a set number of particular components involved in a murder, the more public interest in the killing. Although each paper has its own predilections, the following are generally shared: if the victim is a child, female, attractive, if there is celebrity involvement, if there are multiple victims and/or lots of nasty violence, all of these add up to increase coverage. This all means that a considerable amount of column inches is devoted to very few murders. One other component often overlooked is that if a murder happens in London it is more likely to become a national topic for general debate. The murder of an unknown middle-aged man in Bradford is unlikely even to get mentioned in the national newspapers, unless there is something especially gruesome about the way he was killed.

When there is the possibility of media interest SIOs will seek to use it to help the investigation. It is part of their training to do so. Professional journalists are brought into police staff training courses so that aspiring SIOs can go through the motions of briefing the press and making an appeal to the television cameras. To quote Campbell again, explaining what he thought about handling the hunger of journalists and the public for information on the investigation: 'What do you want to appeal for? What do you want to explain? The media will make up a story if you do not give them some information. Once they do take an interest it is difficult to get out of the vortex once you are in it.'

It is interesting to compare the attitude of the British police with that of the police in other countries to the media. In Britain, that many-headed beast has to be fed continually to prevent it devouring the investigation. In the recent inquiry into the disappearance of Holly Wells and Jessica Chapman in Soham, there was a conscious policy of giving the assembled international journalists one new nugget of information each day in an attempt to keep them at bay. In France, by contrast, there is a blanket silence on an investigation until after it has been closed, and even then little information is allowed out. Israeli police officers have told me that they would never use an appeal to the public for information because it can generate more calls than can be coped with.

There is little doubt that, in some cases, the appeal to the seven million or so viewers of programmes such as *Crimewatch* can produce important results for the police, especially if there is specific information for people to respond to, such as the serial number of a stolen object, or the sighting of a getaway car. But when the trawl is a more general one, asking viewers if they can remember anything of relevance, it is an open question whether the small army of police officers who deal with information coming in from such appeals would not be better employed in the more focused search for information from local sources. *Crimewatch* itself is proud to list the high proportion of cases that achieve some benefits from being exposed on its programme, probably as high as one in four, but I know of no comparison of how these benefits compare with other less broadband appeals.

For Hamish Campbell there was little he could do other than respond to the media interest as best he could. Jill Dando was a television presenter who took part in *Crimewatch*, a programme devoted to drawing on the public to help solve crimes. But what the media wanted most of all was a good story. I remember offering a script to a film company once in which the culprit turned out to be just an ordinary person with a banal grudge, rather than the exotic international network of intrigue that the protagonists in the film had assumed to be responsible. The scriptwriter I showed it to said that the audience would feel cheated by such a dénouement. They would want to learn that it was all even more complex than they could have imagined, not less so. As far as the media were concerned an international conspiracy with hired assassins and terrorists would make Jill Dando's murder really interesting. They pressed this possibility on the police.

For the police the professional hitman option was an interesting possibility. Major murder inquiries typically make the careers of the detectives involved. The subtler the investigation, and the cleverer the solution to the crime, the more kudos attaches to being involved in the inquiry. Beyond these career benefits it is just more interesting to be investigating an international conspiracy, or an underworld campaign, than some local nutter who has taken a shot at a celebrity. There were therefore considerable pressures on the SIO to follow up obscure or exotic explanations for the murder. Just as in a fictional whodunnit the villain needs to be particularly clever, devious or evil to highlight the skills of the detective, so in real-life investigations I have found the police will often concoct complex stories to explain the criminal's actions, making themselves seem especially insightful and intelligent. The police searched widely for her killer, but the man convicted of her killing lived a few streets away from her. Should the police have been so surprised that the murderer was almost a neighbour? Against the plethora of possibilities Jill Dando's death raised, the police shied away, as they still do in cases being investigated today, from recognising and using the power of even some of the simple ideas behind geographical profiling.

INFORMATION OVERLOAD

Perhaps the most significant problem making it so difficult for the police to get to grips with the relevance of the place and locality of the killing was the public enthusiasm for the investigation. This was generated by the heady mix of attractive pictures of the victim, her celebrity, and media interest in the case. The inquiry therefore had to put enormous resources into sorting through the glut of facts, suggestions, indications and names that came pouring in. The police see this as a resource to help their investigation, on the general principle that the more information they have the better. But from time to time they have recognised that certain information streams are producing very little of value. They have seen that what would technically be known as the 'noise to signal ratio' was so poor that it was more likely to hinder the inquiry than help it. For instance a poorly informed newspaper report may stimulate hundreds of irrelevant calls from the public. The investigation team would therefore have to decide to give lower priority to these calls. The risk is always there, though, that something crucial is being missed, especially if the detectives are not exactly sure what they are looking for.

Every information source has dross in it, whether it is the hiss on your radio, the fuzziness of the picture on the TV, or the background chatter that interferes with getting the gossip from a friend at a party. If the dross is so great that it takes more effort to filter it out than to get the central message, then it may be that other forms of communication channel should be used.

Hundreds of phone calls and written messages flooded in to the police. More than 2,000 possible suspects quickly filled the database of 'nominals' who become the centre of any large murder inquiry. A mountain of other possibilities for where suspects might be found quickly piled up. How could the inquiry team sort all this out?

One thing about human beings that modern psychology has taught us is that we have a very limited capacity for processing information. Many of our mental processes have the central purpose of enabling us to cope with the vast amounts of information that is available to us all the time. We do not actually receive a great deal of this potential information. We selectively attend to aspects that we decide are crucial. The criteria that lead to those selections may be less than fully rational, depending rather on emotions, habits, or rules of thumb that have got us through in the past. On a normal basis this can be effective, but when dealing with the overload that is at the heart of a police investigation these strategies for coping can be counter-productive.

Part of the problem of dealing with the information overload by ordinary routine is that it can lead in totally the wrong direction. Investigators do not do what a chemist might do when trying to identify an unknown compound, or a botanist who tries to find the name of a plant he does not recognise. The chemist takes little note of how the compound came to be brought for analysis, other than taking into account some suggestion that it is poisonous or a query over whether it is an illegal drug. As with the botanist, there will be a range of options available and a set of objective tests to carry out that will lead along a path to identification. The professional botanist and analytic chemist will not be sidetracked by how expensive, exotic, attractive or important the object is, except perhaps in the urgency with which the tests are carried out.

But police officers trying to identify a criminal get sidetracked all the time by all those aspects of people that they deal with in daily life. Rather than describe what happened and, importantly, where, using that description to lead to possible suspects in as direct a way as possible, making the minimum of assumptions, they seek to understand and explain.

The starting point for this explanation in the Jill Dando murder inquiry, as in most other investigations, was to focus on the actions involved in the killing, trying to make an assessment of what actually happened there on her doorstep, and why.

WHAT HAPPENED?

You would think that when a person is shot dead in daylight on a public street with people around, and with an ambulance crew there within minutes, it would be reasonably straightforward for detectives to get a clear picture of what happened and how the body was found. After all, even the most casual reading of detective novels brings home the mantra that nothing at the crime scene must be touched. But, as Hamish Campbell is at pains to emphasise, it was extremely difficult for him to determine what information, whether photographs, descriptions, or videotape, did actually record the original murder scene as left by the killer. The traditional wisdom of all police investigators is that what is left at the scene in some ways represents the killer. It could have indicated, for example, whether there had been a struggle, how close physically the killer got to Jill Dando, whether there had been any theft involved, and whether she had faced him or had been killed totally unaware of what was happening. Any particular scenario would at the very least have been food for speculation about whether she knew her killer, whether there had been any attempt by the killer to threaten or control her, and even – as unlikely as it was on the doorstep – whether there had been any sexual activity.

Campbell discovered that none of the murder scene was untouched. As much as police officers and ambulance crew are trained to leave a crime scene as pristine as possible, they had all left their trail. I have heard this so often from senior investigating officers on many different murder inquiries that we have to recognise the powerful urge people have, whether police or not, both to see for themselves what has happened and also to help as best they can. It is not uncommon for policemen's fingerprints and boot marks to be found at a crime scene they deny having gone into. This not only increases the work of the forensic team in eliminating all irrelevant traces, but also makes it much more difficult for the inquiry to reconstruct exactly what happened.

To complicate matters, when the ten or so people who were actually there before the body was moved were interviewed, every one of them gave a different account of exactly where Jill Dando was lying, the angle of her head and the distribution of objects around her. This shows that it was almost as important for investigators to recreate the scene immediately after her death as immediately before – who arrived first, what they did, and then what happened – so that the initial position of the body could be determined. As Campbell put it, there was a need 'to create a time-machine' that went back to the body being found and then back further to the moments before, then the hours, days and years before that.

'Time-machine' technology is still very primitive, although with CCTV and the increasing number of other electronic records it is improving all the time. Within 24 hours of death the inquiry had most of the key information: who had been killed, where, how, when, and what with. In all this, however, the bullet in the bullet hole was the only thing not tampered with by those who had first got to the doorstep. Everything else had been moved. But importantly, however gruesomely, this bullet hole could be put together with the entrance and exit wounds in her head to locate the position Jill was in at the time the shot was fired.

She had been killed whilst forced down onto her doorstep as she was about to open her door, with a single shot to her head from a 9mm weapon. It was quickly established that this was not a commonly used weapon, and was mostly used by firearms clubs. Furthermore, and quite remarkably, the killer had got very close to Jill Dando. He had been seen. He had not worn any mask or crash helmet. Most curiously of all, there had been only one shot, and apparently no one had heard it.

Hamish Campbell drew on a psychological adviser available to the police for all serious crimes. In this case it was Adrian West, a clinical psychologist who has worked for many years in Ashworth Special Hospital assessing, and occasionally helping, offenders who are sent there because they have been classified as mentally ill. One of Adrian's tasks was to find out how unusual an incident this was by trawling through Home Office figures and academic publications, contacting colleagues and drawing on his own considerable experience in advising murder inquiries. He concluded that this was a virtually unique event.

Adrian drew attention to the well-established fact that even those people who kill strangers typically do not travel very far from their homes to kill. However, this was not given a great deal of emphasis by the inquiry, or related to the more general studies of the journeys other criminals make to the crime scene. The importance of place in understanding a crime was low on the inquiry team's priorities in making sense of this apparently senseless killing. But there was information available to give weight to the considerations of place. In the 1990s I had supervised a police officer[6] who was examining the patterns of murder for a Master's degree. He had looked at the distances stranger murderers travelled from home to kill in the UK. One sub-group travelled on average 525 yards. Nine out of ten of all the killers he looked at were familiar with the area in which they killed.

3. THE SIGNIFICANCE OF PLACE

SUSPECTS MULTIPLY

One of the recurring facts of the case that Hamish Campbell returned to over and over again was that Jill Dando's neighbour Mr Richard Hughes had been just a few yards away from her when she was shot. Hughes had heard five sounds that became almost a mantra for recreating in Campbell's mind the last few moments of her life. There was the car engine, and the sound of the car alarm as she set the car lock. Then there was the sound of her footsteps up the path, a scream, then the clanging of the gate. These sounds added up to provide an account of the moment of the death, but curiously there was no sound of a gun or of a car being driven away.

Everything unfolded from these moments, searching back into Jill Dando's life. All the people with whom she had had direct contact and the thousands of people who had an indirect interest in her, through logging on to websites using her name, or by making contact with the BBC or the police, were considered relevant. This added up to thousands upon thousands of people. Within those there were people who may have had some knowledge of her movements and whereabouts; 2,400 people provided statements that related to her presence in the community around Fulham and Hammersmith. Nearly 200 CCTV cameras were also thought possibly to have relevant information of significance to the investigation. The array of electronic information that is now available does not daunt the police. They put more police officers on to the inquiry, drawing them away from other activities considered of lower priority.

The police information magnified itself as the inquiry continued. A man was seen in the vicinity with a mobile phone, so this led to the scrutiny of mobile-phone users. It turned out that there were more than 80,000 such phone users who had made calls around the area where Jill Dando was killed on that fateful morning. It was possible for the police to trace and exclude many of these people.

Then there were all the people that Jill Dando worked with or had contact with on various occasions. Could they reveal anything of relevance? Could they throw any light on a secret part of her life that would explain why somebody would kill her? She had many friends and associates who were close to her over the years. In police jargon, they all needed to be traced, interviewed and eliminated.

THE PARADOX OF MOTIVE

There is a curious mixture of obsessional determination and wild speculation that characterises most major murder inquiries. This one was no different. Whilst trawling through all the information available, the investigating team were constantly trying to identify why the crime had occurred and see if that could help them to focus their attention. The media were already speculating that a hired hitman had killed Jill Dando because of her public prominence either in fighting crime or in supporting the cause of the Kosovan refugees. In either case, with hindsight, we can see how curious a notion that was.

Gunning down Jill Dando would make very little difference to the solving of any crimes or to the power of *Crimewatch*. Indeed, most criminals would realise that it would have the opposite effect of generating such a huge public interest and police presence that it would bring great pressure to bear on anybody who had perpetrated such an act. She was also a female presenter, in a rather secondary role to Nick Ross; it would not gain much support from even the criminal fraternity to pick off such a vulnerable and irrelevant target.

The Balkan connection turns out to be even more bizarre. Before the shooting she was not seen as a symbol of any particular importance. As a presenter of travel programmes and assistant presenter on a monthly crime programme she could hardly be seen as the appropriate target to declare an enemy of the state. Again, as with the criminal fraternity, the choice of a vulnerable woman who had not herself carried out any particular acts of derring-do or military power would be seen as quite unhelpful for any propaganda purposes.

The power of 'motive' as a device for helping to cope with circumstances which are difficult to understand is remarkable.

Most detectives, and all crime writers, believe that if you can understand the motive for a crime this will explain why it happened and will lead you to the identity of the culprit. The papers want to know why because that makes for a better story. The courts and juries need a motive. What this means is that if the jury can be offered a classical story of hate, vengeance, jealousy or greed, then they can fit it into the existing templates of how murders happen.[1] Giving some purpose or objective to the killer's acts turns those acts into a narrative that people can make sense of. It also helps people to deal with the anxiety that surrounds any killing – the anxiety that the killing may be random and therefore we may be the next victims. As Hamish Campbell admitted, he 'got stuck with "why"'.

Yet many psychologists are uncomfortable with the whole notion of 'motive' because it can mean so many different things. It can be the objective or purpose of an action, as when a person has a motive of financial gain. It can be a habitual reaction that is unconsidered, as when a person strikes out whenever insulted. The personality of the perpetrator makes for another type of explanation that sometimes sits under the heading of motive: 'he's a nasty character who hates women'. Deeper psychological explanations are also called 'motives', as illustrated by someone being described as acting out some compulsion derived from internal conflict, possibly relating to his early childhood experiences. The problem is that all these different sorts of explanations run into each other and at any point in time no particular process may be dominant. There will be layers of reasons and explanations for what we do. Different ones will be brought to the surface for different situations. Certainly most of us, a lot of the time, would have great difficulty in being clear as to exactly what the motives for our actions were.

Careful consideration of how the notion of motive is used in daily life produces the rather intriguing paradox that we tend to search for motives only in those situations where we have got no idea of why things happened.[2] If the events have a normal pattern that relates to what we see on a daily basis then we do not search for a motive. It follows that once police start debating the motive for a crime it is a sure sign that they are having great difficulty in solving it. Although the progress of their case will be helped if they can eventually form a view of why the murder happened, and any evidence for this will be of great value in convincing a jury, investigators have to guard against getting caught up in pointless speculations about 'motive' that will happily take them round and round in circles.

In a murder inquiry some consideration of the normal patterns of behaviour – who tends to do what, where and when – may be a productive way forwards. But this clinical consideration does not give detectives a feel of any type of psychological understanding, or control of the event they are examining. There is therefore a tendency to come back to asking why that person was at that place at that time, returning to the crime scene over and over again. In this case, as Campbell put it, the question was to decide if it was a professional killer or 'chaos theory', by constantly asking 'who gained from her killing?'

THE SIO'S DILEMMA

The pressures on an SIO are enormous, and the more the murder investigation is in the public view, the greater the pressure. Not only must he deal with the demands of the investigation in the immediate here and now, but he also has to have a view over his shoulder to the way his actions may be looked at in the future. As Campbell put it, 'All our work is scrutinised.' From the initial coroner's inquiry into the death, through to possible case reviews by external police forces, or even challenges in court or at appeal level, and on into the possibility of a subsequent public inquiry or complaints from the various people involved, the SIO has to be focused and determined, ready to argue the rights of what he is doing with everyone from his chief constable through to junior detectives who are confident that given half a chance they will solve the case overnight. He has to be bold enough to deal with challenges from detectives out on the streets who will say to him, 'That's not the call I would make.' As Campbell recognised, 'You have to make your own call.'

The consequences of the report on the Yorkshire Ripper inquiry, the Byford Report,[3] with its criticism of lack of system and limited strategic planning, still ripple through police forces. But the much more recent Lawrence[4] inquiry came up with very similar criticisms fifteen years later. This shows there are still some fundamental problems in the management of police investigations.

The way experienced SIOs like Hamish Campbell see it is that, 'As an investigator you have to make choices. There are only so many people, so much money and so many hours in the day.' There is also so much happening that there is the constant problem of, 'How do we know what we have done? Everything is pressure. Everything is rush.' There are other issues to be dealt with as well. In the US it is often the case that only a couple of police officers are available to investigate a murder and that if they do not get some significant progress in the first day or two the case will be put on the back burner. In Britain the problem is almost the opposite, especially with a high-profile case. 'What are you going to do with 60 police officers?' Can the SIO be sure that every officer is doing what he has been asked to do? Will the officer recognise the appropriate clues when they are offered to him? When he knocks on the umpteenth door to ask a possible suspect about his whereabouts on the day in question, will that crucial officer be alert enough to determine if the answers he is getting are important to the investigation?

THE PLAGUE OF COINCIDENCE

The pressure on the investigating team for a result in the Dando murder, urged on by public interest whilst all the time being aware that any ineffectiveness of the inquiry would be picked up in later reviews and challenges, was magnified by the vast range of possible suspects and the mounting calls from the public, all of which provided ever more actions for the police to follow up. A team of 60 police officers was carrying out these actions. It is impossible for the senior investigating officer to be sure of exactly what each of these 60 was doing. Even the priority they assign to each individual task given to them has to rely to some extent on that person's own judgement of the urgency of that task. This all becomes ever more problematic as time moves on, traces go cold, and recreating where people had been and checking that out grows ever more difficult. Campbell saw that:

Nine months later I have to have the belief that one officer will come across the right individual. When they knock on the door do they get it right? You have to hope they do. But in many cases they pass him by. Always the puzzle; can you really guarantee everyone knows and does the same things?

Perhaps one of the biggest challenges in a large team of detectives is that what they know can be as much influenced by word of mouth, late-night chat in local bars after the day's work, and what they read in the papers, as by the detailed briefing from senior officers. If the rank and file of police believe the culprit is a hired hitman working for international terrorists, then being given the task of checking out a local man who has been acting strangely will not be seen by them as a high priority.

In the absence of a clear direction for the investigation it is also constantly under threat of being derailed by the build-up of plausible but irrelevant suspects. Have you ever been looking for a post box as you drive along and suddenly become alert to every red object in the environment? This psychological phenomenon of being particularly alert to signals in the environment as they become relevant can get out of hand if all that defines a signal is that it is suspicious. As Campbell put it, 'People become compelling just because you look at them.'

There were plenty of people to look at. Eight people were close to Jill Dando, and every one of those eight could be seen to have links to crime. But given that one in four or so of the male population has some sort of criminal record those links to crime may have been inevitable. They identified 32 boyfriends for this attractive woman, but how confidently could they be eliminated from the inquiry? One was found to have some violent offence history. An informant named two people: known criminals whose actions seemed suspiciously linked to the murder. Campbell remembered that, 'The more we looked at them the more compelling they became.' But as it turned out the crime they were planning was totally unrelated.

This is the plague of coincidences. The next-door neighbour had bought a car identical to Jill Dando's. Was he obsessed with her? Or was the owner of that car the real target for the killing? As I have found in just about every investigation I have looked at, a very plausible suspect always turns up who is not the culprit.

The dilemma of thinking that every person caught in the police searchlight could be the killer is compounded by the problem of base rates. In the Washington Sniper investigation a white van had been seen near a number of shootings. In the investigation into a series of rapes in Manchester the police quickly spotted that all the victims were students. In the Dando investigation the police had a report of a blue Rover car in the vicinity. All these aspects of the circumstances surrounding a crime can take on a huge significance and lead the investigation totally astray, unless investigators understand that there is a background set of chance probabilities. The vans and cars could have been there at any time, nothing to do with the murder. Most young women in that part of Manchester were students, so that aspect of the victims could have been a coincidence of the location rather than a focus for the offender.

These complications meant that Barry George's name was sitting in the lists the police had for twelve months before he was seriously considered as a possible murderer.

CLEARING THE FOG

By November 1999, six months on, Hamish Campbell realised they were still no closer to Jill Dando's killer. He took a brave step and decided his whole approach needed to be redrafted. It was a momentous decision to say, 'Let's ignore *why* she was killed. Instead let's ask, what elements can we follow that would lead us to the killer?'

He had been a detective for twenty years and, from the beginning of the inquiry, had been determined to make it as systematic as he could. He had established a procedure of giving all the suspects a score based on their criminal history, any indication that they had a firearm, why they had come into the inquiry and how often they had been named. It may seem like hindsight, but if I'd been asked for advice on this trawl, I would also have urged him to include how close the offender's residence was to 29 Gowan Avenue. The investigating team did not take this principle on board. They had 1,900 suspects to consider and from these 98 got a top score. Hamish discovered that 6 months into the investigation less than half of these 98 had been approached by police offers in their classic TIE procedure, in which they Trace, Interview and Eliminate likely suspects. Campbell set about making sure these high-priority suspects were attended to.

A very experienced US homicide investigator, Bob Keppel, is often called on to help murder investigations because of his reputation as a profiler. He likes to quash detectives' uninformed belief in the magic of profiles by responding to a request for a profile with the comment, 'D'you want a profile or to solve the case?' His point is that in a great many murder investigations the culprit's name will have already been recorded somewhere in the investigation files during the first few days of the inquiry. It is a matter of an intelligent search through this information to find the culprit.

THE SIGNFICANCE OF PLACE
The detailed reconstruction of Jill Dando's life made it clear to Campbell very quickly that 29 Gowan Avenue was not really where she lived. Indeed she was planning to sell that house after her imminent marriage to Dr Alan Farthing, with whom she was already living in Chiswick. The police had painstakingly recreated her last journey. This made it clear that she had stopped and got out of her car four times in 120 minutes on her drive to Gowan Avenue, not counting stops at traffic lights, which are a Hollywood favourite for assassination locations. She was killed at her fourth stop. The police team discussed why she was killed at the fourth stop and not any others.

29 Gowan Avenue had become little more than an office for Jill Dando. She was only returning there to refill the paper for her fax machine – an interesting indication of the limits of her celebrity, if this was a task she was doing herself. But her killer had been seen hanging around near her door for a few hours earlier in the morning, or at least a number of witnesses had seen someone acting suspiciously in the street from the early hours. She had not been accosted in the street, where presumably his act would have been more visible and she

might have got away. He followed her in through the gate. He did not wait for her to go inside, where the chance of being seen or his act being discovered would have been much smaller. Was this because he did not know her and was not sure if he could get past her door? This was not a man confident in his ability to shoot even a vaguely moving target. He forced her to the ground on her doorstep, killed her with a single shot, and was off.

Barry George's presence was littered in several places around the police investigation, but the difficulty of finding this deadly needle in the piles upon piles of information the police had collected can be gauged by the fact that it was seventeen days after the shooting before Barry George's name was noticed. By then the inquiry team had received 1,100 messages directly and 1,300 letters, as well as numerous other pieces of information, offered to other police forces and directly to the BBC. Yet, like the great majority of people who kill a person they are not living with, his home was less than half a kilometre away from that of his victim. This startling fact emerges again and again in murders, but its simple power can be so easily masked by police determination to 'leave no stone unturned' and to follow every possibility no matter, or perhaps especially because of, how exotic it is. George's home was almost due east of Jill Dando's, but he had also made his presence known at a local advice centre less than half a kilometre north of Gowan Avenue, and a minicab office he had approached was a couple of hundred metres to the west of Jill Dando's doorstep. Other sightings had a man looking not unlike George around the triangle marked by these three locations.

Early in his inquiry the details carefully collected by Hamish Campbell's team made it very clear that the killer at the scene had not used a car. There were speculations that a car may have picked him up later, but that seemed a remarkable risk for such a planned assassination to have taken. So the most likely scenario was of a man on foot: a man who knew enough about Jill Dando to know her official residence, but not enough to know she actually lived with her fiancé some miles away.

It is perhaps not surprising, but nonetheless often ignored by the police, that offenders who walk to where they carry out their crimes tend to live closer to those locations than those who travel there by car. In one study of German serial killers[5] those in vehicles were found to have travelled six times as far, on average, as those who got to their victims on foot. Many other studies have shown similar results. Of course these are average figures and there will always be exceptions. Detectives do not look for an average person. They search for the one individual who is the culprit. That person may be the statistical outlier, the exception far from the average. But it is in the nature of averages that there is a greater chance of any examples from the population being more similar to the average than being very different from it.

2. BARRY GEORGE'S AREA OF ACTIVITY

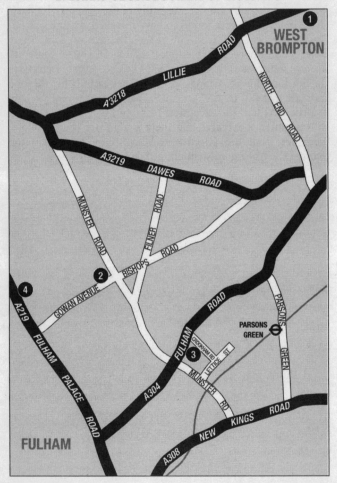

1. Hammersmith and Fulham Action for Disability, Beaufort House, 49 Lillie Rd, London SW6

2. Jill Dando's Home, 29 Gowan Avenue, London SW6

3. Barry George's Home, 2b Crookham Rd, London SW6

4. London Traffic Cars, 325 Fulham Palace Rd, London SW6

4. CRIME IN ITS PLACE

BARRY GEORGE'S HISTORY IN THE LOCALITY[1]

Barry George was in the list of priority suspects because a call had been received from a disability advice centre which he had visited on the Wednesday, asking what time he had been there on the previous Monday, the day of the killing. George was known to the staff at the advice centre, but his actions in returning on the Wednesday made them suspect that at the very least he knew something about the killing. So when they got no initial reaction from the inquiry team they called the police back, but in the police log the second call was from a different address because the building was on a corner. All the police had in their records was a note of a man behaving oddly who may have had some knowledge of relevance to the investigation. He was in the crime environment around the appropriate time. That was all they knew. The killer, interestingly, had been willing to hang around the murder scene for most of the morning, apparently without the pressure of a job to go to. This was an employment bureau reporting him in, knowing his date of birth because he had been registered there. Hindsight offers wonderful views.

Once the police started to consider him as a possible suspect they began to look at his criminal background. I still do not understand why major inquiries do not, as a matter of course, put on a map the location of all people known to live in, say, a mile of the crime scene who have committed crimes that could be related. Of course there are huge civil liberty issues that need to be addressed in how this is done. There are also very real problems of making sure the information is accurate and up to date. But given the resources that go into a major inquiry it has to be one option that is worth following through, because it is unusual for someone who does not have in his background some previous offence history, often for violence, to commit a very serious violent crime. People do suddenly kill others with nothing in their past to presage the violence, but they are very rare.

In Barry George's case it quickly became clear not only that he had a criminal record for indecent assaults and attempted rape, but also that many of these offences had occurred in the area he had mapped out as being of significance to him. He had also been arrested for assaulting his wife, showing how embedded his violence against women was. His history of stalking women in the area was also relevant, as were the thousands of photographs he had taken of women, some in Gowan Avenue. He had approached women and grabbed them on their doorstep. He had been known to follow women since the early 70s when he was 18–19. He had occasionally been stopped, and was known to have stolen women's underwear. He had followed them from their office; some he had even attacked. He had been accused of indecent assault just north of Gowan Avenue.

His interest in celebrities, which took a violent tone, was revealed when he was arrested in the grounds of Princess Diana's residence, Kensington Palace, in commando gear and carrying a knife. The triangle that marked out George's domain did not centre on his home, but on Gowan Avenue. That much was clear from the details of his assaults on women in that area and the many photographs he secretly took of them. His doctor's surgery had been three doors away from Dando's house. This was the territory in which he lived out his private adventure, with his home 500 yards from the crime scene.

GEORGE IN THEIR SIGHTS

When the police first interviewed Barry George it became clear that he had no family links to the victim. He said he had no knowledge of guns, and claimed to have been at home at the time of the murder. Yet a year later it seemed odd that this individual was known to have been around the murder scene, from his own attempts to establish where he was on the Monday morning and eventually from CCTV pictures.

In his cautious and thorough manner Campbell was still prepared to find evidence that would eliminate George from the inquiry. He lists 'what we should not have found when his home was searched: a shoulder holster, a magazine about guns – but he said he was not interested in guns. Should not have found condolence cards for Jill Dando. He said he did not know her.' That put him 'slightly in the frame'. Then there were the hundreds of photos of women developed from film found in his house, including photos of girls on Gowan Avenue. It turned out his doctor's surgery was at the end of the street, which also gave him knowledge of the area. With this, 'George comes very rapidly into sights,' as Campbell put it.

The crucial decision was made to stop all other action and focus attention on Barry George 'a year behind' with the investigation. This produced damning evidence, including firearms residue in his clothes identical to that on Jill Dando's head. An item of clothing he was thought to have worn on the day of the murder was identified. Two women identified him as having been in Gowan Avenue on the day of the murder. There were also fibres from his trousers on Dando's coat. He had changed his alibi from claiming he was at home at the crucial time to saying he was at the advisory centre, but CCTV records showed he could not have been there then.

These were all too many coincidences for the jury, even though they had no knowledge of his previous offence history in the area.

PUTTING CRIME IN ITS PLACE

The pressures on senior investigating officers should not be underestimated. When a murder has a high media profile this pressure increases not just from the demands from all and sundry for a solution but because of the huge amount of information and actions it generates. From the calm of the notional armchair, once the solution is obvious, it is easy to say how the investigation could have reached its conclusion more quickly. So there is no intended criticism of the very thorough investigation that Hamish Campbell managed if I speculate on how a behavioural scientist with a knowledge of criminals' spatial activities might have approached finding Jill Dando's killer.

What if the effort to deal with calls coming through from *Crimewatch* and other media appeals had been turned instead to careful inquiries in the vicinity of the murder, as would have happened with any other murder investigation? Would the significance of the crucial information that helped to draw attention to Barry George have been recognised sooner because there would not have been so many other distracting pieces of evidence to deal with?

What if in this investigation, and indeed in any other large-scale inquiry in the public eye, some proportion of the detectives assigned to the job – it could even be a very small proportion, two or three – were to be tasked with considering all possible suspects in, say, a mile radius (most police officers still seem to think in imperial measures)? If there was clear evidence that the offender was a traveller – as was apparent in other cases considered in this book – then this aspect of the investigation could be very limited. But in those cases where the victims are unlikely to have travelled far, or where there is evidence of a walking offender, or detailed local knowledge that puts the offender's habitat firmly in the locality of the crime scene, then surely there is enough research evidence to add power to the SIO's elbow, so that if he does feel he has to turn over every stone at least someone is looking under the stones around the corner.

Let me hasten to add that this will not always work. In the very thorough investigation into a series of rapes in Bath, the police have followed these guidelines very carefully but have still not found the culprit, although they have DNA that would provide clinching evidence the minute they got close to him.

Yet criminals do often reveal how far they have travelled from how and where they commit their crimes. The killing of Jill Dando had some of the hallmarks of a local, confused criminal. Dr Adrian West, the 'profiler' who advised the police on this case, did recommend that they should not ignore the possibility of a local man. His analysis of the crime indicated why he thought the killer could have lived not far from Jill: the lack of disguise, the fact that the crime was committed in broad daylight, the strange coincidence that she had only returned to change the paper on her fax machine – no one planning with care would have relied on this chance break in habit. The single shot was an unlikely MO for a hitman, for whom leaving his victim alive is the greatest risk. Walking to and from the scene also opened the killer to public awareness in a way that no 'professional' was likely to countenance.

The steps along the pavement that took George to kill tell us more than just his familiarity with the locality. They show the limited world he inhabited. He wanted to strike out at a woman who was in public view. Years earlier he had been found in the grounds of Kensington Palace (Princess Diana's residence) in commando gear, carrying a knife. He craved links with celebrity, changing his name to imply he was related to Freddie Mercury, as he had earlier changed his name to imply he was an SAS officer. Yet his limitations, so typical of so many killers, kept him now to within a few hundred yards of where he lived. It was Jill Dando's lack of a celebrity lifestyle, whilst appearing on the cover of *Radio Times*, that made her available to such a limited man. If he had not sought out people to try to strengthen his alibi at the careers centre and the minicab office, his name might not have got into the police system. If he had not hinted to friends and associates that he was a suspect and might know more than he was letting on, the police might not have taken their suspicions of him so seriously. If his decision to kill had been more developed and less a consequence of the opportunity he had become aware of in prowling around the Gowan Avenue area, he may have found a target further from where he lived and made it much more difficult for the police to build up a picture of his movements. The role he created for himself as clever suspect and secret killer eventually caused his downfall.

Hamish Campbell, who had puzzled over the murder for two years, was never sure, in the end, if Barry George really knew what he was doing: 'I think George was a very angry man. He had this ability to flare up. If women rebuffed him he would react. He spent his life in conflict with others. He had a poor gun. Was it an accident coming out of the sad, lonely life he led, walking the streets?'

BARRY GEORGE THE KILLER?

'Jill Dando was a central figure in many people's minds,' warned barrister Michael Mansfield, defending Barry George. But whilst it may have been a justifiable fear that the jury would desire to find a culprit even if the evidence was weak, 'a desire to see someone pay', as Mansfield put it, reflecting the age-old search for a scapegoat for any crime felt to be a public outrage, Jill Dando's public significance may also have been the best explanation for why Barry George killed her.

Barry George's life story unfolds like that of many violent criminals. From his earliest days it was clear he had difficulty relating to others. Because of his behavioural problems, he spent most of his education in special schools. It is also possible that his incipient epilepsy combined with low intellectual abilities to make it difficult for him to control his emotions and appreciate how others were reacting to him. His unacceptability in conventional schools may also have been a product of the hard time his father gave him, aggravated by the acrimonious divorce his parents had when he was thirteen. As in all human actions, the causes are invariably a mix of many factors. The death of his elder sister during an epileptic fit must also have made Barry George feel vulnerable, if not actually cursed.

In the special schools the children around him would have sensed this vulnerability. They doubtless sought relief from their own confused emotions by bullying and taunting him. Unhappy with his own identity, he was nudged into alternative personae. He tried to create fictional personal narratives, but ended by deluding himself so far that he could not always tell where the truth lay.

Barry George seems to have gained respite from his feelings of inadequacy through an absorbing interest in the lives of celebrities, gaining satisfaction and attention from a declared fascination with Gary Glitter and then later on Freddie Mercury. He found pleasure in thinking himself into the lives of these people – so much so that in his teens he told people his name was Paul Gadd, Gary Glitter's real name.

There is no indication that he ever tried to contact Gary Glitter or any of the other people on whom he later focused his attentions. But the extent of his fascination with celebrity was revealed when he changed his own name by deed poll to Steve Majors, a conflation of the names Lee Majors and Steve Austin, the Six Million Dollar Man. These alternative life stories moved between the starry dazzle of Gary Glitter and other pop stars and the macho muscle of SAS officers and Steve Austin. Clearly he was always searching for a secure identity distinct from his own, which he found so uncomfortable.

His inability to recognise how others saw his strange behaviour took on sexual overtones when, in his early twenties, he started accosting women in the street, trying to chat to them and molesting them when they did not respond. This eventually led to rape and a 30-month prison sentence, which doubtless fostered the image he was nursing of himself as a tough action man. This was reflected in a growing number of ways. He was arrested at night in the grounds of Kensington Palace with a poem for Prince Charles. He joined the Territorial Army under the name of Steve Majors, until he was asked to leave. Once his criminal contacts had been cemented by his prison sentence he acquired a handgun. He even followed through with an attempt in front of TV cameras to carry out the stunt of roller-skating over a row of double-decker buses, which resulted in injuries and concussion.

But his search for a celebrated identity was never just about action-man power. He wanted to be seen as someone of significance, recognising the world of pop music as a major source of accolade. When Freddie Mercury was in the news Barry George again changed his name by deed poll, this time to Barry Bulsara, taking Mercury's real surname. But later he swung back to the action-man narrative, calling himself Tony Palmer after the SAS man who abseiled into the Iranian embassy in 1980.

His attempts to establish contacts with women became increasingly alienated. His photographing of 419 women on 2,500 rolls of undeveloped film seems to have been yet another persona he was trying on, but it is difficult to know if he was aping David Bailey or one of a number of US serial killers who posed as photographers to gain access to their victims. What is certain is that this photography occurred in parallel to his accosting and assaulting many women near his home. When he was spurned, as he always was, he sometimes turned away and sometimes showed his anger. Did Jill Dando suffer from his attentions and rebuff him robustly? Here was celebrity on his doorstep, the sort of contact that he had always craved. Did his action-man storyline lead him to think he must assuage his hurt by killing her?

During his trial various experts offered a number of pseudo-medical terms to describe Barry George's condition. Personality-disordered and psychopath were the favourites. These terms are summaries of how the patient deals with other people, but their medical patina implies they are explanations of what the person is 'suffering from'. Another term gaining in fashion is Asperger's Syndrome. This is thought to be a form of autism, a complex and extremely varied set of ways of finding difficulty in operating in normal society. Those autistic people who are violent from time to time and experience large mood swings, but who do not inhabit as separate and private a world as the severely autistic, are often considered to have Asperger's Syndrome. But as there is no satisfactory explanation for this syndrome and no actual medical markers for it, all it amounts to is the recognition of the co-existence of a bundle of disturbing behaviours. Many people with this diagnosis, moreover, do manage to lead relatively normal lives. It is a label that may describe, but it does not explain.

So we have a man of low intellectual ability who learns from an early age that he has no worth in the eyes of his family or schoolmates, dismissed by his teachers as 'unexceptional in every way' but alert to the images around him of sexual and physical success. As he was searching for an understanding of what the story was around which his life could unfold, he became aware that he was regarded with some significance when he engaged with accounts of popular icons. Doubtless this created a confusion in his own sense of who he was that never seemed to be resolved. Instead he kept trying on many different personal narratives, swinging between pop star and action man, all the time becoming more excluded from ordinary social discourse. A brief marriage to a Japanese woman failed. He spent months in prison as a sex offender. All of this was pushing him to search for personal storylines that would take him out of the self he found so painful. He had spent twenty years without any success in work or relationships, but had found relief in adopting the personae of various celebrities that exuded glamour or masculine power.

The police trawl through thousands of records and consider many possibilities when they carry out a major murder inquiry. The names of all the conceivable suspects are listed. These days psychological research, my own included, supports this task and helps to give the police pointers to where they should look for the needle in their electronic haystack. But even with all these possibilities detectives are still human beings with the limited capacities we all have to process information and make sense of senseless acts.

How could the police have realised early on in their investigation that the cold-blooded act, so like a textbook assassination, was perpetrated by a man who was acting as his own hitman? Many of those in the inquiry team thought that the murder had the hallmarks of a contract killing. But, as so often, experts disagreed over whether the murder owed more to thriller fiction than the hand of a trained killer.

When a much-liked public figure is killed, a complex set of emotions is released in most of us. On the one hand we feel personally affronted by this death of a figure that plays a part in our own mental lives. If we believe her death was at the hands of a stranger, the fact that she was a stranger we knew so well magnifies the vulnerability we share with her. It is much easier for us to come to terms with violence between acquaintances. We can see glimpses of this in our own lives from time to time. It is more difficult to accept the presence of random assassins, who undermine the fabric of social expectations.

Most murders emerge from relationships. It may be the casual contact that explodes into a pub brawl or it may be the result of years of abuse. It may be the consequence of another crime, robbery or rape, in which the victim is an unwilling partner to the antagonist. In all these cases the violence is a consequence of the killer's desire to erase the perceived obstacle that the victim presents, as a source of insult, frustration, threat or competition. We all experience milder forms of the emotions that, when magnified, give rise to these forms of murder; but the cold-blooded killing of a stranger, no matter how well known they are, is anathema.

Hollywood resolves the problem of portraying the cold-blooded killer by inventing powerful, but often implausible, images of crazed fiends, often superficially charming and usually played by British actors, but single-mindedly focused on their deadly task. The reasons why these fictional figures are so determined to kill is never fully explored, but we carry away the image of their resolute obsession and use it to enliven the otherwise vague metaphors of 'stalker' or 'predator'.

It is out of this desire to find a monstrous culprit for so distressing an act as killing a lovely person that there is the quest to label Barry George a 'stalker' and to cast him in some role best suited to the big screen. But it is hard to see the 41-year-old admirer of people as varied as Gary Glitter, Freddie Mercury and Lee Majors as having a persistent fantasy that he could only enact by killing an attractive female TV presenter. For the sake of simplicity Barry George has been described as 'stalking' hundreds of women, but what he did can more precisely be described as following, not stalking. A stalker is obsessional, compulsive and focused. If a stalker is violent, the violence emerges out of threats and pleas and there is no doubt who the target is.

With most victims of assaults by strangers, it is an accident of where they are and when that produces the vicious coincidence. In this case, Jill Dando's celebrity presence in the area that was Barry George's domain gave her being there, at that time in that place, a special significance to him. The distractions generated by the victim's celebrity status were significant in generating the information overload the police had to handle. It seems highly likely that those same distractions caused Barry George to form a plan to kill her. A hired hitman working out an Eastern European vendetta, or revenge from organised crime, is far more in keeping with the significance of the victim in the public eye, putting it on track for an ITV script, or possibly even Hollywood. Such a killing demands subtle resources, deep undercover information and all the skills of a prime-time TV detective. Arresting a local, middle-aged sex offender, who walked past Jill Dando's home on the way to his GP's surgery for treatment for his epilepsy, is all too banal for such an important murder.

5. MEMOIR OF A KILLER

A PICTURE OF INNOCENT LOVE

> Wen ana came back from Jens ana said told Jen I hame
> goWing to have your Baby Will my World had
> slowdown but ana I Was on cloud nine she Was so
> happy and Joyful all ana did Was keept Kissing Me and
> saying I Love you for ever and ever My Darling it Was
> the Baby I hade to sort IT out With ana but not now ana
> was to happy but Was ana pregnant I hope Not I had to
> sort my Marriage out I had to Marriage ana she Was My
> special angel I got out My Guitar and sat on the step of
> the of the VAN ana sat By Me I playd ana sang to ana[1]

A mawkish, rambling, semi-literate passage describing a young man apparently reliving the delight of Ana, his mistress, on hearing she is expecting his child. In the tradition of the novelette, he expresses his torn feelings about his marriage and his painful hope that his lover is wrong: that she is not really pregnant after all. Nonetheless, romantic that he is, he shares the joy with his 'special angel' and serenades her on his guitar in time-honoured fashion.[2]

It is clear that the writer has little education. His spelling confusions, missing words, lack of any punctuation and inability to understand the use of capital letters also indicate that he is not very bright. An IQ assessment of 84 puts him in the bottom five per cent of the population. People with such limited capability find conventional schooling irksome and, unless they have very special teachers, will just cause trouble and avoid lessons as much as they can. For them any sort of abstract concept, such as truth or honesty, love or responsibility, is very difficult to grasp. But, as the excerpt shows, such lack of academic ability does not prevent him from providing a convincing, plausible story.

If we ignore the spelling and lack of punctuation, it is possible to see that the flow of the ramblings has an elegant form to it. Even in this short excerpt, the subject's native skills of storytelling can be seen. Many a novelist would be proud of the way the central theme is nicely introduced. Ana reports on a conversation she has had, and in so doing puts their secret out in the open, with all the potential embarrassment that implies. The emotional significance of this revelation is captured in the sensation of the 'world slowing down', enhanced with starry-eyed Ana being on 'cloud nine'. Having established Ana's happiness, and how much she involves the author in her joy, a dark chord is struck. Our hero has 'to sort it', the capitalisation of IT indicating the significance of the unborn baby. We are led into the problems of his marriage and the need also to 'sort out' that. These gloomy tones, though, are not allowed to settle. Ana is an angel who needs to be worshipped.

The memoir is not easy to read on the page, but once we get over that there is the even more difficult challenge of determining what psychological sense it makes. How can we interpret it to tell us about the thought processes and personal landscape its narrator inhabits? More than the story that is being told, we need to look at the characters, the roles that are assigned to them, and especially the mood that seeps between the words. Reading it this way, glimmers of the intense, charged atmosphere the author lived in can be sensed. Most of what he describes is emotional. A feeling emerges of a secret, private perspective on the world, driven by the writer's desires and his need to 'sort out' events that challenge the way he wants to live. Not long after the events he describes, the author killed Ana. Four years later, he killed the wife.

This tale of a star-crossed lover trying to 'sort out' his marriage and pregnant mistress is taken from the memoir written by Frederick West – one of the most notorious serial killers of modern times. He wrote it when in prison awaiting trial for the murder of twelve young women, including his first wife and two daughters. West was arrested on 25 February 1994 when the body of his daughter Heather was found buried under his patio. Soon after, nine of his victims' bodies were found buried in the basement of his house and garden at 25 Cromwell Street, Gloucester.

How could he have killed so many people without it being noticed? This poorly educated, intellectually dull man lived in a small English town where many people knew him. He regularly came into contact with police officers and the social services. Yet he managed to kill his own wife and daughters – and possibly another twenty young women – without being caught. The Ana he described himself serenading so lovingly was one of his first victims. If it had not been for the determination of one police officer searching for West's missing daughter, this murderous life might have continued to this day. Beyond the question of *how* West managed to evade detection for so long, hindsight requires us to find the clues that could have pointed to the house of death that West had created.

Part of the explanation for his effective deception lies in the unlikely mix of a rambling, limited intelligence with an inherent savvy. He knew how to tell a tale, but many of those who met him were lulled into believing his stories were true. People thought he was harmless because he lacked fluency and was inarticulate, and also because he had a sense of humour. The deceit he wove with his romantic tales helped Fred West to kill repeatedly, without detection, over a quarter of a century. Beyond the nine victims concealed in Cromwell Street, others were buried in the fields of Gloucestershire, around Much Marcle, where he grew up in the 1950s.

His mumbling speech and convincing lies could only be the start to unravelling how it was that his murders remained uncovered for so long. To understand how he avoided raising the suspicions of the many officials who questioned him about his children, or even of the magistrates who dealt with his early assaults on women, we need to get closer to the way Fred West protected his murderous existence. It was not by sophisticated cunning. He was not a clever killer who developed a well-articulated, deviant philosophy, using his intellect to tie investigators in knots. He survived for so long because of the world he created for himself. He did not have to be a subtle actor, working out his part and learning how to play it. His actions were a natural part of the landscape as he saw it. To understand what he did and how he got away with it for so long, we have to try to draw some picture of how West saw others. We also need to see him the way he wanted to be seen himself. Central to his evil successes was the place he built to house – literally and metaphorically – his distorted world. This was West's 'web', the weapon he used to entice and trap the vulnerable young women whom he would sadistically torture, rape and murder.

HOW DO YOU GET INTO THE MIND OF A KILLER?

Getting access to the personal, internal world – the inner narrative – of a serial killer is extremely difficult, not least because these men (they are rarely women) often have only a confused view of who they are and what they are doing. In the case of Fred West it is even more difficult because he had a great problem formulating any clear account of what he had done and why. Murderers often experience psychological difficulties in finding words to express their inner experiences. But an even bigger problem is that every account they give is for one audience or another. Even the rambling monologue is a testing out of what can be said. It is a moulding of how the killer sees his life's course: an attempt, for those who will later study it, to give it some acceptable shape.

This inner narrative is one form of map that we all carry with us as a record and guide to who we are and what we do. It is not a solely geographical map, although that forms a part of it, but a picture of our life – the plot of our identity and what has happened to us. As I explain in more detail in Chapter 13, amateur sketch maps of places are distortions of cartographic reality. It is these distortions that tell us the biases in a person's perceptions. The same is true of the metaphorical map of his life that a serial killer draws when he tells his personal story. The differences from reality as others see it reveal how he deceives himself about who he is and what he has done. The episodes in his life he considers noteworthy may be quite different from those anyone else is aware of. The account he gives of who the key people were for him, and what their significance is in shaping his feelings about himself, is likely to come as a surprise to those who only know the killer from his actions and have not seen into the warped internal landscape that he inhabits.

Paradoxically, even if the warped maps that criminals draw – whether geographical maps or plots of their life stories – are produced in order to provide a particular picture for an audience that may be suspicious of them, the differences from reality reveal what is special about the world in which the killer lives. The form of the map and its biases can also help us to understand how he was able to present such an unthreatening picture of himself to all the victims who trusted him. It is the character he creates in describing himself and his life that he will have presented to those young women before he drugged, abused and murdered them. The self-deception the distortions uncover also helps us to understand how he lived with himself for so long.

THE JOURNAL AS A SOURCE OF INSIGHT

When I heard that Fred West had produced a journal while in prison, I thought it could give some very helpful insights into how he thought about his life and victims. It is rare indeed to have any first-person account from a violent offender that is neither edited when published for public consumption nor an obvious attempt to declare his innocence. The document West produced is what he wanted to say in his own words, more or less as he would speak. He wrote as he was looking towards his trial, when the police were identifying more bodies and the world's press was reeling from the horrors he had perpetrated. His wife Rose had been arrested and charged. To add even more significance to his journal, a few months after he started it he killed himself. Surely the thoughts he had committed to paper in the last weeks of his life would help us to understand the roots of his vile actions and the routes that he followed to such depravity? Would such thoughts perhaps also explain why he killed himself?

I therefore set about the involved task of gaining access to Fred West's journal. This was no easy venture. One of the curiosities of English law is that when a murderer dies without leaving a will his property becomes the responsibility of a legal institution known as 'the office of the Official Solicitor'. This institution then has the task of maximising the benefit to his estate for the murderer's heirs. This meant that rather than make the journal freely available to *bona fide* researchers, as would be done, say, with the letters of Jane Austen and many other similar literary archives, I had to negotiate for the right to study this material. Eventually a price of £600 was agreed, with strong limitations on how much of it I could publish, so that other commercial possibilities would not be compromised.

Despite its potential value and significance, it was remarkable how casually the Official Solicitor stored this document. When the photocopy first arrived the opening page was missing and then I discovered the closing pages had been left somewhere else.

Once I had the full document together I worked with research assistants to understand what it consisted of and to begin decoding the idiosyncratic spelling and modes of expression. The first thorough reading of Fred West's manuscript was a real surprise: there was none of the obvious bravado or posturing I'd expected. He did not explain the murders as acts of vengeance or justice against victims who had got what they deserved. Nor were there any attempts at philosophising about human nature to show his privileged understanding of right and wrong. Much more astonishing was the absence of any reference to his crimes. There was no mention at all of the death of his victims, even though a number of them do have significant parts in the egocentric ramblings about his own experiences. It would be a mistake, though, to dismiss the document as casual jottings written to pass the time. The care he put into the writing means it does tell us more about Fred West than he probably realised.

THE 'AUTOBIOGRAPHY'

When West had settled into solitary confinement in Winson Green prison in Birmingham, with the endless hours that are prison life even for such an infamous inmate, making up long days with little to bother him other than the remains of his conscience, he set about writing his memoir. He may have been encouraged to do this by his solicitor, Howard Ogden, who was clearly conscious of the commercial interest in the life and times of this notorious killer. But West himself was aware that he had become internationally significant. He soon sacked Ogden when he thought the solicitor was planning to sell his life story. He wrote to his wife that, 'You will be Mrs West all over the world.' He was proud that the public eye linked her closely to him. He encouraged his family to sell their stories to the papers to make some money and even scratched on the wall of his prison cell, 'Freddy, the mass murderer from Gloucester'.

Doubtless he did not realise he was following a tradition many hundreds of years old. True-crime literature grew out of the sixteenth-century confessions of people about to be hanged, sold by the prison chaplain as moral tales to educate the masses. Such confessions had strong religious origins, such as those at the heart of the profoundly honest *Confessions* of Augustine, who wrote in the fourth century about his misbegotten youth and finding religion.[3] It is from tracts such as these that the whole idea of expiating sins by making a clean breast of them has emerged. Indeed, this is a practice many psychologists still see as fundamental to effective psychotherapy. Other confessions take on a more salacious air, warping the genre to create sensationalist accounts that will titillate others.

Fred West may have thought he was involved in a combination of the confessional and the sensational but what he produced reveals a deep depravity that is the very antithesis of Augustine's confessions. This depravity is not revealed in any sensational account of his many evil acts, however, but rather through his attempt to present himself as a lover and hardworking husband surrounded by wrongdoing but never touched by it. This enables us to understand how, by creating a self-image that was anything but a 'true' self, he could hide his own vicious debauchery even from himself. He could use the face he put on for the world to camouflage the trap he had constructed to enable him to continue killing unhindered for so long.

It is difficult to imagine what you would feel and think if you were on your own in prison, being interviewed every few days about the most horrific murders, hearing yourself speaking of hacking up bodies in order to dispose of them more easily and almost casually mentioning how you had cut off fingertips to avoid identification, all the time knowing that your notoriety was filling newspapers around the world. You might think of trying to tough it out, boasting about your audacity, as many notorious criminals have done. Just possibly you might take the tack of an abject, conscience-stricken admission of guilt, although I've never come across a serial violent offender who has done that. It is more likely that the arrogance, self-centredness and lack of fellow feeling that had taken you this far would make it possible for you to think about writing about your life as you saw it.

West was 53 years old when he decided to write his autobiography. He told his son Stephen that he would write a chapter about each of the women in his life. Laboriously handwritten in Biro on over 111 pages of lined prison paper, it turned out to be more of a memoir than a systematic autobiography. Fred was almost illiterate. He wrote his journal as a flow of thoughts, spelling words as they sounded in his Gloucestershire accent, often spelling the same word in different ways. His punctuation is haphazard, so it takes considerable effort to read, then still more to make sense of it.

What is even more remarkable about the journal is that it does not connect at all to what was happening to him around the time he was writing it. During those months in prison he had frequent meetings with his solicitor and interviews with the police. He slowly began to admit to one murder after another as police investigators dug up his garden and cellar to discover the remains of his victims. Although he changed his story many times, it was clear from these interviews that he remembered much of what he had done: why he had cut the bodies up, how he had disposed of them. The journal ignores all this.

These 111 pages must have taken him a considerable effort to write. It shows a man not used to putting thoughts down on paper, straining to give the account he wants to be heard. Yet there are few corrections to the text as it rolls along. He prepared written drafts to copy from, and thought carefully about what he was going to write before he set pen to paper. If he was unhappy with a section, he crossed out whole pages and started again. This is not a casual document; it is not the result of scribbling to pass the time. It is a carefully prepared, determined attempt to tell the story of his life as he saw it. It also needs to be regarded as a form of testament, because he killed himself not long after he wrote the final pages. He is declaring who he is and what has been important in his life – or perhaps, more accurately, how he wants to be seen and which incidents he wants people to know about.

THE CONTENTS OF THE MEMOIR

Fred West's memoir mainly describes episodes in his life a quarter of a century earlier, starting in the late 1960s in Glasgow then moving to the caravan site where he lived in Gloucestershire with his first wife, Rena. West recalls a variety of incidents: he writes of running over a young boy with his ice cream van in Glasgow, of needing to escape back to Gloucester, and of a fight with 'yobs' who were associates of Rena.

The focus of the account, though, is his being loved by Anna McFall, whom he calls Ana. The first 32 pages deal mainly with their time together in a caravan near Gloucester when she was around eighteen years old. A second section is entitled 'Shirley', which he apparently intended to be about Shirley Robinson, a young woman he met in Gloucester. This second section presents his time with her in Cromwell Street, punctuated with episodes about his wife Rose and Rose's father, but he drifts back into his memories of Anna, making much of how happy they were with his two young daughters. This section weaves around descriptions of Rena's promiscuity and a party Rena took him to where young girls were sexually abused. West killed Anna in 1967, Rena in 1971 and Shirley in 1978. Both Anna and Shirley were pregnant by West at the time he killed them.

Nowhere is there any mention of the deaths of any of his victims – Anna McFall and Shirley Robinson just cease to be mentioned on the page – and nor does it give any hint of West's involvement in any killings or related activities. The form of these presentations is surely an indication of how he wanted himself to be seen in relation to the terrible actions he had committed. Should the memoir therefore be dismissed as a concoction that has the primary purpose of weaving yet more confusion and deceit to mislead others about the horrors he perpetrated? Although that is undoubtedly part of its mission, I do not think that is the only way we should read it. He was trying to explore his own personal narrative and, by writing it down, make sense to himself of what his life had been about.

The effort and determination with which he wrote his 'autobiography' suggests he was also trying to exorcise some ghosts. His self-delusion here, as throughout his life, was the very opposite of 'searching for his true self'. He certainly was not finding God. It is because West's self-delusion persists in these most personal and final of pages of his life that they allow us to understand the twisted design he constructed – walking without let or hindrance a path so dreadfully violent and depraved that the lexicon of horror soon runs dry in trying to describe it.

VARIETIES OF CRIMINAL AUTOBIOGRAPHY

The unique aspects of West's 'autobiography' become clearer when compared with those of other violent men. We can get the measure of Fred's writing by seeing how very different it is from the many other criminal autobiographies that are available.

In reading these accounts we have to remember that most people writing a memoir must consider his or her life important enough, with sufficient significant incidents, to make it noteworthy. There are some compulsive diaries I have read that record when the writer got up and whether they had their hair cut. But those are records for the author's personal use – attempts, possibly, to keep obsessive control of a reality that feels as if it might fall apart.

There are also the grand diaries of people who see themselves as part of momentous events, recording their experiences not because of their own worth, but in order to leave to posterity an account of what they have witnessed. Some diaries written by convicted offenders are written as declarations of innocence. I have read, for example, the lengthy, fluent account written by Kenneth Bianchi, one of the men convicted as a 'Hillside Strangler'. In its two hundred carefully typed pages, it describes his life story so as to show he could not possibly have been guilty of the murders for which he was convicted.

Of course, some serial killers give very lengthy interviews to provide a biographer with the account they want recorded of their deeds. Ted Bundy, who killed over thirty women during the 1970s, is very often quoted in textbooks that discuss his killings. That is because he was willing to talk to the many researchers who made contact with him. He saw the notoriety his actions had generated and wanted to bask in its flame, all the while hoping it would prolong the time until his death sentence was carried out. He even offered to contribute to the investigations into the Green River Killings[4] but had remarkably little to say that was not immediately obvious.

Then there are pseudo-philosophical treatises like those of the Marquis de Sade, often involving fictional descriptions in narratives that are used to make some claim of a special value to depravity and to argue the virtues of sin. Ian Brady,[5] the Moors Murderer, recently had such a spurious treatise published. His purpose was to exonerate his despicable activities and to defend his disdain for others by showing off his reading of philosophy.

Perhaps the most obvious abuses of autobiography are the accounts given by gangsters and violent offenders who want to be regarded as part of some villainous yet glamorous sub-culture. These men use their autobiographies to posture. They boast about the logic of their crimes, how they were defending some criminal moral code or getting rid of some low-life, or striking before they themselves were attacked. In these episodes the victim is never fit to live and the author, showing no remorse, is always in the right.

Such personal life stories tell us more about such violent criminals than they realise. They show us the black and white world they live in, one that almost caricatures the good and evil of adventure stories. Even more importantly, they reveal the role they assign themselves as fighters for pride, honour or justice. Their autobiographies are constructions, based on the reality of experience as they see it but nonetheless creations to reflect a storyline that invents the author as the hero of his own drama.

Fred West's memoir is none of these. It is at once more subtle and devious, but it also shows his remarkable naïveté. He probably thought there might be some way he could detract attention from the absolute horror of the torture and murders he had got away with for so many years, an assumption doubtless bolstered by a lifetime of being regarded as a small-time villain who was never suspected of being a serial murderer. What he describes is fictitious at many levels. Even the women he describes as doting on him had expressed their fears of him to others. Anna McFall had made it clear she was going to leave him and Shirley Robinson had hidden in her friend's room because of her fear of Fred West and his wife. The story he presents is his attempt to concoct a world as he would like us to see it, but in these inventions he tells us much about his distorted perception.

HAPPY FAMILY LIFE
The primary aim of the memoir appears to be to paint a picture of domestic happiness around the important women in his life, showing how this was punctured from time to time by the aggressive and deviant actions of others. There are frequent mentions of playing with his children and the loving relationship he had with the two lovers he focuses on: first Anna, when he was living in the caravan then, ten years later, Shirley, when he was living in Cromwell Street with his second wife, Rose. He describes a typical 'idyllic' scene:

> So we play with the girls by the river and then walk home. Anna got cakes for us all from work. We put the girls to bed, we kissed them, and said prayers with them. Anna said 'I am going to be your wife and have your babies.

In actuality, the scene he describes was far from idyllic. His first wife, Rena, who was the mother of the two girls – only one of whom was Fred's daughter – was moving in and out of his life. Very soon after the events he describes, he killed Anna McFall, who was pregnant with his child. There were also many terrifying, violent sexual assaults of young women and girls – most, if not all, carried out by West[6] in the area around the time of his supposed idyll with Anna.

It should not be forgotten that he was writing about events that took place more than two decades earlier. It is extremely unlikely that he could remember the details of daily life from that long ago. It is much more plausible that what he was doing was conjuring up some generalised image of the life he wanted to remember. This is the image of the hard-working family man whose main pleasures were playing with his young daughters and enjoying the love of the women in his life.

RECREATING SEXUAL ACTIVITIES

This idyllic vision, though, is paper-thin. Descriptions of his tranquil play and prayers with his little girls frequently give way to accounts that have a much more intense sexual quality. And when he tries to describe Anna's love for him, he cannot resist recreating images of sexual arousal:

> you Do Not have to ask Me When you Wont Me to be
> With Me Just have Me I hame yours you Just undress me
> no one Else ever Will, I Will Make shor of that When I
> said I Was yours I Ment it. So I got out of bed and
> undress ana Slowley fold it yp and put it on a chairby the
> Bed ana Body felt like silk and a smill of spring flower
> ana said this is Me doyou still Love Me I said Yes now
> you can put Me to Bed I put my harms a round ana and
> Kiss on the lips it Was so Wonderful but strange to be
> Kiss By a angel that
> Loved you

Here Fred West is creating an erotic dream of sex whenever he wants it with an attractive young woman. For a man who found it so difficult to write, he does remarkably well in feeding in the details to imply how loving and conventional this sex scene is. He tells us he folded her nightdress 'slowly', thereby creating the impression of genteel, languorous sensuality. He mentions kissing her 'on the lips', a comment that only becomes noteworthy if you ask where else he might have kissed her. Then we have Anna asking to be put to bed, again creating an almost childlike air of innocence. West is building a picture of conventional, consensual sexuality. He is telling us that his relationship with Anna was caring and reciprocal and above all lacking in any deviance or depravity. This shows he knew how to weave such a web of deceit. The account also reveals by what it hides. He knew that his violent sexual assaults, in which binding and torturing young women were commonplace, were what would lead him to be convicted. He does not deny these actions directly, but instead recreates the image of harmonious sexual relationships, implying that he was not the sort of man who took part in the sadistic sexual attacks that probably caused the death of his many victims.

His natural skill at spinning a yarn is also apparent in the reference to Anna's touch and smell. We can hear in this writing how he would have lured susceptible young women, often yearning for some human warmth, into what seemed to be a cosy, even loving atmosphere. This apparently harmless man, seemingly doting on his young children, was barely able to string a coherent sentence together but could nonetheless imply deep, if rather banal, emotions laced with sexual innuendo and flattery. The way he tells this story helps us to understand how Anna McFall, a vulnerable teenager five years his junior, could have initially been swayed by his sentimental chat and his pretence of being a happy family man.

But the most important message he builds this scene around is that Anna was a willing lover, offering herself to him. The idea that he could rape is pushed out of view not by a crass denial but by the much subtler process of describing how a young woman wanted him and his baby. He is using the ploy of many criminals throughout history: 'Why would I want to take that when I already have all this?'

This is a picture he paints over and over again in his memoir. Across the 111 pages he describes 'making love' and 'having sex' on average at least once on every four of his lined paper pages. Interestingly, though typically, he 'makes love' with Anna McFall but usually 'has sex' with Shirley Robinson. He writes that Shirley had told him she was a lesbian, and that the initial reason he had sex with her was out of curiosity:

I hade Never Made Love to a Lesbian Wonderd What it Wood be Like so I said yes

There can be little doubt that for most men (and probably quite a high proportion of women) freely available undemanding sex is a common fantasy. But West shows in his memoir, as he insisted in police interviews, that for him this was no fantasy. In his own mind he had lived in a world where consensual sex was readily available from attractive young women. Such sexual availability was of great importance to him from an early age partly because it was never curbed, and was moreover even actively encouraged within his family. Many of the other incidents he describes when referring to the actions of those around him were also sexual: voyeurism, incest, prostitution and 'parties' in which drugged young girls were sexually abused. For an ill-educated, not-very-bright man for whom existence probably did not make a lot of sense, the satisfaction he got from sexual activity was paramount. It gave a dominant focus to his life. As his son Stephen said, 'Everything was sex for Fred.'

Fred West had learned early in his life that his sexual desires were there to be satisfied. Sex became his driving fascination. This was not sex as anger or enjoyment of sexual power; it was the crude indulgence of his urges in any way he could find. When he found in Rose a mate who shared his lack of any inhibitions and wanted to push the boundaries even further, he needed to create a place in which those indulgences could be satisfied unimpeded. A quick attack on a strange woman out alone may have sufficed when he was younger, but as he honed his appetites this would no longer satisfy him. He needed to spend time with his victims in order to indulge his obsessions. He wanted them available whenever he felt the need. They had to be quite powerless, so that his only concern would be his own satisfaction. Throughout his formative years he had found that all this was possible, provided it was kept within the bounds of family and home. He had to create a habitat, a special place, into which he could entice unsuspecting victims and gorge his sexual craving without fear of disturbance.

6. THE SUSTAINING WEB

ACCEPTANCE OF DEVIANCE

Beyond the family idyll and the erotic scenes with Anna and Shirley, the memoir also presents West's pretence of being a moral guardian against people doing wrong. He describes a number of incidents that are clearly deviant and usually illegal. Some of these describe episodes involving his first wife, Rena, but they mainly deal with activities in Cromwell Street with his second wife Rose, her father and, in this case, Rose's sister Glenys:

> one Night Bill ask Me to take Glenis home With his van so on the Way I said to her do you have sex With other Men she said o yes I said and With your Dad yes but he pays Well I said do you no he is haveing sex With Rose she said yes he give her money to. so it Was for Money is daughter Was doing it for

Looking behind what is actually written, we can see once more the implications carried in how the events are presented to us. This subtlety is especially clear in his account of Glenys's reaction to having sex with her father, who was also regularly sleeping with Rose.

As a way of showing this was not part of Fred's own normal activities, but yet another illustration of the criminal activities of others, he manages to imply the incest was something he stumbled upon. He neatly sets the scene as a confidential setting to which he did not normally have access – one night when, unusually, he is giving Glenys a lift home. In the course of this he implies he discovers the significance of the promiscuous depravity and incest, which of itself he takes as a matter of course. The explanation of these actions is what he wants to tell us – a father paying his daughters for sex.

He leads us to believe that the participants in this took it for granted as acceptable. The response he assigns to Glenys's 'o yes' is full of the innuendo of ready acceptance, even an enthusiastic endorsement of the commonplace. The financial essence of the transaction is also captured in the comment that any labourer could make of his employer: 'He pays well'. West is indicating that the immoral people he is describing, who sink to the especially low depths of incestuous prostitution, surround him.

Yet his moral stance here is far from secure. In so far as he uses punctuation at all, West seems to use full stops like other people would use paragraphs. He ends the final comment with a full stop and moves on immediately to another incident. This means that we must take as the main critique, the reason why this incident was so revealing to West, the way in which he concludes this episode: '[Bill's] daughter was doing it for money.' He details that both Glenys and Rose have sex for money with their father, and elaborates on Glenys's defence that the money was good. The prurient quality here is not about incest but about the financial nature of the transaction. The incest of his wife is passed over; Glenys's promiscuity 'with other men' is not commented upon.

West's account of this episode shows the extent to which he accepts the depravity he was part of. Rather than any comment on the incest as such, for him the most notable part of the events, to which he draws attention, and elaborates, is that daughters were paid to have sex with their father. It seems West wants to tell us that what made this unacceptable was that it was a financial transaction.

West follows on immediately from this conversation with Glenys to describe another incident with his father-in-law, Bill Letts, in which West accidentally happened upon him peeping on girls having a bath:

> I Look up to the roof at the back of the cafe ther Was Bill he hade sacking over him By the bathroom Window, I said What you doing up there he sais SHSS he cam down to Me he said I pick up two young Girll in Bristol how Wer caming to Gloucester and they stay the Night and there haveing a bath to gether if you get up on the roof you can see them I said No Way I hame not in to that

West is telling us he is not a pervert. He says he is 'not into that', but he does not suggest that he challenged Bill at all. There are many accounts that West was very much 'into' voyeurism, even setting up cameras in 25 Cromwell Street to be able to watch others engage in sex. But here he describes the extent of the trouble that Bill went to in order to be able to watch the girls unseen, as a way of implying his own distance from such activities.

The sections dealing with the promiscuity and sexual deviance of others contrast strongly with his accounts of his own sexual conquests. These are all rose-tinted, showered in love and delight, utterly distinct from the tawdry voyeurism and casual incest he sees around him. Although this is transparently an invention to cast the best possible light on his own activities, the detail and conviction with which he writes of his own sexual exploits shows that he believed he had had loving relationships with these women. These were women whom he knew he had killed, cut up and buried.

The misdeeds of others, which are contrasted with his own heavenly love life, are not presented with any sense of great moral outrage, but rather with a feeling that it was naughty and somewhat unfair for the rules of the game to be broken in that way. This is a very concrete level of morality. It is a knowledge of what is right and wrong but no understanding of *why* something is right or wrong. A morality that works by such simple rules is not a deeply held set of beliefs. It ends up making anything for which you do not get caught acceptable. Typically this is the morality of a child.

If you can build a place in which your own concrete morality rules, then you can, without conscience, present a totally different picture to the rest of the world. It is easy to convince yourself that what you tell and show others is an acceptable part of the game that need not be connected to what you do within your own house. But to maintain this division between the private and the public face, you must have control over your domain. This domain is a web, a vulnerable structure that you build stealthily, and is consequently difficult to move.

A HIDDEN WORLD WITH ITS OWN RULES

The bizarre, abnormal and highly sexualised universe he created in Cromwell Street does emerge from West's journal, even when he is describing what he seems to think shows his own moral stature.

> I had a accident on a priss at Work and Wint to hospital for treatment. I stopped at home to see Rose it Was about eleven p.m. Rose Was in Bed so I Went in to the Bedroom to Rose I didnot put the Light on in the room. I sat at the bottom of the bed I Was telling Rose What I had did to my hand at Work then anna cam runing down the stairs, and said to Rose Grampy going to sleep With Me anna had Not seen Me anna thought I Was at Work. Rose said go back to Bed hes Not going to eat you he only going to f— you. Rose said to anna I ham shor you Will Love that. I said What going on. Rose said anna bean going out with Dad for Mials ana drinking so she sould give him her body to play With I said to Rose your Dad is out.

Once again we see West's implication that it was only by accident that he tripped over this revelation when, unseen in a dark bedroom, his daughter Anna Marie unwittingly let him know what his wife had known all along. West is also indicating here, by the way, that he intended his memoir for publication, putting the coy 'f—' in the midst of what most people would regard as an outrageous scenario. West's reaction is not to berate Rose but just to make Bill leave:

> I Wint up stair to him and said What going on anna Was With Me Bill said Rose said anna could sleep With Me, but anna playing up I said What ar you on about I said to Bill your out of this house in the Morning.

However, it is far from a serious punishment. He is to leave 'in the morning'. Also, Bill's argument that Anne Marie's mother sanctions the sex, but it was West's daughter who was to blame for 'playing up', is never commented on. West does not wish to explore this can of worms, implying that it makes no sense at all – 'what are you on about?' – and gives Bill his marching orders.

Let us not forget we have here the writings of a man in prison for having inflicted the most brutal and heartless assaults on young women for a period of over a quarter of a century. The police were digging up bodies in the basement and garden of his house on a daily basis. He was briefing his solicitor and being interviewed by the police in preparation for what he must have known would be the most intense trial. Yet in writing a memoir that was clearly intended to provide some sort of exoneration for his actions, the strongest example he can pull out of his own moral fibre is to tell his father-in-law to leave in the morning because his daughter does not wish to have sex with him.

West shows further how he understood the actions that were needed to cope with this terrible state of affairs:

> I Went With anna to her Room, anna told Me Rose had
> been sleeping With her Dad and Now Mum got Men
> coming from the pub at night When your at Work, and
> Mum told Me to sleep With her Dad so he didnot go
> down stairs to Mum Room.

He uncovers the fact that the reason for Anna Marie sleeping with her grandfather was to free up his wife to take in clients. Again West expresses no concerns about this state of affairs and clearly does not see any need to raise the matter with his wife. It is more of an administrative problem to be solved so that Anna Marie can avoid doing something she does not want to do.

> I Went and got the key to anna room and told anna to
> lock her Door, I Went back to Work, When I got home
> in the morning, Rose and her Dad Was in the kitchen
> haveing Breakfast he Live Well. he said to me haveI got
> to go I said yes, Wer can I go I said to the cafe ther Was a
> flat on top of the cafe you can go there so he Went there

Anna Marie was just to lock herself away and Fred could then go off to work. In the morning he dealt with the matter.

Not by exposing Bill to the police, or making sure he never came near again, but merely by moving him to the flat above their café. His only comment about his child-molesting father-in-law is a sarcastic aside that he 'lived well', meaning he had a cushioned life in contrast with Fred, who apparently worked all the hours available.

It might be argued that Fred West was afraid of going to the police or fearful of authority in general, but he knew he had created a sealed world that the authorities could not penetrate. When it suited him, however, he was only too happy to imply he was a stalwart citizen and report wrongdoing:

> I Was told that Bill hade bought a gun I Went and ask to see it, it Was a hand gun it Look real one he allway had it With him so I ask the police to have a Look at it I Was told later that the police hade it of him

It seems most likely that, given the apparent animosity between them, West was afraid that Bill might use the gun against him. Bill had not mentioned it directly to Fred, who 'was told' about it and had to 'ask to see it', learning later that his ruse had been successful and the police had taken the gun away. He would use the authorities to his own ends whenever he wanted to. Early on in the memoir he describes a visit from Social Services about his children:

> the Man from the children departmint came on time but What a Waste of time he Was and space he Was. ana and I ask him to help us to get a house he said No but he could put the children in a home ana Was geting up set so I ask hime to Leave and Not to come back. so he Went, the children had Never been so Well Look after

The deprivations of the two young girls he had in the caravan, who were looked after by the seventeen-year-old Anna, and the way they were moved around between Fred and Rena, are now well documented. Here West is using the children as a bargaining ploy to get a house. When this is clearly not working he is very ready to frighten away the 'man from the children's department', and does so with apparent ease. The quest for a house and the role of children in the ploys of West turn out to be perhaps the most revealing aspects of the memoir.

THE THEME OF BABIES

Although the journal recounts tales of promiscuity and incest, and is spiced with many episodes of love-making and repeated incidents in which Fred West is the innocent victim of violent circumstances, it always comes back to two themes. One is the time West spent with his children, looking after them to save them from their predatory mother, and how they were shunted back and forth between them, ending up in the loving care of Anna.

The other theme, most curious and, I think, most significant of all, concerns the constant references to Anna, and later Shirley, wanting his baby. Fred West claimed to have fathered 42 children. There is no evidence he ever used contraception, so this is perfectly possible. Yet he took little interest in his many offspring, not even always remembering the names of their mothers. In fact, outside the imaginings of his memoir, he was often only too happy for his first wife Rena or the social services to take the children off his hands from time to time. Yet over and over again he takes the opportunity to mention that Anna and Shirley wanted to have – and were going to have – his baby. For Anna, he claims the baby was an expression of her love for him:

> ana telling Me she loveed me and Wonted My Baby I put
> my harms a round ana and Kiss her We then Made Love
> We Wer in heaven

West was more puzzled about Shirley's reasons for wanting a baby:

> so We hade sex I said you ar not to tell Rose she said No,
> sherley said I Wont a baby, I said What for your a
> Lesbian she said I have a Girll friend in Bristol and We
> Wood Like a baby. I said no baby, a baby has to hove a
> Mother and father Not two Girll. Whatabout When the
> child going to school.

But even here he quickly moves to thinking about the difficulties of maintaining the secret world he thought a lesbian couple would need. The main problem would be what would happen 'when the child went to school' and presumably revealed the unorthodox household she was living in. As his writing progressed, though, Fred claims that Shirley had significance for him because she 'was having his baby':

I Went to see shirley 2 or 3 time I Mist her We got on so
Well together and shirley Was haveing my baby

The theme of Anna's desire to have West's baby is also a constant refrain. He mentions her planning her dates and that they did not use any contraception. There are over twenty mentions of Anna's desire for a baby and of her conceiving across the 111 pages. When he mentions Shirley, much more briefly, her desire to have his baby crops up at least ten times.

I've puzzled long over these asides and comments about Anna and Shirley bearing his children, and how it preyed on his mind, alongside the meandering, repetitive descriptions of looking after his children, playing in the park, and having tea and breakfast with them, with many 'kisses and cuddles'. These are all set against the backdrop of his dense, dark, interior world: his attempts to recapture the sexual excitement he had had with Anna and Shirley whilst maintaining a Mills and Boon image of love, but all the time trying to find opportunities to indicate how hard done by he was; his being beaten up by 'yobs' and taken to sex parties he didn't want to go to; his trying to control the rapaciousness of his wives and father-in-law.

What is going on here? We know his children were subjected to the most terrible tortures, strapped to their beds, living in fear of their parents and sexually abused from an early age, with the added terror of what Fred and Rose would do to them if their suffering were ever discovered. What was West doing by presenting this cereal-box advert picture of happy family life with an 'angel' who was going to bear his child?

No psychological assessment is available of Fred West. It would have been a brave and extremely competent psychologist who could have got him to confront his actions and explore their implications. West would have taken every opportunity to evade, distort and invent whatever he could if he thought it would let him off the hook for that day. He had admitted the murders to the police but never really admitted to himself that he had done any harm. I can only think that he bolstered his protection of his psyche from total meltdown by maintaining in his own mind the bucolic image of happy family life which is the constant refrain that he returns to over and over again in his journal.

Yet nagging away at that image was the memory that the creation of this domestic paradise was intertwined with Anna McFall carrying his baby. This baby would have been another child in his household to contribute to the image of the happy family atmosphere. Yet he had killed Anna before she had even delivered the baby. This dead baby was a wound on the canvas he was painting that became inflamed when he remembered the same thing happening with Shirley Robinson. He had killed both of them at a time that he was trying to portray as one of heavenly joy because of their pregnancy. He must have remembered how totally he had destroyed that joy by killing them. His fascination with Anna's baby and its significance to him was gruesomely demonstrated when Anna's body was disinterred. The baby had been cut out of Anna after her death. West had buried it next to her.

THE SUSTAINING WEB
His memoir makes it clear that when he originally left Gloucestershire for Glasgow he soon got out of his depth, and had to escape back to the area he knew well – where his family would keep quiet about his violent assaults and where the leisurely pace of small-town, mainly rural life would keep the pressure from the authorities light enough for him to deal with. The caravans in which he set up home with Rena and Anna gave him the independence to start inventing the narcissistic world in which he could explore his sexual appetites. But even if the anonymity of the caravan park kept him away from prying eyes, the limited, essentially temporary space crowded his desires. The crammed flats he stayed in with Rose also constrained their freedom of action.

Fred West, aided by his wife Rose and supported by her family and the clients for her sexual services, needed a controlled environment – a lair within which he could do as he pleased. He could only sustain the myth of happy domesticity that would keep the authorities at bay and ensnare vulnerable victims if he had a place of his own in which to build the castle of his dreams. 25 Cromwell Street gave him just the setting he needed, at the same time providing somewhere safe to bury the bodies.

What emerges from West's journal is the closed, incestuous, unthreatened, protected world he created for himself, most particularly when he got to Cromwell Street. The self-centred nature of this world is clear in one remarkably simple way: he never explains who any of the characters are in the story he creates. Any person writing for a public audience knows that the strangers he is trying to communicate with will need to be told who the main characters are, and what their relationship is with the author. But Fred West is oblivious to this. He assumes the reader knows who everyone is. It takes close reading and some careful research to work out whom he is writing about. Across his poorly handwritten pages, West presents a picture of himself to the world with apparently total conviction. By believing this invention, and separating off in his mind this fictional domestic bliss from his vile actions, he was able to continue to create this secret world convincingly. So plausible was this world that when people called round from time to time looking for young women, he and Rose were able to convince them of their own innocence.

The more I read this autobiography the more aware I become of the remarkably skilful and clever way he used his incoherence and lack of fluency to create the image of the bumbling yokel, devoted to a happy family life. He knew with a streetwise native wit how to tailor the image of domestic bliss, allowing him to concoct a seductive world that would simultaneously be attractive to vulnerable young women and delude the authorities. It needed to be a world he had total control over; like a spider's web, almost invisible until its prey is trapped in it.

His home had to be the focus of his criminal activities, its dark core, for psychological reasons as much as for practical ones. His memoir is obsessively concerned with the small world of his family and particularly the attempt to mingle erotic memories with declarations of love from the women he remembered. Feeling and believing that he had once lived such a carefree existence gave him the illusion that he could build it again. It was the very existence of his house – that he could extend and shape, with rooms for his children and lodgers, cellars and places to keep his tools – that gave him the confidence to continue with his depravity. The psychological power of the house came from the way he could impose upon it his vision of the golden age of domestic bliss that he had had with Anna McFall.

SUICIDE

Fred West lived a life of unimaginable evil and confessed to many horrific murders, never showing any shred of regret or remorse. He seemed to think that he was one step ahead of the police, changing his story from one interview session to the next. He hinted at other revelations that would support his innocence. It is easy to see why he might have believed that he could walk free once again. At 53, he could look back on a life in which he had been able to get away with the murder of young women year after year. From his earliest rape of his 13-year-old sister (for which the charges were dropped), on to the derisory fine of £25 for the violent torture and rape of a young woman to whom he had given a lift, and his frequent contact with Social Services, West had found that his bumbling, meandering chat could take in officials and young girls alike. In his journal he had even concocted a world of innocent love in which he was the hardworking husband and concerned citizen trying to do the best he could amidst incest, promiscuity and violence. Why then, after six months in prison, did he commit suicide? He was found hanging behind the door of his cell on New Year's Day 1995.

Fred West had indicated to a few people close to him that he was feeling desperate about his plight. The son who visited him reported tearful visits. These tears never seem to have been for his victims but for himself.

He was aggrieved that the wife to whom he had professed undying love (although his journal is full of accounts of cheating her), and for whom he had without doubt killed some of his young sex partners, had turned away from him and would not even look at him when they stood in the dock together in court. But as important, perhaps, was the fact that the police had taken his house apart, brick by brick. The foundations of his world had literally and symbolically been dug up. The web he had created had been destroyed.

His house meant everything to him. The memoir shows what he wanted to create there and how this focus to his life provided so much support for his egotistical yearnings. With the destruction of his house he had nowhere to go. Suicide emerges out of a narrowing of the mental focus,[1] a feeling that there is no way out of the black impasse in which one feels trapped. It is also characterised by a distortion of memory in which everything one looks back upon is seen as negative and painful. Many people who commit suicide cannot remember anything about their lives that is joyful. Fred West, natural storyteller that he was, did not seem to finish his memoir with any strong flourish. There is no summing up of his life or his mission. Amongst the single sheets, notes and letters he left, it is impossible to be certain of the last thing he wrote. His journal seems to end rather as it began:

> I would have lik'd to know about ana passed but ana
> would not tell me and allways siad her live began when
> she met me in glasgow what moor could I ask for in life
> to be loved by an angle ana and I wnet back to the tanker
> ana went home to sandhers lan

It is as if he just abandoned the journal at this point. A few days later it seems he decided to kill himself, and wrote a letter to Rose saying he would be with her in the afterlife. Perhaps the effort of creating the world of his journal eventually broke through his defences. He saw how destructive his life had been and how, through his own evil actions, he himself had ensured that the heavenly love he had aspired to with Anna McFall could never be.

7. DARKNESS VISIBLE

'WHERE I COULD FEEL AT HOME'

Fred West and his memoir educate us into understanding the profound personal significance that the home can have for some criminals. We can see how the mixture of psychological and practical import enables this physical location to become the motor for their criminality, the heart of their personal journey from which they set out and to which they return. It can be a haven in which the murderer gains respite from the adventure on which he has been engaged – or, as in West's case, it is the object of their journey itself. The purpose for killers like West is to people their lair with potential victims who will be manipulated into playing a role in their vicious dramas.

West's memoir shows the intense, emotionally charged, supremely egocentric, highly sexualised inner world of Fred West. To sustain this he needed to build a place that would facilitate his crimes. Such a web had to seem benign, even inviting. With his cheeky turns of phrase and sexual innuendo, this rambling, apparently inarticulate local may have seemed unthreatening – but possibly quite exciting – to impressionable young women. We know that this web was virtually invisible to those around him. The memoir, both in what it neglects to tell us and in what it so overtly sets out to tell us, reveals the hidden world of Fred West. If only there had been eyes to see, the very invisibility of the web he created was a major clue to its existence.

For serial killers who are building a secret domain to inhabit, the only hint of their activity is people going missing. But all too often no one notices that these victims have disappeared. Killers like Fred West become highly skilled at spotting possible victims who could disappear without leaving tell-tale traces on police maps. No record is held that the person has not been seen for some time, and no body is found.

For West and many other serial killers their home is at the core of their criminal activity. As we have seen, many other criminals do not travel far to commit their crimes. West's intense account of his own vision of his family life goes some way to explain why most criminals do not journey beyond the bounds of the familiar. It is due to more than criminal laziness and familiarity with the opportunities for crime around the home. We need to get beyond the general idea[1] of a 'comfort zone' in which the offender feels most at ease. This begs the question of what gives rise to this 'comfort' beyond familiarity with the area and knowledge of the possibilities it offers for unprotected victims.

John Wayne Gacy had been operating in a rather similar way to Fred West during the 1970s, burying under the floor of his house or in its garden the adolescent boys he raped then killed. In total the bodies of 32 youths were found in and around his ranch-style house at Norwood near Chicago. Gacy's murderous career has become the subject of many films, in part because this Junior Chamber of Commerce 'Man of the Year' was apparently such a stalwart citizen. He epitomises the criminal who has a more than acceptable public persona – he performed as Pogo the Clown at children's parties – whilst living a deadly private life. He turned his house into a hidden world into which he could lure victims. Over and over again people searched for those who had disappeared but it took the local police a long time to trace them all back to Gacy.

A decade before West was arrested, Dennis Nilsen also created a black hole from which many of his victims never escaped. He was a quiet clerical officer in the Department of Employment whose promiscuous homosexuality went unquestioned. Between 1978 and 1983 he picked up gay men in Soho bars and took them back to his house. But he didn't just pick up any men he fancied. Like Fred West, he had an eye for homeless young people, offering them a drink and somewhere to stay. He killed them as they slept and then dismembered their bodies so that he could dispose of them. He started by burying them in his garden and then, when he moved to a flat, he hid the bodies under the floorboards and tried to flush body parts down the toilet.

Remarkably a number of victims survived being attacked by him, but they were so much part of a nefarious underworld that their experiences never saw the light of day. At least fifteen young men were not so lucky; Nilsen managed to kill these unfortunate victims and dispose of their bodies. He was only exposed when the smell of his blocked sewers led to the discovery of the body parts.

The 1990s opened with reports of the Milwaukee murders in which Jeffrey Dahmer was revealed as perhaps one of the most deranged serial killers of the late twentieth century. He killed seventeen young men who he brought back to his apartment. He moved within the gay community, notably the bathhouses where untrammeled promiscuity was the norm, finding young men who would return home with him. His violence and drugging of the youths he picked up had had him banned from a number of these places over the years. Within this unseen society warnings certainly circulated about Dahmer's dangers, but the disappearing young men were not linked to this apparently urbane, well-educated, blue-eyed, blond 30-year-old.

Dahmer managed to present such a convincing account of himself that the police actually returned one of his victims to him for his care. Dahmer had drugged Konerak Sinthasomphone as part of the routine he had developed to control his victims. When Dahmer went to buy some beer Konerak, in a highly confused state, managed to escape. The police were called to help a very dazed youth wandering the streets 'butt-naked'. But Dahmer, coming out of the store, coolly said that Konerak was his lover and had had too much to drink. Despite the protestations of neighbours, who did not trust what Dahmer was saying, the police took control[2] and helped to return Konerak to Dahmer's apartment, insisting that their long-standing expertise should override the suspicions of mere members of the public.

Once the police had left, Dahmer, as he had with his other victims, strangled Konerak, had oral sex with the corpse and then dismembered the body. He kept the head in the freezer and the torso in a 57-gallon drum in his bedroom. The head was eventually stripped of its flesh and prepared as a skull to join the other mementoes on the 'shrine' that Dahmer was creating.[3]

As with so many other serial killer investigations, there were many occasions when Jeffrey Dahmer's killings came close to being detected. Gacy, Nilsen, West and, as we shall see, Dutroux, did not live in some hidden backwoods where no one knew them. They were known and there were suspicions about them that were not acted upon. But we need to understand why there was the reluctance to act. It was because there was no co-ordinated map of the suspicions tied into known disappearances.

This invisibility grows out of the killers' focus on their own dens. They bring their prey back to the world they are creating as much in their heads as in their houses. We have read how West built this image of himself and his family life. Jeffrey Dahmer also indicated the importance to him of the inner world he was creating. He needed to enshrine his fascination with bodies, especially dead bodies, and brought his victims into his apartment for the early stages of that ritualistic creation. He was planning to build a reliquary that would display the various reminders of his deadly sexual conquests. When asked what the purpose of this display was he replied that it was 'a place where I could feel at home'.

These invisible abductors and rapists are not confined to the last century. In April 2003 the police arrested John Jamelske, a 67-year-old who had not had a job for over a quarter of a century. He had built a concrete dungeon under his house in the wealthy DeWitt suburb of New York, consisting of two rooms twelve feet square and eight feet high. Hundreds of beer bottles that he had collected hid the steel door that gave access to the underground tunnel from his house that led to the bunker.

There he kept women he had abducted for months and, in some cases, years. Controlling every aspect of their lives, he raped them as often as once a day. Eventually he let most of them go, confident that he had frightened them so much that they would not report him, or that they were so marginal in society that if they did they would not be believed. In a sad parallel to the neighbours who tried to save Konerak, one of Jamelske's victims, a 53-year-old immigrant, reported that when she informed the Syracuse police that she had been held captive, 'They pounded the table with their fists and said I was ... making up a story ... if someone gets kidnapped, they don't come home alive.'

Jamelske was also alert to victims whose disappearance would make few ripples, including youngsters who had run away from home, a drug addict and an immigrant whose poor English would feed the racial prejudice of any authority figures with whom she came into contact. As ever, the separateness of the different agencies served his invisibility too. One victim spoke to the Syracuse police and the other to the sheriff's department of Onondaga County, where Syracuse is situated. Neither department had any knowledge of the kidnapping reported to the other within these overlapping jurisdictions, so neither could add up the blips on the radar screen that might have indicated a common source.

All these ensnaring serial killers manage to create lairs out of which no information escapes. Like astronomical 'black holes' they are dense, imploding places that tear apart anything that enters them. Therefore if these places are to be located, we must learn from astronomers and use the very lack of information that reveals their presence. It was the social worker looking for the West's missing daughter, on whom there was no information, who opened the lid on 25 Cromwell Street. To detect their earliest crimes and identify these murderers we need better, co-ordinated pictures of what crimes are happening where. These criminals can show up on virtual images if we compile them effectively.

THE CREATION OF WEST'S BLACK HOLE
A short walk from the centre of the old city of Gloucester, Cromwell Street is an unprepossessing, quietly seedy little street built at the turn of the century to house shopkeepers and office workers. It now has a strange gap in the houses halfway down one side that is a pathway through a pleasant garden, much used by local children on their bikes. This gap, next door to a Seventh·Day Adventist church, is made all the more incongruous by the bollards that stop motorists using it as a short-cut, and the odd tourist who stops to look at this hole where once a two-storey terraced house stood. The gap in the houses, like a missing tooth in an old man's smile, seems all the more unexpected because this is not a town still recovering from bombs of the Second World War, like other cities in Britain that took two generations to finally fill in

long-forgotten scars. The scar here is the product of a much more focused, evil activity. This is the place where 25 Cromwell Street once stood.

The house Fred and Rose had lived in earlier, in Midland Street, is in a much more run-down area, on the other side of a major road, cutting it off from the town. You can readily see how Fred and Rose would feel they were moving up-market to be nearer the city centre and to be somewhat more anonymous and unchallenged, just a short walk from the main shops. Fred did not keep out of view, though. This was not the anonymous stranger next door. Chatting to people around Gloucester, especially in Cromwell Street, generates many spontaneous comments about people whose mothers were offered a bed at number 25, people whose friend married into the West family, or people who turned down a late-night offer of a lift from Fred in his van. Many people have their Fred West story.

When the police told West they were digging up his patio his reaction was remarkably dismissive – he asked if he could go home and commented that they should be sure to put the patio back the way it was. It is easy to see this as an attempt at humour but it also reflected the way West's house was the special world he had carefully structured it to be – the place within which he could continue his debauchery with Rose and anyone they could entrap.

West made no reference in his memoir to the many young women who he brutally tortured for sheer pleasure and then raped and murdered. His journal is devoted to descriptions of his apparently loving relationship with two women who became pregnant with his children. This does not mean he had forgotten the many women he had killed. It is rather a reflection of the cruel distance from his victims that carried across into all his relationships. Between sessions writing his journal he was also being interviewed regularly by the police. During that time he confessed to many of the murders. He remembered them only too well. When the police took him back to the basement in Cromwell Street to point out and explain who was buried there he spoke of seeing his victims as happy spirits. This was how he thought of them, ignoring the terror of their murder and dismemberment.

Curiously his memoir is a public display written as an expression of how he wanted others to see him. His confessions to the police seem to have been something more private that he did not think of as being heard outside the interview room. The absence of any reference to any of the killings in his memoir and the way he ignored even mentioning most of his victims can therefore be seen as having direct parallels in the lack of any outward sign at the time that the crimes were happening. The house held its secrets until a specialist search team arrived at Cromwell Street with a warrant. They had no idea of what they would unearth. Over eleven days the house was taken apart. The remains of nine young women were found buried in the garden, under the patio and in the cellar. No one will ever know exactly how they died or the extent of the suffering they endured.

The house became so notorious and the concern of the local authority over the ghoulish interest it could create so great that the house was demolished and converted into a path and garden between the terraced houses.

As Karl Marx pointed out in the rather different context of *Das Kapital*, what distinguishes the most sophisticated bee from the most lowly architect is that the architect first builds his constructions in his head. Fred West, lowly builder that he was, had a mental image of what he wanted to achieve and 25 Cromwell Street allowed him to construct that image in reality. A builder by trade, he had turned his house into a private world for debauchery, into which he and his wife Rose could lure his victims and control them before killing them and burying their bodies. Rose had a room upstairs where Fred could watch her having sex with the men he brought home for her. There were microphones around the house so he could hear his family.

He maintained a cellar – a dungeon, really – where he imprisoned and sexually tortured his victims, including his own children, and eventually buried some of them. Every floor of this anonymous house told stories of violence, of fear, of murder: the bedrooms where victims were tied up and abused; the cellars where others died and were buried. Like other secret killers he created his own small, deceitful worlds, literally building his own hidden territory in which he could violate and kill his victims then hide the bodies. These serial killers form a distinct type. They do not commit their crimes on their travels, and nor do they maraud outwards to find opportunities for rape or murder. They do not find targets in places in which crimes are possible then return to their base. They entice their victims into their lair: their home that seems so ordinary, welcoming even, but that is the hidden focus of their dark activities.

The house is the main witness to their hidden depravity. Eventually it is this web they have constructed that reveals their guilt, giving up its secrets, when it is eventually questioned.

FINDING BLACK HOLES

Astronomers tell us there are certain cosmic bodies – vast, dense collapsed stars – so massive that their gravitational fields drag in not only all the matter in their vicinity but even light itself. In the taste for graphic labelling that marks astronomers out from other more down-to-earth scientists they call these stupendous collapsed suns 'black holes'. It is difficult for me as a psychologist to fathom what a 'white hole' would be, but the colour of these holes signifies that nothing can get out of them: no information of any sort. Against the darkness of the sky, black is the colour of invisibility.

These extraordinary phenomena are so far beyond our daily comprehension that no sooner had they been described by scientists than they became the stuff of fantastic fiction. Such indulgence in exotic storylines typically ignores the fact that black holes would tear solar systems apart and, more importantly, they neglect the most remarkable aspect of black holes – that they were discovered at all. How did astronomers searching the heavens become aware of these hellish points? If no light escaped from them then how could they be seen? The method of discovery was as unexpected as many criminal detections. At the very core of swirling cosmic stellar activity nothing could be seen. It was this absence against the backdrop of activity that forced them to realise something special was happening where nothing could be perceived.

Astronomers play tricks with the stars all the time. They create images that capture the background buzz of energy in

3. WHERE FRED WEST'S VICTIMS DISAPPEARED

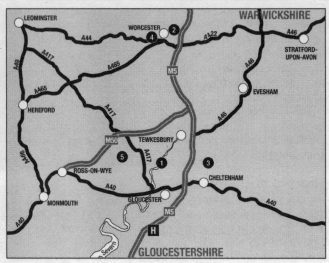

1. Caroline Owens, November 1972. Last seen on the outskirts of Tewkesbury by the Gupshill Manor Public House

2. Carol Ann Cooper, November 1973. Was abducted from a bus stop in the Warndon area of Worcester.

3. Lucy Partington, December 1973. Last seen near a bus stop in Pittville, Cheltenham

4. Shirley Hubbard, November 1974. Was abducted by the River Severn in Worcester

5. Juanita Mott, April 1975. Was standing beside the B4215 near Newent

H = Fred and Rose West's House at 25 Cromwell St, Gloucester

the sky and colour in the high points. If there is a gap in the energy emissions it can look like a pinprick on the cloth of the sky – a black hole. It was the absence of anything visible at the very heart of violent turbulence that got astronomers interested.

Eventually they realised they had to look at these points of absent energy in new ways and started in the 1970s to measure the energy emissions from these pinpricks in the canvas of the heavens. They did not measure light as we know it – there was none – but that powerful yet invisible energy known as x-rays. The staggering discovery, like that of the bodies buried in Fred West's garden, was just how much of this secret light there was to see, desperately escaping from the turmoil of the imploding sun that had dragged everything else in with it except for these strident wisps at the end of the spectrum.

The similarity of the discovery of black holes to the discovery of the West murders is both instructive and awesome. Young women had disappeared from time to time in and around Gloucester, where Fred and Rose West were living. They just vanished from the known universe. No one seemed to notice their disappearance. As in any other city – Chicago, London, Milwaukee, New York – there are always casual visitors staying in hostels and working in cafés, passing through. Some have troubled pasts, and it is no surprise when they apparently run away. Others have long since lost regular contact with anyone who cares about them. The police may not be informed. If they are people for whom serious concern is expressed it may be extremely difficult to trace their movements in the anonymity of an open and free society. The register of missing persons merely records a sad absence, not the presence of a crime.

Following the lead of astronomers there may be other information that could point to the hidden turmoil that may be destroying these missing lives.

If the disappearances of young women around Gloucester over two decades are considered and all located on the same map, an important picture emerges. In 1973 alone three girls went missing, prompting a police search which revealed nothing. One was Lynda Gough, who went to live with the Wests. They told her parents that she had moved on, but in fact she was buried under the rear extension. Fifteen-year-old Carol Ann Cooper, who lived in a children's home, went missing in November after getting on a bus in nearby Tewkesbury. They had abducted, abused and murdered her.

Lucy Partington was less anonymous than many of the other victims. A university student and cousin of the novelist Martin Amis, her disappearance eventually affected a wider audience when her cousin chose to contemplate its effect on him in his autobiography. She vanished on her way for a bus in Cheltenham. Her remains were dug out from under 25 Cromwell Street.

If these and other similar disappearances over the same time period had been put on a map it would have shown that they were not random. They cover a distinct region with many disappearances actually in Gloucester itself, and follow Fred West around like a black trail. He had a pregnant girlfriend while he was living at a caravan park just outside the city. He buried her body in nearby countryside. His step-daughter from his first marriage disappeared from the house in Midland Road on the outskirts of Gloucester, where she was living with Fred and Rose. When her mother turned up they killed her too, burying her in nearby fields.

It is hard to believe they got away with all this. Why did the police not notice? Part of the answer has to be that he managed to make himself almost invisible in the small city. He chose his victims carefully from those young people who would not be quickly missed and then killed them as soon as there was any sign that they might draw attention to him.

There may be a way of identifying the location of offenders by using the idea that where there is a consistent absence of information this must indicate the presence of some influence causing that absence. We need to look at the missing data in new ways. Is there something similar about the victims – about how, where and when they vanished? More importantly, does the geography of their disappearances point to a centre of hidden activity that may only be seen from what is absent?

It would seem that often it is rumours that are the alternative form of energy which leads to the discovery of these deadly black holes. It was rumours that alerted a diligent detective constable, Hazel Savage, to visit Cromwell Street in search of West's daughter Heather. She persuaded senior officers to get a warrant to dig up the garden to find the girl. Only then did the grisly evidence start to emerge: the bodies of nine girls, including Heather.

When murderous criminals are so careful that nobody even realises they have killed anyone, there is nothing to put on a map. Without the pattern of activity there is no 'criminal geography' to profile. But if the absence of information about each missing young woman had been collated with the absence of information in the other cases, perhaps it might have pointed to the black hole in which these victims had been trapped and killed.

There may be many more bodies lying out in the fields and deserted farms around Gloucester. Those involved with the case, including West's son, suggest that there were many other victims: at least twenty. There are stories about officials attending the Wests' sex parties, and a mystery over hundreds of records of missing young women that themselves went missing. A geographical profile might suggest areas in which the police should look for more victims. But only if the police re-open the case and seek out more information will those missing victims have a chance of some final dignity.

THE CIRCLE OF CRIME

map of woe, that thus dost talk in signs
Shakespeare, Titus Andronicus

It would be hypothesized that no matter what scale of distances he travelled, on average his location choices would tend to be within the same range. In other words there would be the possibility of distinguishing offenders in terms of the general size of the area over which they operate.

Lundrigan, S. and Canter, D. (2001) 'A Multivariate
Analysis of Serial Murderers' Disposal
Site Location Choice',
Journal of Environmental Psychology,
21, pp. 423–432

The sense that heroism and effective action are absent, disorganized or foredoomed to defeat, and that confusion and anarchy reign over the world, is the archetypal theme of irony and satire.

Northrop Frye (1957) Anatomy of Criticism,
Princeton University Press, p. 192

8. A FRAUGHT INVESTIGATION

'MUCH HAS BEEN WITHHELD'

An attractive young woman, serenely dressed in the dark colours of mourning, stands in the dock charged with murder. Her trial will eventually change English law. Her conviction for poisoning her husband will lead to many innocent men being freed after serving long prison sentences. But at the moment the judge, only a few months later himself locked away as insane, is summing up the case against Florence (Florie to her friends) for the benefit of the jury.[1]

It is the heyday of Victorian hypocrisy, and the judge is appalled by the pretty Florence's love affair with another man and the cuckolding of her husband, the stalwart cotton merchant, James Maybrick. The crowd in the small courtroom, tucked away at the end of the grand St George's Hall that imposingly defines the centre of Liverpool, had been baying for Florie's blood when the trial started. But as the story unfolds – one of insult and abuse by her husband, who was twenty years her senior – the mood of the mob changes and the biased judge becomes their target, so much so that he has to escape the building in disguise.

These were severe times. People in authority were completely confident about their opinions. A loose woman was regarded as evil enough to have murdered her husband so that she could be free to be with her lover. Florence Maybrick was sentenced in 1889 but the public outcry against this injustice went unheeded by Queen Victoria even after the incapacity of the judge became public knowledge. It was fifteen years later in the new century, with a new king, that she obtained a pardon. The great injustice she had suffered led people to realise that a more reliable form of appeal was necessary and the appeal court as we now know it was set up, eventually leading to many high-profile judgements being found to be unsafe.

She may have suffered from prejudice as well. She was after all an American who had caught the eye of an older man when he was returning across the Atlantic to Liverpool. It was not difficult to see the penny-dreadful story in her actions. She could be portrayed as a gold-digger who had used her undoubted attractions to seduce the cotton merchant in order to gain a foothold in good society and some income to go with it.

Juries are not immune to such naïve speculation. Quite the reverse: they actively search out a plausible storyline to make sense of the facts before them. So when the judge spelt out the case against Florence they could see no alternative explanation and she was convicted. When the jury returned its verdict, which many had expected to be in her favour, she was given the traditional opportunity to respond. Her statement reverberates down the centuries in a way that perhaps she did not fully expect: '. . . much has been withheld which might have influenced the jury had it been told. I am not guilty of this crime.'

What none of them – the judge, jury or waiting crowds – could have possibly realised was that a totally different story was playing out before their eyes: a story far more bizarre and far more significant in the annals of crime. It now seems very likely indeed that the man Florence was convicted of killing, her husband, was Jack the Ripper, the vicious killer of at least five prostitutes in London's Whitechapel in the space of a few weeks in the autumn before he died.

FORGED DIARIES

There have been many claims as to the identity of the Whitechapel murderer, including most recently the bizarre suggestion that it was the painter Walter Sickert,[2] based on little more than the fact that he had painted scenes not unlike those that had been published in newspapers around the time of these most notorious murders. But none seems more outlandish and patently less plausible than the suggestion that Jack the Ripper was a pillar of the community who lived nearly 200 miles away from where the killings took place.

The evidence for this most unlikely of culprits has started to mount ever since a journal was found in 1992 purporting to have been written by James Maybrick, giving a first-person account of the deeds of Jack the Ripper. When this journal was published in the book *The Diary of Jack the Ripper* with a detailed commentary by Shirley Harrison, an established journalist and biographer, everyone assumed it was a forgery.

There was still the collective memory of the fiasco of the 'Hitler Diaries'.[3] In April 1983 the world's newspapers were agog with the discovery by the German photo-news weekly *Stern* of 62 secret diaries written by Adolf Hitler, together with 300 of his watercolours and other fascist archive material. The late Sir Hugh Trevor Roper, a distinguished historian, had not only vouched for their authenticity but had commented on their historical significance. But then their author was ignominiously unmasked.

The 'Hitler Diaries' were, after all, part of a long history of forgeries that have fooled experts. Perhaps the most audacious was in the late 1700s when Henry Ireland, whilst still in his teens, forged a whole new Shakespeare play that was performed at a Drury Lane theatre. An American counterfeiter in the late 1920s, Joseph Cosey, forged thousands of documents purporting to be in the hands of US presidents, which still circulate undetected today. Versions of Mussolini's diaries were written so skilfully by a 75-year-old Italian woman that Mussolini's own son, Vittorio, agreed that the writing was his father's.

The similarity, though, between these well-known fakes and 'The Diary of Jack the Ripper' is not as close as many have assumed. The 'Hitler Diaries' were so badly forged that the Gothic initials on their cover read TH instead of AH because their forger could not read Gothic script! Hugh Trevor Roper quickly realised the diaries were forged the minute he saw the original documents, and apologised for having been cajoled by the editors of *Stern* into lending support to their claim to authenticity on very flimsy evidence. As soon as Konrad Kujau, who forged the 'Hitler Diaries' and pictures, was unmasked, he became something of a celebrity. There is still a trade in his work, notably his pictures, which are technically much better than anything Hitler could have done. Ireland's play contains appallingly bad poetry and has a plot so poor Shakespeare would not have given it a second glance. It is the content of these documents that gives them away so quickly. It is that authentic mental process that is so difficult to falsify.

Tapping into the genius of Shakespeare or the inner turmoil of a serial killer demands much more than most forgers can provide.

The 'Ripper Diary' is in a different dimension from that of the Hitler or Mussolini 'diaries'. It poses a many-layered set of challenges, worthy of a novel in the best post-modern tradition. First we have to consider its origins. How did it come to be discovered and presented to a publisher? That may or may not help us to form a view on another central decision to be made. Did James Maybrick write it or not? The third layer of questions is about whether the diary is describing actual events that its author experienced. The Whitechapel murders were so widely publicised in their day, and ever since, that most of the details were widely known. What if the document was written as an exercise in getting into the mind of the notorious killer, or even a plan for a novel or the like?

These give us four broad possibilities with a number of subplots that could be spun off from them:

1. *Total invention*: It was not written by James Maybrick or Jack the Ripper.
2. *Maybrick's fantasy*: It was written by James Maybrick who was not Jack the Ripper.
3. *Jack the Ripper stitching up Maybrick*: It was not written by James Maybrick but was written by Jack the Ripper.
4. *The truth at last*: It was written by James Maybrick who was Jack the Ripper.

PROVENANCE

The first complication is the provenance of the diary. If it had been handed to Michael Maybrick by his brother James on the latter's deathbed and then presented in open court in 1889 as part of Florie's trial, the debate would not have stopped, but it is unlikely there would still be shelves of books exploring the possible identity of Jack the Ripper well over a century later. The origins of the diary and how it came to be published is a whole subplot in its own right that threatens to overshadow the main storyline from time to time. In absolutely the best tradition of forged documents, when the diary first came to light it had been given to one Michael Barrett by an associate in a pub who had since died. Barrett, who had been a merchant seaman, barman and scrap metal dealer, was the man who took the leather-bound volume to a publisher, claiming he knew nothing of its origins.

Needless to say, the story did not finish there. Michael Barrett later came forwards to swear on oath that he had written the diary. By this time he had gone through a painful divorce from his wife Anne,[4] to whom he had been married for sixteen years. She counteracted by claiming the document had been in her family for more than a generation and that she had arranged for Barrett to get it 'via a third person, with the hope that he would take an interest in it and use its contents as the basis for a fictional book'. Anne further hinted at her possible connections to James Maybrick by revealing the possibility that Florence Maybrick was her great-grand-mother, through an illegitimate child that Florie may have had as an unmarried teenager.

The attention thus turns, momentarily at least, to Anne and Michael. Could he have forged the diary? Could she be part of a larger plot? Anne had diplomatically described Michael as 'ill' and admitted how destructive their marriage had become at the time she had had the volume passed to him. Were we seeing some marital squabble played out through the pages of a notional 'Ripper Diary'? Could Michael's 'illness' have been part of a great scheme to forge the document?

One aspect of this that I realised was open to exploration was to see how readily a document like the diary could be forged. Barrett was keen to prove his authorship and even turned up, uninvited, at an international conference I was holding on investigative psychology. He declared to all present his credentials as the author of the diary. The audience was fascinated. One of my police officer colleagues who was there was ready to arrest Barrett on the spot for the crime he had confessed. I counselled caution.

Michael agreed to take part in an experiment. I asked him to write some more of the diary for us to look at. At the same time I asked two of my students who were very interested in the diary, one British and one from the USA, to invent some more of the diary as well. We then subjected all of these examples to linguistic analysis for comparison with the 'original'. Now, I am the first to insist that these forms of linguistic analysis are far from foolproof.[5] They are very rough and ready indicators of similarities between texts, especially when the material available is so sparse. What was interesting about the results, though, was that all three people produced reasonably plausible renditions. Michael Barrett's was the one that had the fewest linguistic links to the 'original' and my American student's had the most. Once again, we are thrown back to the document itself to determine if the storyline it portrays is more likely to be the imaginings of a late twentieth century, unpublished scrap metal dealer, or a nineteenth-century Liverpool cotton merchant.

JAMES MAYBRICK?

A related and rather fundamental question is whether the journal was written in 1888. James Maybrick died on Saturday 11 May 1889. The diary closes with a great flourish: 'I place this now in a place where it shall be found . . .' and is dated 3 May 1889. The last known murder ascribed to Jack the Ripper was on 9 November 1888. Many people would assume that dating the diary would be the definitive test, and one readily available. We read all the time of artefacts thousands of years old being dated with great confidence. The late nineteenth century is so recent that there exist many scientific records of what was in use, and what had yet to be discovered. Surely inks, papers, handwriting styles, vocabulary and the wear and tear of time would be open to expert analysis? It turns out, however, that the mechanics, paper, handwriting, chemistry and so on examined by forensic scientists can be mimicked and invented in various convincing ways. Furthermore, as Shirley Harrison reveals very clearly in her search to test the diary, the experts do not always agree in any case. Even the matter that most of us might assume to be the most straightforward, the dyes used in inks in 1888, turns out to be contentious. So there is no definitive demonstration that the document could not have been written at the time of the Ripper murders.

The debate around the diary therefore relates to how closely it links to what is known about the Whitechapel murders. All the pundits seem to agree that the facts relating to the Ripper murders are correct. Shirley Harrison also presents evidence that some of the details of the murders that have only come to light in recent years are correct within the diary. So the Jack the Ripper side of the equation has not been faulted. That does not mean the diary is genuinely the writing of the killer, but from a psychological point of view the historical accuracy of the diary encourages me to turn my attention to the way it is written, and to ponder whether that is how such a killer might have recorded the details for himself and posterity.

We therefore have to turn back to the possibility that the diary is a reasonable reflection of what Jack the Ripper might have thought, and plausibly relates to what he actually did. From a psychological point of view these possibilities are very interesting indeed. If the diary had been shown to have little relationship to what was known about the murders in the East End of London in 1888 then we would either have to assume that those murders did not reflect the linked actions of one man and were a series concocted by the police at the time, or that the document was an outrageous invention, like Ireland's pretend Shakespeare play.

The second problem, though, is deciding whether it is the work of James Maybrick. That is no easy matter. Very little remains of any writing that can be claimed with confidence to be genuinely in his hand. If this is a secret document written clandestinely, the handwriting may capture aspects of Maybrick's character not known to anyone else, and be far different from his normal, formal style. Is the journal of Fred West the sort of document that those who knew him would have expected of him?

A FRAUGHT INVESTIGATION

'The Diary of Jack the Ripper' clearly has to be approached with extreme caution. Certainly when it was first shown to me I was deeply suspicious. These suspicions were further fuelled by the remarkable way in which opposing camps so quickly formed, advocating or denigrating claims as to the authenticity of the 'Ripper Diaries'. This is a common problem that I have found in all areas of crime speculation. Commentators get heated about the rights and wrongs long before the facts have been fully collected. Opinions are offered, but are derived from the personal values and beliefs of individuals rather than any reasoned argument. For example, the 'Ripper Diary' has been argued to be a fake because all the facts in it accord with those that are known. Such evidence of historical verisimilitude is of course taken by others to imply it is genuine. Instead of the steady drip of systematic research that such a document would demand if its historical importance were to be determined in the academic field, with a consensus slowly emerging after careful consideration of all the facts, there has been a feast of claim and counter-claim, fed by expostulations from every bizarre sort of 'expert' that could be got hold of.

The investigation of this diary is fraught with the same problems that a major criminal investigation faces if it is badly managed. There is an overload of information that no one settles down to systematise, and which throws up many intriguing possibilities. In the case of the diary the information includes serial killings in the US before the Whitechapel murders and spoof diaries written at the turn of the century.[6] Coincidence and enthusiasm feed off each other so that in this maelstrom of possibilities the more searches that are made, the more intriguing will be the associations that can be built. Coincidence is taken as proof. Association is taken as cause.

CONFIRMATION BIAS
In early studies of how people come to inappropriate conclusions from the evidence they seek out, psychologists, as is their wont, gave people simple judgements to make.[7] One example was to ask people to work out the 'rule' behind the sequence 2, 4, 6 and to see what information they would seek to check if they were correct. Like me, and most respondents, you would probably offer the number 8 as the next in line to see if you were right in assuming the rule to be 'increase by 2'. This is seeking evidence to confirm your assumption. A more scientific stance is suggested by offering the number 97. If this were accepted then it would disprove your hypothesis

and offer the simpler possibility that the sequence involves any increase in the number. We are all prone to this 'confirmation bias' and it is a challenge in all police investigations to overcome the psychological tricks it plays.

Shirley Harrison's thorough exploration of the provenance and likely authenticity of the diary is sadly replete with this difficulty. It therefore provides yet another fascinating example of the difficulties that any investigation faces, let alone one with so many added layers of complication.

She puts aside scepticism to discuss the document on the assumption that Maybrick wrote it. I realise that it makes the writing less engaging and more difficult to follow if the writer constantly draws attention to the fact that *if* Maybrick had written it then certain points would make sense, but that is a caveat that we constantly need to be reminded of. She certainly does not follow the scientific tradition set up specifically to reduce the impact of the confirmation bias, of seeking alternative explanations for the evidence she garners in support of the diary's authenticity. If a documented event can be linked to some general statement in the diary then it is accepted. To take just one example, the diary contains the comment:

The bitch has written all
tonight she Will fall

Shirley Harrison finds a reference in Florence's trial to her having written to Maybrick's brother Michael about the white powders James was taking. These were the arsenic and strychnine to which he had become addicted. Michael reported at the trial how annoyed James was when confronted about this. But this hardly counts as 'writing all' and we are left wondering what 'fall' was wished on her. Harrison implies that Maybrick's changes to his will may have been the consequence, but that is hardly the vicious act of a violent killer.

This is not meant to be a condemnation of Harrison's detailed collection of all the possible facts that might relate to the contents of the diary. Rather I am drawing attention to the phenomena that are seen over and over again in police investigations. The intense poring over the details of a case and the search for any possible links throw up many coincidences that can take on a significance they do not warrant. In the case of the diary there is the great difficulty of separating clear, simple objective facts, like the reference to an assistant in Maybrick's office by the name of Lowry, from interpretations of possible meanings comments in the diary might have. For example, the fundamental assumption made by Harrison that Florie is the 'whore' in the diary and her lover Brierly the 'whoremaster' is not an objective fact. Nonetheless, despite these cavils, I have still to see any indication that the contents of the diary are incompatible with other known facts. There are a few references in the diary that could be open to verification but have not yet been verified, a sure sign that this one will run on and on.

DIARY TESTING

I was first approached by Paul Feldman to comment on the diary.[8] All I remember of that was his unremitting advocacy of the diary's authenticity. It was impossible to get any clear or detailed information about its provenance, or the tests that had been carried out on it. I quickly became familiar with the strange world of 'Ripperologists' – a surprisingly large group of enthusiasts engaged in heated debate about anything to do with Jack the Ripper. The claims and counter-claims of the advocates and critics of 'Maybrick's Journal' were so vociferous that it was not really feasible to enter into sensible dialogue with most of them. Those early harangues became ever more confused as they were overlaid by comments on the 'Ripper Diary' from astrologers, graphologists and a small army of psychics. I looked in vain for some systematic rigour, some knowledge of how science works, but the opinions of psychics, graphologists and astrologers were presented in the same confident sweep as those of chemists, historians and document specialists.

Shirley Harrison reports, for example, how impressed she was by the 'performance' of a graphologist, Anna Koren, who had travelled all the way from Israel to London to look at the diary; Harrison claimed with unquestioned naïveté that the graphologist had had no prior knowledge of Jack the Ripper before she got to see the document. Interestingly, Harrison reports that Koren looked at the diary in her presence and then gave 'confirmation in writing' of the original 'off-the-cuff assessment'. Anyone who has studied how psychics and others of their ilk (which certainly includes graphologists, who claim to derive personality characteristics from the style of a person's handwriting) work,[9] will be aware that, if it is available to them, they look for cues from the person to whom they are giving the report; even if such cues are little more than changes in breathing patterns, they still let slip increased interest. I am not for one second suggesting this is chicanery. I know from direct examples that these folk are often no more aware of what they are doing than their clients. They merely feel they are responding in a considerate way to the interest of the people who pay them.

One of the interesting differences between real experts who base their opinions as much as possible on scientific findings and those pseudo-experts who people the astrology and psychic columns (which seem to be particularly prevalent on the women's pages of newspapers and magazines) is that the pseudo-experts typically offer clear and categorical views with great confidence. By contrast, scientists are aware of the weaknesses of their opinions and will often be less certain. The open debate around which science evolves also brings to the surface disagreements between scientists until principles are established that the scientific community can agree upon.

Shirley Harrison had turned to a document examiner, Sue Iremonger. Document examiners[10] are very different from graphologists. They often have a background in physics and are merely concerned with the form the letters take, seeking to determine how similar are the shape and sequence of line strokes that make up letters from one example of text to another. They give evidence in court and, like all true experts, will often not be able to come to a clear decision one way or the other. Unlike graphologists, they make no comment on the *personality* or *character* of the author of the text, but limit their opinions to the similarity in the letter shapes they are looking at. Sue Iremonger was unable to say with confidence that the writing in the diary was like any examples of writing that were available that could have been penned by Jack the Ripper.

When commenting on Iremonger's report, Harrison revealed the sort of bias that I have seen in all too many investigations. She declares how impressed she was with the psychic meanderings of Anna Koren, but comments wryly on the lack of validity to the much more objective examination by Iremonger – the examination that did not support her claim that the diary was genuine.

There is another phenomenon, which I have seen in police inquiries and indeed solicitors preparing a case for court: searching out the opinion that is wanted. If the opinion from one expert does not give this answer another expert is turned to. Unhappy with Iremonger's response on the handwriting, Harrison offers her own opinion alongside those of other people with experience of looking at handwriting in a criminal context. Yet we are not presented with a test of other graphologists who might challenge what Koren had to say. When I did a study some years ago of how graphologists formed opinions of the same material, I found that not only did they not agree with each other on the opinions offered but nor did they even deal with the same aspects of the handwriting.

This latter point is more important than is often realised. For any systematic procedure to be evaluated it is essential to know what it is based upon. That is the starting point for science – a clear definition of what is being examined. This is often referred to as 'measurement' or 'instrumentation', but it is more fundamental than that. It is the description of the relevant features of the matter under study – those that are to be considered. The chemical tests on the inks of the diary revolve around the presence or absence of particular chemical compounds. There may be debate over how the compounds can be identified, then whether the compounds are present or not, and there may then be further dispute over whether such compounds were used in inks available in 1888, but these are all scientific arguments that are ultimately open to test. These tests take time and effort and therefore cost money, and so are not as attractive as someone who will wander in and offer an immediate opinion that fits what the listener wants to hear. This is especially true if the person commissioning the tests has only limited funds available.

At one gathering around the diary I witnessed a psychic swinging a pendulum over the document, intoning, 'Was this written in 1888 ... 1889 ... 1890?' whilst apparently well-informed, intelligent people watched without even a smile to cloud their gullibility. This confusion of serious science with hocus pocus has masked the growing body of scholarly and objective information accumulating about the diary. The proposal that astrologers, psychics and graphologists should be taken seriously in evaluating the diary has tempted me to dismiss it and to see it as one more component of the myth of Jack the Ripper: another millennial, New Age flowering, half fiction, half fantasy. Yet when I decide to get on with something more befitting a professor of psychology, I am brought up against the fact that so far no scientific or historical evidence has been produced to indicate with confidence that the diary is a fake. In true scientific tradition the hypothesis that it is genuine stands until the proof that it is not becomes available. (The hypothesis that it is a fake, of course, also stands until it is proven to be genuine.) The lack of such proof raises the possibility that James Maybrick wrote the diary as a record of his exploits as Jack the Ripper.

One consequence of this possibility that has to be emphasised is that if the diary does contain the genuine outpourings of a Victorian serial killer, it is a unique psychological document which can be studied to help us get into the mind of such a killer. This can be compared with what we know of killers today, as well as throwing new light on the mental patterns that give rise to these crimes. It does therefore seem worthwhile to struggle through the quagmire of anecdote and specious opinion to see what sense can be made of this curious document.

9. PROFILING THE DIARIST

One important complication that runs through the inquiry into this manuscript is that if the diary of Jack the Ripper is a total invention, then who wrote it? That is subsidiary to the central questions, but the route along which it takes us throws light on the primary issue. It also leads us into explorations of why such a document may have been faked. Let us pin some pointers down. If we have here a sophisticated descendant of the 'Hitler Diaries', then it is written as part of a commercial enterprise, that had some ideological support. There were indications, for example, that *Stern* was only too happy to re-invoke reference to Germany's fascist past. Another context is the creative delight of a novelist in exploring the world of Jack the Ripper. Then there are the more subtle and surreptitious possibilities of attempts to frame James Maybrick, either by the Ripper himself or someone else who had no contact with the Ripper.

We can get rid of one of these possibilities fairly quickly. The Ripper would have had access to much more damning and less time consuming evidence than a misattributed diary. He could have left property from the crime scenes hidden in Maybrick's house for others to find.

All the other possible authors, though, would have left their particular stamp on the diary. It is therefore time for me to join the debate and put in my pennyworth, but rather than looking at the historical accuracy or scientific evidence for the authenticity of the diary I feel it is important to look at what the document tells us about the person who wrote it.

Having bad-mouthed psychics and the like, I feel the need to explain the basis for my offering such thoughts. All I am doing is drawing attention to aspects of what is written that seem to me self-evidently to support views about the diary's author. We would need extensive scientific studies to check whether many of the views I offer stand up to close, experimental scrutiny. The reader therefore needs to decide for him or herself whether the matters to which I draw attention make any sense.

What sort of a person, or team even, could have come up with the unlikely notion of a Scouse Ripper? Psychological offender profiles of Jack the Ripper are ten a dollar, but what would be the profile of the hoaxer who perpetrated such an inventive scam?

The first point to come to mind is that the author of the diary, be he hoaxer or fraudster, was a remarkably ingenious man. (Most crime and the majority of frauds are committed by men, although fraud does attract more women than other crimes, but even these women – contrary to feminist aspirations – are often secondary to their male partners.) When I first read the diary I was struck by how unstructured the writing was. It is not really a diary in the usual sense at all, but more of a journal of thoughts and feelings, or even at times a notebook recording sketches of half-hearted doggerel. There are no clear or regular dates. It meanders from thoughts to accounts of events to plans for action. In the same section that describes the most horrific post-mortem mutilation there is the search for a rhyme scheme. The delight in the murders is juxtaposed with mundane comments on relatives and acquaintances.

This is inventive psychological writing of the highest order. My suspicion is that most people who sat down to write a convincing diary about another's life would want to place the publicly known events of that life clearly for the reader to see. (This would be an interesting student project, to see how convincingly a fake diary could be generated.) I think a fraudulent diarist would normally have to take the public events as a starting point and build the diary around them. But our fraudster is much more cunning than that. The diary deals with the feelings of the writer: a record of what he feels dominates them, rather than of his actions. The things noted in the diary are those that would be of interest to the author. It does not focus on what others have seen him do.

Many serial killers write autobiographies and some keep a journal. These typically capture the self-centred, narcissistic focus that drives these people to such disgusting excesses of depravity. Fred West's memoir is full of the trivial detail of daily life, dotted with casual references to the outrageous sexual exploitation of his children and larded with gooey declarations of love. Pee-Wee Gaskins[1] describes with glee how he killed babies by sexually assaulting them, implying in a mock sermonising tone that his pleasure in this justified his actions. Charles Manson keeps a manic, self-centred diatribe going throughout his extensive correspondence. Sadly, there are many more examples in the archives. They are all leagues away from the ponderous seriousness of those who write about Jack the Ripper. Indeed, few novelists could capture the all-embracing egocentricity with its mix of gloating irony and self-pity that is this diary.

The 63 pages are intensely focused on the diarist. With the exception of the rare mention of his children, other people are just foils against which he reviews his own reactions. At times it is as if he is using the writing as a way of trying to make sense of his own existence. Very tellingly he writes, 'The man I have become was not the man I was born.' This could be a remarkable, indirect clue from the faker that he is not what he claims, or a rather more conventional plea from a tormented man to consider that something has driven him to his current state.

There is another rather more objective test that psychologists have fashioned to help determine the authenticity of an account. It has been graced with the rather grand title of 'Criteria Based Content Analysis'[2] (CBCA). What it amounts to is a list of the aspects of an account that indicate its truthfulness. The approach was developed to help sort out whether children were lying when they gave accounts of sexual assaults and has been used in many courts, especially in Germany, where it originated. The applicability of CBCA to accounts given by adults is still a contentious issue. Its utility when dealing with an expert in invention and lying, such as any experienced storyteller and especially a novelist, is even less certain. But at least it provides us with a framework for considering how convincing the diary might be if presented as a genuine statement.

CBCA aspects are taken to reveal the density of experience on which an account draws. The fundamental assumption is that an invention is always more likely to lack the sort of detail that a genuine account would have – the sort of detail that would be more likely to come from genuine experience than fabrication. Of course, creative writers unconsciously tick off the criteria for making their invention seem genuine as they work, but less effective imaginations do miss a few tricks. The point most often missed is the almost irrelevant detail, or casual aside, that embeds the narrative within a particular context, especially when that detail does not really move the storyline forwards and may actually undermine its obvious purpose. An example would be a rape victim mentioning that after the assault she was worried about being late for work. This might be taken to indicate that she had not been seriously traumatised by the assault, but is the sort of thought that occurs when the mind is on automatic pilot.

The author of the diary is a particular master of the casual aside, the irrelevant detail that implies a person whose mind is not entirely on the events he is describing – a person who seems to be writing to sort out his own feelings, not just to tell a story. He may be bragging about having fooled the police, yet there is still the need to record how cold his hands felt. Amidst the gruesome writing about removing body parts is the domestic aside of wondering 'how long it will keep'. Because these specific comments are apparently derived directly from the diarist's immediate concerns whilst writing, they bring the reader back to thinking about the person writing, not just his deeds. It is therefore a powerful literary device if used effectively, but can easily turn into self-parody.

The author of the diary has a particularly clever way of keeping these irrelevancies consistent with the character he is creating. We are given a man who thinks nothing of murdering and mutilating others but is nonetheless psychologically vulnerable. He is desperately concerned with his own state of health and determined to get rid of intrusive thoughts about his children that might distract him from his campaign of murder. After the most violent outburst he notes that 'the children enjoyed Christmas'. Through these asides a surprisingly insecure protagonist is created. No steely, emotionless Hannibal Lecter is he, but a man who misses his brother, is astonished that he has not been caught, and is dependent on his 'medicine' – but finally a man who eventually becomes obsessed with his own actions and their consequences.

The literary profile of the perpetrator of this fraudulent diary, if such it be, is already revealing some distinct characteristics. Here is a subtle writer who is determined to envelop us in Maybrick's thoughts and feelings, even if that introduces ambiguities into the details of his actions.

He is also remarkably crafty in the way he develops his fiction. If you had not been told these were the actual writings of a notorious serial killer, the opening pages would not have made you any the wiser. There are only oblique references to indicate that the author is engaged in nefarious activities: 'Time is passing too slowly, I still have to work up courage to begin my campaign.' The danger of being discovered is hinted at: 'I am beginning to believe it is unwise to continue writing.' (What a brilliant technique, by the way, for keeping the prurient reader interested!) We get an indication that the actions of the diarist cannot be specified too precisely for fear of discovery. There are emotional words that raise more questions than they answer. The opening paragraph reveals an inner turmoil – 'I long for peace of mind' – and introduces the curious term 'whore master', showing an anger with someone who although execrated as a 'whore' is still of great emotional significance to the writer.

The opening paragraphs lead us further into an intriguing world of subterfuge and emotional tension with just the necessary sexual undertones to raise our interest without giving too much of the plot away. We are hooked by the time it is clear that the writer has a 'campaign', although we are not told explicitly what that 'campaign' is; but sex and violence, those great recipes for public interest, are never far from the surface. Only once our interest has been raised does this skilled storyteller begin to feed in connections to a world we might recognise.

There is a further subtlety in the way the diary has been concocted. It is not clear at the beginning what it is dealing with, other than the possibility of an attempt to plan some dangerous 'campaign'. Indeed what we have appears to be the second half of a book that has had the opening pages torn out. The first page we have of the diary does not even start with a complete sentence, but rather with what seems to be the end of a sentence from the previous page: 'what they have in store for them they would stop this instant.' It carries on as if following an earlier idea: 'But do they desire that? My answer is no.' The reader is required to work out the missing prior phrase – 'if they knew' – that could have started the sentence at the bottom of the previous page. (Also worth noting is that this device of carrying sentences over pages is kept consistent throughout the manuscript.)

Here is someone having a discussion with himself, and we catch him in the middle of it. The discussion is about nothing less than whether his targets would wish to change their lives if they knew the consequences their caution would have. As such it has a dramatic power on a par with that of Hamlet wandering on stage, in deep thought about the purpose of existence, uttering the most famous line in all literature: 'To be or not to be'. All serious authors take special care of their opening words. To start such a significant text in the middle of a sentence is little short of genius.

Of course, that could have been a happy accident due to the document being damaged over time and pages going missing through mishandling. But the actual volume is rather tidy. The pages are not scuffed or dog-eared, and there are virtually no blemishes on the paper itself. The earlier pages have been removed in a determined, if rather crude way. So this first page does seem to be exactly where the author wants us to start reading.

The reader is led on by hints of the danger of actually writing things down, but then we are given the strangely ambiguous phrase 'to down a whore'. This is almost a hunting term, as in 'the dogs downed a fox'. Its true significance is indicated by the suggestion that the act of recording it is dangerous. That ambiguous caution continues throughout the diary, but after a visit to Manchester and the apparent strangulation of a 'whore' the accounts get ever more explicit and caution is eventually put aside by the diarist to enjoy the delight of recording the experiences.

He measures his pace very well, slowly involving us in ever more gruesome details, capturing a mood of increased anger mixed with pain and delight. What starts as an unclear reference to a 'campaign' gets more explicit with a reference to the purchase of a knife. Then all is made terribly clear when the difficulty of cutting off a head is mentioned. As if that were not enough the diary moves into angry despair: 'I want to boil boil boil', an almost incoherent tirade against himself and the God that made him. Lucid moments of self-doubt intervene amidst a growing refrain that perhaps he should give himself up or commit suicide.

The ending of the work is much more effectively resolved than it would be by a pusillanimous suicide. The author actually asks the reader for forgiveness. The whole document emerges as a justification of his actions, which were brought on by others, and the external forces of 'love', rather than evil within himself.

Only someone who has carefully explored how serial killers see the world could be perceptive enough to notice that in the end they always seek to justify their actions by some means or other. Typically these justifications place the blame outside their own nature. Furthermore, the purpose of writing their accounts is essentially to defend and excuse what they have done.

Most novelists struggle for years to gain the ability to look at the world as if through the eyes of another. Then they usually fail and are only able to give us one of their own perspectives. The diary writer, though, brilliantly captures a sense of adolescent delight in fooling others and getting away with crimes he finds exciting. A melodramatic 'ha ha ha ha', as though written by the vaudeville villain the diarist sometimes seems to aspire to be, is dotted throughout the manuscript.

He also enjoys an unselfconscious thrill in seeing his deeds written about. This fraudster really enables us to get into the mind of a 'Ripper' character and see the turmoil of emotions and tumult of thought that keep him going. As the diary unfolds, the author gives, with developing clarity, the reasons why it is being written at all. What starts as a desire to plan and record illicit pleasures evolves into a struggle to make sense of his emotions and ends as a testament to his deeds which he almost hopes will exonerate him.

This is masterly psychological thriller writing, deftly indicating why the diary is being written at the same time as drawing us into the anger and confusion of the author. These moods are seasoned with playful poems. There is a use of frivolity and dark humour, to highlight the deadly seriousness of the drama, that Shakespeare could have been proud of. Constant anger or polemic would have been tedious and unconvincing, but the mixture of emotional expression and banality keeps the reader mesmerised as by the slight twitches of a snake.

There are moreover just enough hints at facts to allow us to tie the experiences into known events. These historical cards are not over-played. It took Shirley Harrison and her advisers a considerable amount of time and effort to unravel all the references to actual events. A more conventional fraudster would have made sure that the critical events were clearly present. There are even hints at events that have no place in the Ripper canon, like an early murder in Manchester. Could an author who was so meticulous in all his other details have made a mistake here? Or is this a devilish nuance to hint at things that only Maybrick would have known, but which no one else could ever verify? (Indeed, a strangulation would not usually be linked to the mutilation that gave Jack his sobriquet.) It is a clever strategy. If no Ripper crime is ever discovered in Manchester then people will continue to look. If one is found then the diarist is vindicated. Manchester was a forty-minute train ride from central Liverpool in 1888 (it takes nearer an hour these days). It is a plausible location for a Liverpool cotton merchant to visit.

'SO HISTORY DO TELL'

The artistry of the fraudster has been demonstrated. But what of the character he has created for us? Does that give us any more clues to the person who wrote the diary? Most novelists inevitably write about themselves, no matter how hard they try to disguise the fact. So what sort of person is James Maybrick revealed to be in the diary? He is certainly the centre of his own world. The diary is written for his own pleasure but also in the arrogant belief that his views are inevitably of public significance. He does, after all, declare at the end that the point of the volume is to leave a message for posterity 'so history do tell'. This document is meant to be found.

He has enormous mood swings from the heights of delight to the depths of despair. He is an inveterate gambler who gets real enjoyment from taking risks. But his arrogance is based on profound doubts about his own self-worth, especially in comparison to his brother. This seems to be what gives him such preening satisfaction in duping others, such pleasure in showing them to be 'fools'.

Yet for all these explosive emotions and wild mood swings he knows he is able to present himself to others as mild-mannered and is aware enough to recognise that duplicity and gloat over it. He is not uncontrollably impulsive, but plans ahead, enjoying the planning and reminiscence of past acts as much as the acts themselves. This is a man others would recognise as intelligent but not easy to know, because he hides so much of what he feels. There are some well-established British authors who would fit this picture. What have any of them to gain from remaining anonymous all this time?

A subtle novelist capable of giving the feeling of what it is like to be inside the Ripper's skull, but who also knows how to tread softly and pull back from revealing everything too readily, is clearly a master of his art. But the fraudster/novelist had to do more than simply to convince through carefully ambiguous statements. He had to have a thorough knowledge of Jack the Ripper and his activities. There are, of course, far too many books about the Victorian killings, so a study of these might have provided the basis for the prank. But as I found when I tried to put some thoughts together for this book, the plethora of material on the Whitechapel murders is actually the problem. There are huge disagreements about most details, including who Jack actually killed. So the fraudster/novelist would have to have been very heavily immersed in the Ripper literature for some time. He would also have to have had a very good understanding of Victorian England and police investigations in order to distil from all the writings those facts that the experts would agree on. Such a person would be known to the experts and could indeed be recognised as one of them. Having had to plough through many Ripper books, however, I have to say there are not many, if any, that reveal the writing skills apparent in the invention of the diary.

Our profile of the fraudster, then, has narrowed the field down to gifted writers who are also Ripper experts. But there is one more clear indication of the character of the fraudster/novelist/expert.

This is the very clever focus on a Liverpudlian. Jack the Ripper is a London character par excellence. If he is not one of the professionals or aristocrats that crown our image of Victorian London, then we can almost see him as a sort of Dick Van Dyke classic cockney. Liverpool can claim to be the birthplace of many of the metropolitan developments of the last century, from medical officers of health to recalcitrant strikers, but it is not usually thought of as an especially violent city, nor one from which the modern serial killer would have originated. It is a brilliant stroke to spot the trial of Florence Maybrick for murdering her husband, and to decide to work the fiction backwards from that point to invent her alleged victim as Jack the Ripper.

It may be that my own birthplace, a short bus ride from where Maybrick lived and died, biases my opinion, but surely only people from Liverpool are convinced enough of the fecundity of their city and its central position in the known universe to believe that Jack the Ripper could have been a Scouser. Yet number seven Riversdale Road, where Maybrick came to his untimely end (it was number eight for some time) is a quiet place. The lack of tourist crowds testifies that its likelihood as a former residence of Jack the Ripper has certainly not caught the imagination of present-day citizens. So whichever of their number invented the diary, she or he was certainly swimming against the Merseyside tide. The author of the diary was not picking up one of the popular myths of Liverpool and cloaking it with invention.

This Liverpool fraudster/novelist/expert was also, of course, very knowledgeable about the Maybricks and their doings. Florie's trial was of great note in the local press so, once again, tireless research would have provided the depth of insight to be able to scatter references to major and minor figures in James Maybrick's life. A variety of names would be available from the trial but, once again, the author does not over-use them. The outburst against a subordinate in the railing against Lowry is a delightful touch, for example, and further evidence of the control and skill of the novelist. I must confess that if

I were to invent such an interesting walk-on character as Lowry, I would want to develop his involvement and use him as more than a cipher.

The knowledge of inks and paper, of Victorian vocabulary and handwriting styles and the other objective aspects of the diary that Shirley Harrison has so painstakingly examined, were of course available to the fraudster in much the same way as they were available to her. Readers of crime fiction and non-fiction will be aware of the forensic sciences that can be drawn upon. Our fraudster is no Liverpool scally, no slouch throwing a few possibilities together. He has devoted considerable time and effort to getting the diary just right. He would not make the mistake of getting the forensic science obviously wrong.

Our profile of the author of the diary, then, has him (or just possibly her) based in Liverpool with a very good knowledge of the life and times of the Maybrick family. He also has excellent knowledge of Victorian England and the Jack the Ripper murders and their investigation. He can further very plausibly capture and express the mixture of thoughts and feelings that the Whitechapel murderer might have had. Furthermore, he is likely to be a careful scholar who enjoys taking risks. Those who know him very well will recognise a turmoil of emotions deeply hidden by a placid façade. He has access to Victorian writing implements and writing styles, and knows how to use them effectively. But above all he does not display these consummate creative and scholarly skills by writing a gripping novel or screenplay, but produces a personal, meandering document that is so unlike a diary that it finds a publisher almost accidentally.

This is a person so fascinated by Jack the Ripper that he has devoted a large portion of his life to trying to be him. A person who gets such delight in recreating the feelings that Jack the Ripper might have had and such excitement from the stir that the diary might cause, that this shy genius has still not stepped forwards to claim his rightful glory. His story would be a sure bet for Hollywood treatment. (Anthony Hopkins was actually offered the role but turned it down because he thought he was getting a bad name as a villain.)

THE RESIDENT OF RIVERSDALE ROAD

The journal of James Maybrick turns out from these considerations to be very different from any of the other fakes to
which it is compared. No one has made a great deal of money
out of it or indeed tried. So far, furthermore, despite the
obsessive analysis of many Ripper experts and forensic
scientists, not a single fact has been produced that incontro-
vertibly shows it to be fraudulent. In support of the
authenticity of the journal a number of facts have emerged
subsequent to its publication that only the most astute and
thorough forger could have known. It is difficult to believe
that a forger of that capability would not have come forwards
by now to claim the limelight. True, Michael Barrett swore on
oath that he dictated it to his wife Anne; but then she denied
that categorically.

In trying to draw out the obvious characteristics of the
author of the diary, fake or genuine, I have, briefly, drawn up
a picture that others can test for themselves. This picture does
not prove the document to be what it claims to be, yet, the
question still lingers as to whether it might after all be
genuine.

Psychologists and others who study these matters have not
come up with any foolproof method for detecting fraudulent
writing, and certainly not one that is 'geniusproof'. A further
problem, of which my own studies have convinced me, is that
close examination of any human utterance makes it seem
suspect. Watch a TV news announcer as carefully as you
possibly can and see if you think he or she really believes
what they are saying. You will notice little twitches that are
suspicious, or perhaps the complete lack of any hesitation or
doubt will raise questions in your mind. If you give written
accounts to ordinary people and ask them to determine
whether they are genuine or false, the majority will be
assumed to be false no matter how many are genuine. So read
the diary with the assumption that it is a hoax and you will
be amazed at the way some details are spelled out as if to
make us believe it is genuine. Now read it again assuming it
is genuine and you will be struck by what you learn about
Jack the Ripper's thoughts and feelings.

These musings, then, give us two broad possibilities for the authorship of the diary. One is that it was written by a shy and emotionally disturbed genius, who combined the novelist's art with an intelligent understanding of serial killers and had an exhaustive knowledge of the agreed facts of Jack the Ripper and James Maybrick. The other possibility involves a rather different person. He knew how Jack the Ripper felt and had knowledge and experience of his killings. He was also totally familiar with the world of James Maybrick. He fits the personality profile revealed in the diary exactly and had ready access to all the necessary writing materials. He also had a plausible reason for writing the diary. He desperately wanted others to know the secret festering within him. And he lived at number seven Riversdale Road in the late 1880s.

10. MAPPING THE MURDERS

If we treat the diary as at least a plausible indicator of the identity of Jack the Ripper, we return to the central question of what a Liverpool cotton merchant was doing killing prostitutes in London. The most palpable reason why James Maybrick is not an obvious candidate for Jack the Ripper is that he lived 200 miles away from London; and London has always claimed the Whitechapel murderer as its own. Local lunatics or even deranged royals have all been within at least a hackney-carriage ride of the murder sites.

The document is spine-tinglingly aware of this fundamental question and offers some answers. It also throws light on why the police did not locate the culprit despite an investigation that was as thorough as many that still happen around the world today. The Liverpool businessman determines that his campaign should be set in London: 'I finally decided London it shall be.' Here, on the second page of the manuscript, he does not make clear why he has chosen London. All that he does is express his belief that he will not be suspected for going to London because he often has business there.

In these opening pages he does not write about which part of London he will visit, nor exactly who his targets will be, although it is clear that they will be 'all who sell their dirty wares'. There is an interesting juxtaposition in the opening sentence of this paragraph in which it is noted that the 'foolish bitch' has arranged a meeting with a man 'in Whitechapel', but only ten pages later does the diarist make the connection between Liverpool's Whitechapel and London's, as if the connection were something the writer initially took for granted. Why might that be?

The writer is looking for vulnerable targets amongst women of the streets. The Whitechapel area of London was well known in those days for the prevalence of prostitutes; some estimates[1] put the figure as high as 2,000 women who would sell their services. But a man does not plan to visit an area of prostitutes in order to kill them secretly on the reputation of the area alone. He must have had some direct contact with the services on offer. Importantly it is known that when he lived in Norfolk, Virginia, James Maybrick did regularly visit a whorehouse there.[2] This is no proof that the diary is genuine; many Victorian men used prostitutes, as many men do today. The point, though, is that if there had been incontrovertible evidence that he eschewed any such activity this would have been a damning challenge to its authenticity. As it is, we can make the only slightly risky supposition that the diarist had assumed that Whitechapel was the area into which he would travel to find whores he could kill.

Here is a process we see time and again in serial killers. Although they deliberately travel from their base to distance themselves from the crime scenes, they are not travelling at random. They know where they are going because they have prior information about a location's suitability for their purposes, or because they have been there before – usually both. In some cases the information can be gleaned from public sources, which is certainly a ploy that thieves use. One thief who specialised in stealing golf clubs was recently interviewed by one of my students. When she asked him how he knew where to go, he answered in amazement at her naïveté that there are published maps of the locations of all the golfing centres in the country. For the more dangerous activity of killing the criminal would quickly get caught if he did not know the lie of the land and the pattern of movements around it.

A man intent on a campaign of killing also needs to know how the killing is going to work. If he thinks there may be difficulties in fulfilling his ultimate aim he may well try out other possibilities first. The diary describes the first murder as taking place in Manchester, not London. He is learning his trade as a killer. He describes 'squeezing' his victim to death. This is an experience that was not as exciting as he had expected: 'I felt nothing.' This is commonly reported in many forms of premeditated violence with a sexual component. The act is not as satisfying as the prior thoughts about it. It is this search for what was anticipated that urges the offender on: 'next time it will thrill me . . .' He is exploring his urges and realising how much of the pleasure he seeks comes from thinking about brutally hurting and mutilating his victims. He considers pouring acid on them and how he will 'ram a cane into the whoring bitches' mound.' Eventually he decides to 'purchase the finest knife money can buy' and 'to go back to my original idea' of finding victims in London.

The trip to Manchester, and how he contemplates it afterwards, suggest a remarkably controlled killer who is seeking to test himself: 'I shake with fear of capture. A fear I will have to overcome.' Revealed here is a mind that thinks through the implications of his actions and considers how he will deal with his own inner demons. Here is a killer who, whilst developing an account of himself as being driven by unfathomable, bizarre urges, nonetheless reflects carefully on how he will commit his deeds and get away with them. He realises that he has 'not allowed for the red stuff, gallons of it in my estimation'. His first killing appears to have been a strangulation, but he now sees that his satisfaction will be stronger from mutilating and ripping his victims, and so must take precautions to avoid being seen covered in blood.

Whether this is a fake or genuine document, the way he decides to avoid detection is one that detectives should mark well for future consideration in any inquiry in which they are involved. In keeping with the attention to detail that the diary already reveals, the solution is elegant in its simplicity: 'I have taken a small room in Middlesex Street.' Here is the answer to our central conundrum of how a well-known Liverpool resident could commit a series of crimes in London without being detected, and how a man could commit so many crimes in Whitechapel without being spotted. (Although I must hasten to add that we have only the diary's word that Maybrick took such a room. But then what name would he have put in the rent book?)

There is more to this, though, than just a small room. He still has to be able to move around freely at night through the maze of narrow back streets. Like an urban guerrilla planning a campaign he must reconnoitre the terrain and learn it well. He tells us he has done just that: 'I have walked the streets and have become more than familiar with them.' Walking the streets looking for possibilities is extremely common in serial offenders, whether they be burglars, rapists or killers. They may be convincing themselves that this is careful planning, but they are also enjoying the thought of what is to come.

He also lets slip a curious indication that we have only a part of his thought processes here: 'I said Whitechapel it will be and Whitechapel it shall.' But he has not told us that! He has mentioned London as his target and indicated the nature of his victims, but this is the first time Whitechapel has been mentioned. Having come to a decision that it is to be Whitechapel, he now justifies that as a reference to Liverpool: 'Whitechapel Liverpool. Whitechapel London, *ha ha*. No one could possibly place it together.' The area provides the opportunities he seeks and thereby begins to take on a particular significance for him.

The base in Middlesex Street is of great interest. It is a proposal in the diary that has never been mooted in other accounts of Jack the Ripper. Does it make any sense in terms of the locations of the killings?

A LIMITED GEOGRAPHY

When reviewing the murder locations there is always the problem, as in any police investigation, of being sure which crimes are linked. In this case I feel the need to bow to the collective expertise of all those who have devoted so much energy to studying the murders in Whitechapel and accept the five victims – Nichols, Chapman, Stride, Eddowes and Kelly – that are usually agreed to be the full catalogue.

The first point to note is the limited geographical distribution of these killings. This seems always to have been taken for granted. But why would a man seeking out weak women available on the street limit himself to a constrained area in this way? Why would he limit his area of activity to little more than a mile square?

One reason is, of course, the prevalence of possible targets. This means not just nominally available targets but victims the offender knows will be available. A familiarity with and the reputation of the area could both combine to draw him to Whitechapel, but the area of activity is still remarkably limited. There were doubtless other locations in the broader East End of London that would have also offered up vulnerable victims.

4. THE WHITECHAPEL MURDERS AND MIDDLESEX STREET

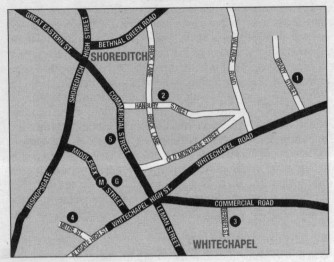

1. Mary Anne Nichols, 31.8.88, Buck's Row, retitled Durward Street (now demolished)

2. Eliza Smith ('Annie Chapman'), 8.9.88, 29 Hanbury Street, near Spitalfields Market

3. Elizabeth ('Long Lizzie') Stride, 30.9.88, Berner Street, Whitechapel

4. Catherine Eddowes, 30.9.88, Mitre Square (half a mile from Stride's murder)

5. Mary Jane Kelly, 9.11.88, Miller's Court

G. Graffito

M. Middlesex Street where Maybrick may have rented a room, 1888

The diary throws some light on the reasons why offenders are sometimes so limited: 'I have walked the streets.' Over and over again the spatial distribution of crimes shows us the sort of transactions that the criminal has with a location. If you are going to get to know an area so well that you can escape quickly from a crime scene then, unless you have been born and bred there, there will be a limit to how far you can explore. The crucial point here, of course, is that a London resident would be likely to have knowledge of a much larger field than someone who had come into the area for a limited amount of time. Ask a person who was brought up in a city to draw a map of it, and compare that with a map drawn by a casual visitor. You will find that they may both have a similar degree of knowledge of a commonly used area of the city centre, but that the visitor will know little else beyond, except those places to which their visit takes them.

We can turn away from the contested diary for a moment and consider the actual locations of the killings and the area in which they happened. About these there is no debate. Hundreds of thousands of visitors each year wander the streets of Whitechapel on walking tours that visit each of the murder sites. The walking tours illustrate graphically how localised the crimes were: the victims were encountered and killed in locations very close to each other. Therefore the sites where each of the bodies was found do indicate places sought out by Jack the Ripper. Careful examination of the distribution of these locations reveals some intriguing possibilities.

The first known murder was that of Mary Ann Nichols in Buck's Row on 31 August 1888. This is a mile or so due east of Liverpool Street railway station, and the easternmost limit to the area in which the killings took place, thus defining a boundary to the geographical range over which the offences spread. After this murder there was some public concern. It is reasonable to assume that a careful offender, seeking to avoid detection, would not revisit the area too soon afterwards. The next murder took place just over a week later, on 8 September. Annie Chapman was killed in Hanbury Street, less than a mile due west of the first offence.

The location of this second offence would seem far enough away from the first for suspicions not to have been aroused in this densely crowded area of Victorian London. But now there was more public anxiety and Jack the Ripper would have to be more cautious. He waited three weeks before he struck again on 30 September, killing Lizzie Stride. This time the location is a little under one mile south of his first crime in Berner Street. Of further interest is that it is south of the main roads, Commercial Road and Whitechapel Road, that bisect this area of London. This accords with the attempt to distance themselves from earlier crimes that we have found in studies of modern-day serial killers.[3] There is a geographical distance here and also a psychological distance from both the earlier crimes, created by the physical and mental barrier of the two busy roads.

However, Jack was disturbed whilst attacking Stride and apparently wanted to complete a 'ripping' murder that night. But having marked out a triangle of offences around a mile or so equidistant from each other, where would he be expected to strike next? We can assume that he was probably limited by the range over which he could travel, but that he also wanted to avoid going to a place where he might be recognised or people might be more vigilant. On this simple logic the prediction would be that he would kill in the only area so far untouched, the south-west corner. There was another killing that same night, just half a mile due west of the murder of Stride. Catherine Eddowes was killed in Mitre Square, which is more or less a mile south of Hanbury Street. The prediction is correct.

There are some other interesting aspects of the location of the murder in Mitre Square. Most notably, it is about the same distance west of the previous murder that night in Berner Street as the second murder is of the first murder. Is Jack the Ripper moving back towards a preferred location? Is he aware of a distance of about three-quarters of a mile that he needs to keep between offences, a sort of 'safe distance' that he feels will keep him away from possible recognition?

With these four murders he has mapped out the four corners of an area that covers Whitechapel. If he is to continue to operate under the same principles, he has limited opportunities. Anywhere he goes now will be less than his 'safe distance' from previous crimes. Of course, he could move out of the area, but if he does not know other areas so well or the journey there, for whatever reason, is problematic, he has to stay in the Whitechapel area. This means that his next crime will be close to one of his earlier crimes. Over a month on from the first killing in Buck's Row, we might assume that this would be the crime location he would be most comfortable revisiting, or some area between here and Berner Street.

Instead, however, the murder on 9 November of Mary Kelly takes place in Miller's Court, not far from the second murder in Hanbury Street, less than a mile north of the fourth death in Mitre Square.

These five crime scenes have marked out a circle that embraces Whitechapel. The sequence of the crimes also shows a tendency to be more towards the western side of Whitechapel. The two killings that took place on the same night are particularly interesting if the logic that Stuart Kind brought to the analysis of the Yorkshire Ripper's crime locations one hundred years later is followed. I will describe Kind's ideas in detail in Chapter 12 but, for the moment, it is enough to mention that Dr Kind drew attention to the fact that the killer must return to some base. Therefore the location of the crimes must be considered in relation to the time of day they happened. Were they committed on the way out from home or on the way back?

In the case of the two Whitechapel murders on 30 September it would be a reasonable assumption that Jack was on his way back from the first murder when he saw the opportunity for another 'more satisfying' killing. If this direction is compared to the direction of the first two murders, of Nichols and Chapman, then it may be proposed that the first crime on 30 September was at the extent of his walking reach, as was the murder of Nichols, the very first murder.

Nichols was murdered at about 3.40 a.m. Is that late at night or early in the morning? Following Dr Kind's logic we would expect that crimes committed late at night would be farther from the killer's base, as he moved ever further from it to search for victims. The very first crime is also likely to have required plucking up courage and lengthy wandering before he felt that the time and opportunity were right. We can well imagine him wandering round the streets into the early hours before finally deciding he could kill and get away. On this logic, that attack at 3.40 a.m. would be seen as late into the night, as far from his base as he could get.

If we make the assumption that Buck's Row is some distance from his base, this would also accord with the suggestion that the journey from Berner Street to Mitre Square was on the way back home. Lizzie Stride was killed around 2.00 a.m. and Catherine Eddowes 45 minutes later. Is this in accord with the hypothesis that the first of these late-night killings was at the end of his search but, having been disturbed, he was returning back to base?

In the best traditions of hypothesis testing we should look at the timing of the other two murders to see if they support or contradict our emerging thesis. The second murder, in Hanbury Street, was just before 6.00 a.m. Is this an indication of Jack on his way out from his base early in the morning, urgently seeking a victim that he could find close to home? Or does it show a man on his way back from a fruitless night, finding at last what he has been looking for? Or even a man at the outer edge of his search area, as far away from his base as is comfortable, when the city begins to wake up and go to work? The most likely possibility, it seems to me, is that it is not too far from his proposed base either on his way back, or on his way out.

The timing of the final murder is much more difficult to pinpoint precisely. For although Kelly's body was not discovered until 10.45 a.m. there are indications that she was likely to have been killed a few hours earlier, making the time of the killing similar to that in Hanbury Street. Would a killer who knew the whole country was looking for him risk being far from his hideaway at a time when this busy area of London was waking up? Or would that time of day be precisely the time when he would be out and about farthest from his base?

These are all difficult questions to answer, but I think reasonable speculation adds up to Miller's Court and Mitre Square being the closest crimes to Jack's base. The direction of return and the time of the offences are plausibly consistent with him wanting to be nearer to the west of Whitechapel than the east when he finished his crimes.

A WHITECHAPEL BASE

One fundamental question, though, is whether his base was in Whitechapel at all. There were railway stations running into Whitechapel and many other forms of transport that would take people in and out. We cannot know with certainty, but from studies I and others have carried out we have made a remarkably robust finding. If the area covered by a series of crimes is circumscribed, then in the majority of cases the serial offender has a base of some sort within that area.[4] Let me hasten to add that this is not true in all cases, and the proportion of offenders who live within this 'criminal range' varies considerably depending on many aspects of the crimes and locations. But as a rule of thumb there is at least a 50-50 chance that the offender lives within the area defined by a circle that joins the two furthest crimes. If the spread of the crimes is great and the criminal thinks he may be recognised in a given location then the chance he lives within this 'circle' increases. If the criminal is clearly targeting a particular type of criminal opportunity then the chance will decrease because it is the opportunity for the crime that determines where he will offend, rather than the location of his base.

There is thus the real possibility that Jack came into the area because of the opportunities available to carry out his mission. But the distribution of the crimes around the small area, together with their timing, also offers the possibility that he had a base in the area. The diary, curiously, suggests both are possible, but this is not the place for a dénouement. We still have some analysis to do.

If we assume that Jack did have a base within the area circumscribed by his crimes, then various forms of analysis are open to us to see if we can find its location. One approach, for example, is to assume that the crimes describe a region of activity spreading out from the base. On this assumption the base would be in the middle of our notional circle. But human activity is rarely so symmetrical, and I have found in many studies that the centre of the circle is not the closest estimate to the offender's home, although the home is frequently not far from that geometric centre.[5] In the case of the Whitechapel murders this would put the residence somewhere a little north of where Commercial Road meets Whitechapel Road.

The disadvantage of using the centre of the circle as an estimate is that crimes are usually unevenly distributed across an area. This gives far outlying points more weight to any computations than they perhaps warrant, drawing the average centre of the circle towards the most extreme point. In other words, the simplicity of calculating the centre of a circle is also its main weakness. The two furthest points typically are used to define the diameter. The centre of that diameter is thus half way between those two furthest points. But if most of the points are close together, and one of them is far away from this cluster – say, because the killer made a rare visit to an old flame in that location and took the opportunity to offend whilst he was there – then that one point will have an inappropriately large influence on the calculations.

An approach that reduces the impact of the rare, distant points is to calculate the 'centre of gravity' of the points. This treats the points like weights and works out where a fulcrum could be placed around which the weights all balance. If mechanical engineering is not your forte, then a straightforward piece of arithmetic can be used to locate the numerical heart of the points and thus the region in which the offender is most likely (but not inevitably) to be based. This is to calculate the average horizontal distance between points and the average vertical distance. Where these distances cross is the 'centre of gravity'.

If you are like some who have read drafts of this explanation, and do not know what I mean by this arithmetic calculation but do know how to compute an average, then the process I am implying here can be described more fully as follows. (If you do not know how to work out an average you have probably already skipped this section when you got to the first use of the verb 'calculate'.)

You need first to fix a point on the map. Somewhere to the edge of the crime locations is easiest, but it does not really matter where. This point is your 'notional zero'. Now draw a horizontal line and a vertical line from this point at right angles to each other. From each of the crime locations now draw two straight lines: one that touches the horizontal line, the other touching the vertical line, but each touching those lines at right angles. These are notional co-ordinates of the crimes on the horizontal and vertical lines. Measure the distance from your notional zero to each of the co-ordinates and calculate the average of these distances. At this average point draw new horizontal and vertical lines into the area of the crimes. Where these two notional lines cross is the average weighted centre of the points – the arithmetic heart of the crime locations.

In the Whitechapel case this brings the hypothesised home location to the west of the centre of the offence circle. We can see now that we are moving into a territory that is not far from that given by our other considerations about the location of Jack's base: this arithmetic centre is closer to Miller's Court and Mitre Square than any of the other murder scenes.

There are limitations to the 'centre of gravity' calculations as well. Those calculations assume that we think about and therefore use distances in a simple incremental way. This can take us into heavy maths, so let me explain it by a simple reference to a common experience. If you were to go to your local shops and the nearest shop was, say, a quarter of a mile away, but someone told you that a shop a mile away was much better, you would say that to increase your journey fourfold the shop would have to be really good. The difference between a quarter of a mile and a mile, in these circumstances, is quite significant. By contrast, let us consider that you plan to go to the pictures and the nearest cinema is ten miles away, but you are told that there is a better one twelve miles away. You may well consider the extra couple of miles worth the bother. Two miles on ten is only a small increase, whereas in the first case three quarters of a mile was considered a lot.

Of course, mode of transport and many other factors influence our judgements in these situations, but I hope I have convinced you that psychologically all distances are not equal. As distances increase so we need a larger change in their size for the change to be noticeable. In the case of the criminal looking for opportunities for crime this translates to meaning that locations closer to his home have more weight than those further away. The significance of this for our calculations of the possible residence of Jack the Ripper is to give even more emphasis in our calculations to those crime locations that are close to each other. There is a mathematical way of doing this that was built into a computer programme developed under my guidance at the University of Liverpool. But with just five points the impact of these calculations is easy to perceive without the need for extensive software. They pull the posited base further to the west, to somewhere around Commercial Street. This reinforces our earlier suggestion that the killer lived somewhere between Miller's Court and Mitre Square.

Which takes us back to the diary. The only specific point it has to offer that has never been open to historical or scientific tests is the claim that he has 'taken a small room in Middlesex Street'. This street is just a few yards west of our posited 'weighted centre of gravity' on Commercial Street and runs from near Mitre Square on Whitechapel Road to near Miller's Court. If the diarist was faking then this is a remarkably good guess. If the diary is genuine then it accords with what we know about the activities and movements of many, but certainly not all, serial killers.

THE WHITECHAPEL CONNECTION

Our analysis of the geography of the Whitechapel murders and their relationship to the significance of Middlesex Street takes us back to what has become known of James Maybrick. The diary and the geographical analysis draw attention to the special significance of Whitechapel for the diarist. It was a place he knew had the opportunities for crime that he wanted and to which he could clearly get comfortable access. Would it therefore be expected that the diarist had extensive prior knowledge of Whitechapel and its whores before he took rooms in Middlesex Street? Or would it be more likely that he had some vague knowledge of Whitechapel that he deliberately extended prior to his crimes?

One significant entry in the diary that we have already had cause to ponder was this: 'I have walked the streets and have become more than familiar with them.' If this was James Maybrick writing, could he have become familiar enough with those streets on fleeting visits to London, popping in to take advantage of the widely known services available on the street? It is difficult to be sure, but it seems to me that it is unlikely that the level of knowledge required to move around at night with the confidence of Jack the Ripper would have been based on rare visits. It is more plausible to assume that he had 'walked the streets' many times, possibly long before the start of his campaign.

That then sets the questions rolling about what prior contact James Maybrick had with Whitechapel. Shirley Harrison presents a considerable amount of evidence that he had many reasons to be in the area. She cites a mistress living on the eastern edge of Whitechapel who was registered as Mrs Maybrick. She draws attention to the fact that his business partner, Gustavas Witt, had London offices in Cullum Street on the western edge of Whitechapel. By this rekoning the walk from his partner's offices to his mistress's house would have taken him on a walk right through the middle of Whitechapel. With only a little detour he could have visited all the murder scenes. But, of course, so could a number of other popular suspects.

'THE MAN I HAVE BECOME'

If James Maybrick was the vile murderer of so many women in the East End of London, the journal that he left is one of the most valuable documents we have to give us an insight into the mind of a serial killer. Its very existence tells us a lot about such killers: their self-obsession; their inner turmoil; the careful planning that becomes a self-perpetuating narrative of the evil character they build for themselves. It shows how this personal campaign that they construct for themselves is directly reflected in the physical as well as the mental journey they take.

If James Maybrick wrote the diary, there are other things about serial killers it tells us too. The diary refers often to his taking some sort of medication or drug and the headaches it gave him, the coldness of his hands and the way the compound also often energised him. Could this drug have played any role in his bizarre narrative? It emerged during the trial of his wife Florence for his murder that he was addicted to arsenic. It was the arsenic found in various locations in the house as well as the hints of it in his body that led to Florie's conviction. This is a curious addiction by modern standards, but arsenic was actually used in many 'pick-me-ups' of the day. However, it was rare for people to take so much that it became an addiction so strong that withdrawal symptoms could be fatal, which is one possibility of how Maybrick came to die. Not knowing how addicted he was, Florie withheld the white powders from him when he was ill, and thereby possibly produced such severe withdrawal symptoms that he died. She was charged with poisoning him, but the irony is that she may have killed him by trying to save his life.

The difficulty for us is to determine the psychological and physiological consequences of taking arsenic in increasing doses over a number of years. When I first heard about Maybrick's arsenic addiction I remembered earlier work I had done on alternative medicines, in particular homeopathy. This widely used form of therapy relies on the idea that a minute dose of a compound will alleviate the symptoms that are produced by large doses of the same compound (an idea that has some analogies to modern inoculation). Homeopaths therefore need to know about the effects of many different compounds. Over the nineteenth century they therefore set about the hazardous task of recording the consequences of taking various doses of everything that they thought might have therapeutic value – what they called 'provings'. At the start of the twentieth century Dr James Tyler Kent brought all these provings together in a fascinating volume known as the *Homeopathic Materia Medica*.[6]

What is special about this archive of the effects of various potions and nostrums is that, because of the holistic nature of homeopathy, it records every aspect of the compounds' effects on both mental and physical processes. *Arsenicum Album*, the white arsenic that Maybrick used, has a dozen pages devoted to it. The symptoms it generates make fascinating reading, but are especially significant when read in conjunction with the diary.

With a bitter irony that can only be fully appreciated when knowing Florence Maybrick's full story, the entry on *Arsenicum Album* (Ars) commences with a reference to it being 'mostly abused, in the form of Fowler's solution'. This is what Maybrick used to take and Florie tried to keep from him; it was found in his house and used as part of the evidence against his wife. When we turn to the account of its mental effects the irony gives way to a bitter recognition.

In the Maybrick diary there are frequent mentions of the writer's hands being cold and the difficulty he has in getting them warm: 'My hands still remain cold.' Dr Kent deals with that: 'The Arsenicum patient [in a restless state] is *always freezing*, hovers around the fire, cannot get clothing enough to keep warm, a great sufferer from the cold' [italics in original]. The headaches, bodily pain and vomiting described in the diary are also all described in great detail by Dr Kent:

> The *anxiety* that is found in Ars, is intermingled with fear, with impulses, with suicidal inclinations, with sudden freaks and with mania. It has delusions and various kinds of insanity; in the more active form, delirium and excitement. *Sadness* prevails to a great extreme. So sad that he is weary of life; he loathes life, and wants to die . . . The anxiety takes form also in restlessness, in which he constantly moves . . . The restlessness seems mostly in the mind; it is an anxious restlessness, or an anguish . . . [original italics].

The diary records that: 'I believe I am mad, completely mad. I try to fight my thoughts I walk the streets until dawn.'

A GOOD ALIBI
It is difficult to set up clear tests that would categorically challenge the hypothesis that the diary is authentic. Certainly all the tests that have been set up so far have failed. Perhaps the most popular challenge to its authenticity – that the Ripper must have been a resident of Whitechapel, and not a traveller from Liverpool – is undermined by the diary itself, as well as the patterns of the crimes on the map. If the murders had been spread across London, or a wide area of the East End, that would have undermined the possibility of the Ripper being a traveller who visited London on rare business trips. If the sequence of crimes had not been circular but along some clear route, that would have pointed more towards a traveller without any base in the area than one who had taken rooms locally. If the diary had portrayed a fit man, or one not showing the effects of arsenic, it would have been sloppy work, given what was revealed about Maybrick's addiction after his death. But even with all these, and many other possibilities for rejecting the diary as a hoax, we are still left with the risk of confirmation bias in recording only the

things that might support its authenticity. What we need is evidence that James Maybrick was not in London on the Friday, Saturday and Sundays when the murders took place – evidence, indeed, that he was a hardworking man who was most unlikely to leave his work on a Thursday evening and return for Monday morning. What James Maybrick needs, like all prime suspects, is a good alibi.

If we take the diary as genuine, a plausible story unfolds. An intelligent man who is besotted with his attractive young wife, but certainly not the pillar of society that he presents to the world, becomes angry with his own inadequacies and, suspicious of his wife, angry with her and the other women he sees as representing her. He turns this festering resentment into a campaign that is halfway between an ironic challenge to the world around him and a desperate tragedy that will bring about his own death after he has carried out his heroic mission. The feelings that he converts into the narrative of his campaign are exaggerated by his arsenic addiction, increasing his restless search for actions that will quieten him.

He realises the risks of his mission and determines to distance himself from those dangers by going to a place to which he has ready access and which also has particular significance for him. He then walks the streets and maps out the area in his head so that he can kill and mutilate as he wishes, having first developed his taste for killing elsewhere. The map of his killing charts his inner journey until eventually his addiction to arsenic kills him. Yet he is apparently such a pillar of society that his pretty young wife gets sentenced unfairly for his murder, with no right of appeal when the facts of her husband's arsenic addiction eventually become public knowledge.

If genuine, the most important message the journal has for us is that even under the intense gaze of the trial of his wife, no clues to Maybrick's secret life emerged. The last page of the diary opens with the words: 'The pain is unbearable. My dear Bunny knows all. I do not know if she has the strength to kill me.' Yet in death, when the only pretence left to him was the persona he had created in the minds of those around him, the other life described in the leather-bound scrapbook was so implausible that even the wife to whom he had confessed his crimes could not bring herself to believe such enormous evil. Was this what she meant when she said before being sentenced, 'Much has been withheld'?

The scepticism of science is essential. The diary may be a fake, but what it tells us certainly does not contradict what we know from other sources about James Maybrick or Jack the Ripper. It also accords with what we can see about how a serial killer's inner narrative is reflected in the geography of his crimes. If the diary is genuine, though, it also raises one final thought. It is difficult to see how modern techniques of police investigation could have caught Jack the Ripper, unless a policeman had known to knock on the door of those rooms in Middlesex Street and recognised the man he was looking for, or had found the diary.

11. LAS VEGAS SURVIVORS

Las Vegas is a brightly glittering grid scratched from the surface of a barren desert. It welcomes with a tastefully spacious airport, one of the busiest in the world, that contrasts with the seedy appearance of LAX in Los Angeles, from which many visitors make the hour-long flight. This oasis in the desert shouts out how different it is from anywhere else the minute you disembark. Passing through halls of one-armed bandits, or 'slots' as Americans call them, you are immediately aware this is a haven for mindless pleasure and effortless excitement, attracting millions of people from all over the world. They mainly come here to play, but many also come here to work, as you discover when you step into a taxi. Every taxi driver, whether born in Haifa or Addis Ababa, Dubrovnik or Belfast, has a story of escape to tell, bringing him to this asylum for sybarites.

Driving along the freeway streaming into the city, all you can see are huge hotels – the largest in the world, as the locals are proud to tell you – fronted by surreal scenes. Hotel Treasure Island boasts a fully rigged eighteenth-century galleon that is sunk by a pirate ship in Buccaneer Bay every ninety minutes. There is a small Venetian lagoon (complete with gondolas), unnaturally clean and odour-free. As you acclimatise, you become aware that there are no clocks in Las Vegas. This contributes to the atmosphere of endless, un-changing time in which nothing of substance matters. The only advertisements carried in the local free newspapers are for call-girls and other indulgences of the flesh.

Inside the huge hotels are endless casinos. There are small sections with tables devoted to games of chance, but most are made up almost entirely of row upon row of slot machines. Because these require little more than pulling a handle and pressing a button for success, these rows are rarely crowded. And hidden away are the serious betting areas where you can gamble on anything.

Las Vegas is one of the most febrile and unstable commu-nities anywhere. With the delight that Americans have in immodest figures, you can readily discover that Las Vegas has a residential population of 1.4 million people, but they service over 120,000 hotel rooms, which host more than 30 million visitors a year. To add to this fluid, party atmosphere, more than 100,000 of those visitors come to Las Vegas to get married.

It would be natural to assume that crime is imported into Las Vegas with its millions of visitors. To some extent this is true; the migration of criminals has certainly increased since neighbouring California introduced its 'three strikes and you're out' law, which means potential long-term imprisonment for even minor crimes, if repeated. But in Las Vegas, as in the majority of places around the world, most crime is home-grown. Step behind the huge hotels and walk a little way from their garish lights and you will find streets of tawdry pawnshops whose windows, filled with wedding rings and family heirlooms, speak of the lives destroyed by gambling. They show how readily trades emerge to take advantage of the failings of fellow humans. Near these shops drunks lie around, sleeping rough. Talk to them and you will find they were once respectable citizens. One I spoke to had been a civil engineer, another a company lawyer.

These street people are the visible tip of the iceberg of crime for which Hollywood has made Las Vegas so notorious. With around 200 murders a year and nearly 1,000 rapes, more than twice as many as Manhattan, and putting the city on a par with New Orleans, the local police are busy. It is a level of criminal activity that does reveal something of the luckless underbelly of Las Vegas.

DAN HELMS

Dan Helms is a crime analyst in the Las Vegas Detective Bureau. Because we share an interest in the mapping of criminals' actions, we were put together on the platform at a conference in December 1999 arranged by the US National Institute of Justice – an arm of the Department of Justice. The NIJ spends millions of dollars each year helping to improve the work of law enforcement agencies across the US. Dan and I quickly found that we shared a desire to use scientifically based procedures as support to police investigations, so we kept in touch after the conference.

Dan has the large, athletic build and lapsed military bearing that hints at his past in the US Air Force. Unexpectedly, in the frivolity of Las Vegas, he is fluent in Arabic from his time in military intelligence. He has a droll, deadpan humour, from which he spins a stream of repartee that would shame many stand-up comics, but he is also the quintessential computer whiz kid, totally at home with operating systems, innovative algorithms and the practice of information technology. He uses his humour, as much as his knowledge of computers, to help him deal with some of the horrors that lurk below the glamorous facade of his patch.

Pinned to the wall behind Dan's desk is a set of photographs of wanted villains. But because this is the detective bureau in Las Vegas, many of the crimes they are wanted for are rather unusual. In addition to the crimes that plague all cities, Las Vegas has its own special brand. There are 'doorpushers', who make a tidy living from the specialist career of finding hotel doors that have not been properly closed. Visitors to the vast anonymous hotels the city is so proud of are eager to get to the gaming tables, and are unaware of the network of criminals dedicated to exploiting every human weakness. As Dan[1] explains:

> The 'doorpusher' is dressed like a tourist and may have a room key, making him/her appear to be a guest. As he walks down the hallway, he lightly leans against the wall, dragging his fingertips. When he passes a door, he gently shoves at it. Now, hotel room doors at Las Vegas resorts are very heavy and very well protected – kicking one in is quite an athletic feat. They are closed by hydraulic springs, which keep them shut. However, very rarely, a door will almost, but not quite, close. The 'doorpusher' finds these by the simple expedient of leaning against them lightly. If the door is not quite perfectly shut, it will open. The 'doorpusher' will then enter and clean out the room of valuables. Probably only one door in every few thousand will open, but this relatively low-risk method of attack pays off enough to support a small cabal of this type of burglar.

Another form of criminal life that has evolved specifically to survive in the immense casinos, laden with slot machines, is the 'tubsnatcher'. To quote Dan again:

'Tubsnatchers' are extremely common. To understand how they operate, you'll have to visualise the slot floor on a busy Vegas casino. Several thousand slot machines are packed together into islands, usually in short rows. There is a tiny space between each machine and its neighbours to either side, and behind your slot machine is the back of another machine, facing the opposite direction. When you sit down in front of a slot machine, another person is directly facing you – but there are two slot machines between you, yours and his, so you don't notice him.

How do you play slots? Well, you insert coins, of course. But how to carry all those coins? Casinos supply plastic tubs, or cups, decorated with their logo and big enough to carry several hundred dollars in coins each. Now, naturally, since these tubs are heavy (with your money!) and you will be in front of this slot machine for some time, it makes sense to set the tub down in the empty space beside the machine. It's right in front of you, and you can keep an eye on it, and of course it's easy to take coins from it every few seconds.

Although there are hundreds of variations, 'tubsnatchers' usually operate from the other side of the bank of slot machines from you. They reach through the space between machines and grab your coin tub from the other side. They are usually very good at waiting for you to be distracted – by winning, perhaps – or at creating a distraction (casino criminals usually work in teams), so that you don't notice the hand, obscured by the large machines, pulling your money away. Even if you do notice, in order to chase the criminal you'll have to go around the huge bank of slot machines that lie between you.

This kind of offender is usually good at managing fast getaways, and also at engineering obstructions for you – so, if you see your coin tub disappear suddenly behind your slot machine, and get up to chase after it, you'll usually find that a change trolley is in the way, or a party of sixty Japanese tourists is taking a group picture in the aisle, or an enormously fat woman has decided to tie her shoe in your path. Something like that. 'Tubsnatching' is more dangerous than 'doorpushing', and yields lower cash returns; but it is vastly faster and easier to do, and requires less intellect. It's fairly common – but also very easy to catch.

This detailed knowledge of the unique foibles of Las Vegas criminals is a prerequisite for understanding the much more serious crimes that happen around the city. Beyond the petty criminals feeding off holidaymakers, Dan also has to deal with crimes that are altogether more serious and vile. He needs to be able to tell if an incident is a consequence of a 'tubsnatcher' or 'doorpusher' progressing to more vicious robberies. Las Vegas detectives must understand how networks of minor criminals operate. For example, the police need to know if a murder has emerged from turf wars between small-time hoodlums, or if they are dealing with something totally different.

If a crime, or series of crimes, cannot be linked to the known felons who have their photographs pinned up behind Dan's desk, then he has to draw on skills that go beyond his local knowledge of particular individuals and their criminal habits. He has to draw on his knowledge of patterns of crime in Las Vegas, using his computer skills to tease pointers out of analyses of the information available to him. A particularly powerful form of such analysis derives from having crime locations inputted onto a computerised map. Dan has special expertise in using computerised mapping and has helped Las Vegas to become the city with the most detailed set of electronic maps in the US. As he puts it characteristically, 'We can locate every manhole cover in this place.' Once crimes have been put onto electronic maps it is possible to look for the underlying trends that may be causing the geographical distribution of the points. This is the process called 'crime mapping'.

CRIME MAPPING

Across the USA a lot of the work supported by the National Institute of Justice is devoted to crime mapping. This consists, in the main, of creating prettily coloured maps showing where various types of crimes have occurred. The commercial potential for selling software that will produce these maps has generated an explosion of salesmen who fund the buffets and keep the coffee flowing at seminars for law-enforcement agencies across the country. It seems that many police forces across the US feel they are starting to understand crime in their area if they can at least get reports of it recorded on a map.

The practical benefits of incessant mapping are still not clearly established but it does appear to be of particular value in the USA because of the country's proliferation of many hundreds of different law enforcement agencies. In Britain we tend to think of 'the police', and are often puzzled by the US term 'law-enforcement agency', but the difference is much more than just a name. In the UK there are 42 police forces, one for every major city and major region of the country. This is taken to its logical conclusion in the case of the great metropolis of London, which even though it houses about one eighth of the British population and accounts for perhaps a third of all crime that takes place in Britain – is serviced by the one huge Metropolitan Police Force, known throughout as 'the Met'. The Met covers an area of 620 square miles, employing about 25,550 police officers. In addition Britain has only a few other 'law-enforcement agencies' beyond the 42 police forces, such as British Transport Police, the Ministry of Defence Police, Customs and Excise and the very small espionage and counter-espionage organisations of MI5 and MI6. This means that a series of crimes is likely to happen within one administrative area. Even if they are spread across police forces, it is not a particularly difficult task to get the handful of constabularies needed to work together.

In the US, things are far more complex. There are highway police and state police, city police and county police; and the curious mixture of Alcohol, Tobacco and Firearms has an agency all to itself. Determining whether a fire was caused by arson is initially a task for the insurance companies, who therefore employ their own investigators. Then there is the FBI, which has a rather complex advisory role, and the CIA, which has an overseas remit which can readily merge into domestic matters; but both are distinct from the Secret Service, which is mainly concerned with the strange mix of forgery and protecting senior politicians, yet can investigate other crimes that drift into its arena.

What this means is that if a mixture of crimes is spread across an area of any reasonable size, they will fall under the jurisdiction of many different agencies, each of which keeps different records in varying ways. Therefore, crimes may not be effectively linked because they often sit on incompatible databases and are being investigated by totally distinct organisations.

I was told by an experienced FBI agent that if a dead body is found at the base of the Washington Monument with drugs in its pocket, there are instantly twelve different law-enforcement agencies that have the right to investigate the case as a possible murder, each with its own independent procedures. Multiply that across a number of different crimes and it is clear what a huge job it can be, especially in large cities, to make sense of patterns of crime. Putting crimes onto a map is one way around this problem, especially if the map is shared by different agencies.

This use of maps to help cope with problems created by the organisation of bureaucracies is still a primitive methodology and gives rise to what the director of the London-based Jill Dando Institute for Crime Science calls 'blobology',[2] the almost mesmeric state induced by the process of inputting dots on a map and creating blobs around clusters of them. What is needed is an understanding of the process that gives rise to the locations of the blobs; but this needs to be done in a context where the bureaucracy has already been sorted out. The unique location of Las Vegas in a desert means that one major police force deals with virtually all the city's crimes. In Dan Helms, they have a crime analyst who is certainly not content just with blobs.

AN EVIL MAN

Crime analysts like Dan are only as effective as the police departments they are part of. In the US the sheriff, who is an elected official responsible only to the community he protects, can have a huge influence on how law enforcement operates. As Dan explains:

> The sheriff of Clark County at the time was Jerry Keller. Keller was a big change for the LVMPD because he actively embraced technology and internal reform. Although some cops didn't like his methods, the changes he introduced revolutionised how the LVMPD did business and transformed the agency from a 'Cowboy Posse' into an ultra-modern police organization (prior to Sheriff Keller, the Las Vegas Metropolitan Police Department was sometimes jokingly referred to as 'The Mormon Gun Club'). Keller often became closely involved in task forces and tried to make certain that special equipment, manpower, and overtime would be provided when necessary.

The context provided by the forward-looking sheriff laid the basis for good working relationships between crime analysts and the police. The work of such analysts will only be effective if there is ready co-operation from informed and intelligent police officers. Certainly the way Dan tells it, the Las Vegas Police Department seems to be blessed with good cops. One such is Debbie Love. Her petite, tanned appearance and the stereotypes blondes have to fight all over the world may lead some to expect her not to be as determined and capable as she is, but her picture on the wall behind the police desk at headquarters, along with other winners of police medals, is a testament to her drive and tenacity.

She has paid the price all police officers pay in one way or another for total commitment to their job. Her forearms are crisscrossed with white scars; some come from knives, and others from the time a half-handcuffed suspect picked her up bodily and swung her round like a child swinging a doll. So although still a fairly young woman, her natural good looks have changed in character – her face is somewhat lined, and her posture ever so slightly bent, as if she were a little tired, or carrying something heavy. The weight she carries is the need to catch the bad guys. As Dan puts it:

She collects confessions like other cops collect patches and coffee-cups, but because of some earlier successes in dealing with crime series, Debbie has confidence in crime analysis and embraces the tools, techniques, and methods which more traditional detectives sometimes shun. She is quick to try new things, but covers all her bases with the best kind of old-fashioned investigative work.

So when a particularly nasty crime occurred it was no surprise that Debbie brought the details to Dan before the case had even been filed. It was an assault, on 1 February 2000, that was remarkable in its viciousness. As Dan tells it:

A very, very, very evil man broke into a woman's apartment in the downtown area. He beat her up to subdue her, then bound her with duct tape and electrical cord to her bed. He beat her further. He tortured her with a cigarette, and a knife, then sexually assaulted her. Right now, you're probably thinking, 'This sounds like a pretty bad fellow,' but we're just getting started. Next, he knotted an electrical cord around her throat, to strangle her, and cinched it with a tourniquet. He tortured her further while she asphyxiated. Then he stabbed her with a kitchen knife, several times.

Still not quite finished, he doused her with an accelerant, then set her, the bed, and the apartment on fire while she was still alive. On his way out, he barricaded her inside the burning room, still bound to the bed, knife still in her, cord knotted around her neck.

You will share my amazement when I tell you: she lived. She extricated herself from the restraints she had been put in. She overcame the weakness caused from her injuries, which were extensive. And she managed to escape from the barricaded apartment that was burning all around her. Which of course gave us a witness to the crime.

LINKING IN OTHER CASES
In places other than Las Vegas that might have been the end of the story. Perhaps a drug-crazed visitor, passing through,

had chanced on this victim, or maybe this was a robbery that had gone seriously wrong and the robber, with all the means of rapid exit available in Las Vegas, had quickly left town. In this case having a small, integrated police force paid off. Discussions between different teams in the LVMPD led to the discovery that the Burglary Squad was looking for a serial burglar, and that the case might be related because of the offender's willingness to break into homes when people were present. It quickly emerged that the Robbery Squad was also looking for a similar suspect.

Examining the evidence from these cases gave fingerprint links. The police officers dealing with rape in Las Vegas also became part of the discussion. They were investigating a series of rapes in the same general area as the burglaries that had parallels in their violence and the description given of the rapist. The linking together of offences culminated in June 2000, when a Tibetan monk was found murdered. A fortuitous DNA link made it plain that the serial burglar, serial robber, and now rapist-cum-murderer were one and the same. Dan was part of the team trying to find this one-man violent crime wave:

> The degree of violence that was employed, and the description of the suspect, were clear enough that we were able to say with relative certainty that we had at least eight events that could be attributed to the same offender. In this particular crime series our offender took things from most of his victims, he was a robber as well as a thug and a rapist. He took cars from two victims and also as you call it a pram, a baby stroller, as he put a victim's large TV in it.

Now all they needed to do was to find the culprit. They had many crime locations and were able to use the advanced crime-mapping procedures that Dan had made his own to examine the implications of where the incidents and associated events had happened. The efforts served the investigation team well.

LOCATING THE OFFENDER

Some of the things the offender stole were later dumped. The dump sites were part of the picture that Dan could build onto his map alongside the actual locations of the assaults and burglaries. The advantage of knowing where the stolen objects were found was that he could work out the route the offender had taken. In three of the crimes, the offender stole then dumped cars. From noting where they were recovered, Dan could put on the map the most likely streets the cars were driven down immediately after being stolen. In one case where a pram was used to transport a stolen TV, the direction that it was ferried in could also be worked out. In all cases, the direction in which the criminal was moving was the same. That allowed Dan to continue the lines of these routes on his computer map until he saw where they overlapped. It defined a triangular area of Las Vegas. The houses the offender broke into were all concentrated around this triangle. The offender appeared to be criss-crossing an area just a few blocks wide, backwards and forwards in a classic pattern that lent itself well to computer analysis.

Many factors can cause such a pattern. The geometry of lines on a computer screen does not automatically tell investigators why that geometry has emerged. If the offender is, for instance, searching out particular opportunities for crime and such opportunities are only available in a limited area – as happens with attacks on street prostitutes – then it is the opportunity that draws the criminal in, as with a commuter going to his place of work. There may also be accessible routes that shape offenders' journeys, creating spatial patterns that have little to do with the offences themselves. In addition to the complication of what the offender may be doing, there is also the number of types of computer analysis available for exploring spatial patterns. Some examine the density of the offences; others focus on the geometric patterns. Yet others pay most attention to the roads along which the offender is most likely to be travelling. All these forms of analysis can generate different results, depending on the particular circumstances of the cases.

In serial offences like this it is often difficult to be sure which individual cases really were the actions of the same

5. LAS VEGAS CRIMES WITH DRAGNET ANALYSIS

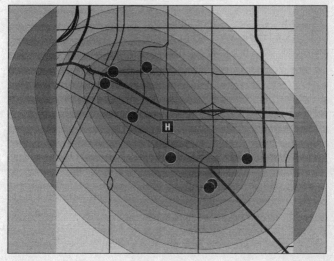

Justin Porter's home location and site of crimes on Las Vegas grid.

person. Unless there is very strong forensic evidence, such as DNA or fingerprints, there is always a degree of speculation as to which offences are linked. Dan therefore selected eight offences he was confident had been committed by the same person. He tested a variety of ways of determining the likely geographical focal point – the criminal heart, as it were. One of the most fruitful was my Dragnet[3] system that I'd let him test out in order to see how effective it might be in Las Vegas. This is based on specific psychological principles about the 'mental maps' of offenders in addition to well-established principles about the typical distances offenders travel from home to commit their crimes.

He fed in the locations of the various crimes and Dragnet came up with a high-priority area that was very close to the area he had identified using other techniques. What he found was that almost every way he looked at the problem he ended up with the same area of the city being the likely base for the crimes. Even the simple expedient of calculating the centre of gravity of the incidents pointed to the same location as the other more sophisticated analyses. They highlighted a tiny area of downtown: an area that contained four low-rent condominium and apartment blocks.

Dan's analyses were so precise that he was able to suggest that just one of these apartment complexes contained the residence of the offender. So confident was he in his predictions that he went even further. He predicted which side of the complex the criminal would most likely live on, based on his analysis of which streets the offender probably used most. As Dan put it:

> I have never been so certain of any prediction in my life.
> I was more secure in my forecast that the offender lived
> in that building than in a forecast that the sun would rise
> tomorrow. I told anyone and everyone who would listen.
> Fortunately, my star is pretty high here when it comes to
> making predictions, and there were plenty of people
> willing to listen. One of them was Detective Debbie Love.

Detective Love's experience as a rape investigator got her the job of lead investigator as part of a combined task force involving several units. Determined to catch this terrible criminal, she was backed up by one of the special Problem Solving Units (PSU) within LVMPD. They are patrol officers, not detectives; however, they wear civilian clothes and drive unmarked cars. The big difference between them and the majority of patrol officers – the ones in uniform – is that PSU teams do not respond to calls for service. They are totally self-directed. Rather than run around from call to call, they try to get ahead of crimes by identifying and solving problems before they get too serious. Dan again:

> They keep themselves busy – very busy. It's fair to say
> that there is sometimes some friction between PSU teams
> and the rest of the department. Detectives sometimes get
> vexed because PSU squads perform investigative work of
> their own; uniformed patrolmen sometimes envy the
> autonomy of PSU and wonder what they're doing, if
> they're not answering calls. But the effectiveness of PSU
> has been well documented.

The PSU provided back-up for Debbie Love as she went to the apartment complex to see if she could identify the man so many different squads in the LVMPD were looking for. In parallel Sexual Assault teams and Robbery Squad teams were involved in canvassing the whole neighbourhood.

HOMING IN ON THE OFFENDER

The house identified was at a busy crossroads a few minutes' drive from the 'Freemont Experience', a shopping mall that links hotels and casinos, that is covered with a barrel-arched roof that dazzles nightly with gaudy flowers and swirling patterns. Behind the mall is a part of Las Vegas that visitors never see, even though it is so near to the 5,000-room hotels. It is the 'backlands', where the people who service the hotels live in run-down accommodation in stark contrast to the gaudy luxury only a short distance away. Here there are one- and two-storey wooden houses crammed together, some boarded up; others have plastic sheeting on their windows to keep out the heat and glare of the desert sun.

Detective Love's search of this area drew on all her experience. She had a description, and the police had formed the view that there was only one person known in the area who fitted it: Justin Porter, a young man who still lived with his mother and who, at the tender age of seventeen, had no police record. Dan tells the story of what happened:

Debbie took the prime target – the apartment complex we identified. Rather than knock on doors, she waited until about 2 a.m. on a day when we had identified the offender as often being active. She spotted the suspect – Porter – moving through the complex and stopped him for a 'chat'. She very prudently called for four other guys from the PSU team to join her at a discreet distance. Because DNA had already been collected and matched, she and the other hunters had swab kits with them, and they asked the subject, Mr Porter, for his permission to obtain a swab. He procrastinated, then insisted that he couldn't give his consent because he was a minor; only his mother could do so. Big mistake! Debbie knocked on the door and woke up Mom, and after a few words managed to obtain her permission, and took the swab. So now she had DNA, and left. Well, it took a while to get the results back – almost thirty days. But they were a match. She (and the rest of the team) knew Porter was their man. She went back to collect him. His mother revealed that her son had left for Chicago – just two days after the swab had been taken. He knew that he was going to be spotted, and thought he could escape justice by fleeing the state.

Debbie Love was not going to leave it at that. Using her accumulated skills and experience she found someone who knew Porter and was willing to talk to her. This uncovered a girlfriend that Porter had in Chicago. It did not take Debbie long to find the girlfriend's address and solicit the co-operation of the Chicago Police Department. They moved with speed and arrested Justin Porter so that he could be brought back to Las Vegas to face trial for 58 felonies, including six counts of rape and one of murder. DNA linked him to the rapes and some of the burglaries, and eight victims identified him as their attacker.

LAS VEGAS SURVIVORS

The ship that is sunk four times a day in front of one of the huge hotels in Las Vegas is a British man-o'-war. The scenario played out – with much shouting and firing of cannon – is of a pirate ship sinking one of Her Majesty's gunboats. It seems to capture the frontier-town spirit, with all the anti-authority determination that enabled people to carve Las Vegas out of the most inhospitable of desert habitats. That spirit seems to live on in the grit of many of Justin Porter's victims. All but one of the many victims he raped, bound and tried to kill managed to survive, often against the odds, and give the police enough information to enable them to tie some very different types of crimes together.

Another mode of survival in hostile settings is to become vicious. The rattlesnake and poisonous cactus are both well adapted to the heat and drought of the desert. Is it going too far to suggest that although Las Vegas now has enough water shipped in from the next state, it is still an emotional and cultural desert? In such a desert, from time to time, vicious forms of life are likely to emerge as a way of coping. When he came to trial, Justin Porter's family claimed he had learning disabilities. In court he smiled and waved at the waiting media. What did he make of the place he lived in? It is surely possible that the mindless excesses around him stimulated some adolescent, atavistic desires that he just did not know how to curb.

As ever, Dan has a clear take on the problems of explaining Porter's actions:

> As to why Justin Porter did it – well, I frankly have no deep answer. I think he just wanted to rape women and rob people. His family knew he was a 'problem kid', but the depths of his malignance were shocking to everyone. When the question of 'Why?' arises, I'm afraid I'm out of my depth. He was certainly involved with a bad crowd, including some serious gangsters – but then again, to our knowledge, none of them committed any acts approaching Porter's degree of depravity. He's something special.

To survive in Las Vegas the police need to understand the unique qualities of its habitat. This requires a detailed knowledge of the special creatures that live there, such as the 'doorpushers' and 'tubsnatchers', but also an ability to detect when some new species has found its way onto their patch. That ability involves the effective pooling together of information from different members of the law-enforcement team. But such information may not make a lot of sense without the interpretation skills that Dan Helms showed. These skills went beyond putting dots on a map. He needed to draw upon psychological principles that help explain why the dots end up where they do. It is the adventure of discovering these principles to which we now turn.

MARAUDING CRIMINALS

In this harsh world draw thy breath in pain,
To tell my story

Shakespeare, *Hamlet*

In the marauder hypothesis the offender is assumed to
move out from his base to commit his crimes then return
. . . This hypothesis implies a much closer relationship
between the location of crimes and of a criminal's home,
such that the further the distance between crimes the
further the distance from home.

Canter, D. and Larkin, P. (1993) 'The Environmental
Range of Serial Rapists', *Journal of Environmental
Psychology*, 13, pp. 63–69

A quest involving conflict assumes two main characters, a
protagonist or hero, and an antagonist or enemy . . .
everything is focused on a conflict between the hero and his
enemy.

Northrop Frye (1957) *Anatomy of Criticism*,
Princeton University Press, p. 187

12. CRIMINAL GRAVITY

Justin Porter was apprehended in Las Vegas in August 2001 after investigators drew upon discoveries that had been made in the fight against cholera in Victorian London a century and a half earlier. The curious chain of scientific breakthroughs from past to present, forgotten and rediscovered, included along the way advice to the British police on how to avoid the mistakes of the Yorkshire Ripper inquiry. It eventually led to myself, a social psychologist with virtually no background in the study of crime, unexpectedly helping to catch a serial killer and rapist. From that I developed procedures that found their way to Las Vegas. Such are the convoluted ways of science, especially applied science that must find a route across many disciplinary boundaries.

CRIMINAL GRAVITY

The lynchpin in this historical chain was Stuart Kind, who recently died at the age of 78. His obituary in a number of national newspapers[1] emphasised how he drew upon his wartime experiences, forty years earlier, to develop a procedure that pinpointed where the Yorkshire Ripper was likely to be living at the time the police were searching for this killer.

I find it curious that a career that spanned a major slice of the twentieth century, encompassing the directorship of the Home Office Central Research Establishment at Aldermaston, and then being head of the forensic science laboratory in Wetherby, as well as other professional accolades, should all be subordinated to a fortnight's work that did not, as it turned out, in any way influence the course of the investigation. On his death, media attention did not give pride of place to the great contribution Kind made to the development of systematic, professional forensic science services in the UK, but rather to a brief interlude in which, almost by accident, he invented what a few years later was seen as the origins of present-day geographical profiling.

When 55-year-old Kind was assigned to the Yorkshire Ripper enquiry, the term 'offender profiling' had not yet found a place in FBI vocabulary, and no one in law enforcement circles had carefully considered how maps of crimes could reveal the inner working of criminals and where they might be based. Yet Kind's early analyses in 1980 set out on a track that others eventually also stumbled upon. My own initial explorations in the same direction had a somewhat different starting point. But, when I rediscovered his work over a decade later, his writings greatly encouraged me to pursue my initial ideas because I knew that on this track I had good company.

I also realised that I had probably been asked to help the Railway Rapist enquiry in the hope that I would do for them what Stuart Kind had offered the Yorkshire Ripper enquiry a few years earlier. Yet, with the lack of openness sometimes typical of police officers who ask outside experts for help, his work had never been mentioned to me. I had to make similar discoveries from scratch.

In his somewhat eccentric autobiography,[2] Kind describes in detail how he came to map the crime locations of the man the police had been looking for over a period of five-and-a-half years. From his description it is clear that his whole approach had roots in the provision of scientific advice to police investigations and a determination to use any logical means to help an investigation. For although he came into police work as a biologist, who had served as an RAF navigator during World War II, he saw himself first and foremost as a scientist whose job it was to bring the systematic collection and analysis of data into areas of police work that had previously relied on custom and gut instinct. Most of all, his cantankerous unwillingness to accept foolhardiness in his colleagues was channelled into forcing the data he had before him to speak to him and reveal its secrets.

He recounts how on 1 December 1980 he was despatched to Yorkshire with four senior police officers. Not quite sure why he had been selected, but probably because he was the one most easily spared from his job, he was pleased to take it on 'not least because I learned that my boss would have liked the appointment for himself'. He even 'delighted in reports

. . . of his [boss's] discomfiture in the matter'. From such very human foibles do significant events emerge.

The initial task of the team that was sent to Yorkshire was to review the investigation to that point. This included the difficult task 'of sifting masses of data, produced over a period of more than five years by many different police officers working over a wide geographical area under varying conditions'. What this sifting enabled him to identify was that 'the series of offences stretched from an assault in the town of Keighley on 5 July 1975, to a murder in Leeds on 17 November 1980. In between these two crimes there ranged a series of fifteen other attacks which were believed to be the work of the same individual.' Thirteen of these attacks had resulted in the victims' deaths.

Dr Kind describes the attacks which had sent waves of panic over a wide area: 'during the hours of darkness a woman would be approached and struck on the head with a hard instrument which in many cases, from the nature of the injuries, appeared to be a hammer. Thereafter the victim was stabbed to death, sometimes with a few, but often with many, blows.' The viciousness of the assaults and their being widespread over such a long period of time put great pressure on Kind and his team to produce some response. Presumably, the looming arrival of Christmas was also in their minds. They consequently issued a preliminary report seventeen days after their arrival.

Kind's major contribution to this report was a close examination of the locations and times of the attacks. 'I decided to apply the mind of the navigator to see if it would yield any indication of the base of operations of the Yorkshire Ripper on the assumption that, throughout the series, he had used the same starting point.' He also considered the time of day of the attacks, postulating that the killer would 'return to base as soon as possible after any attack and before police activity had been stimulated by the incident being reported'. This gave rise to the further assumption that 'in order to minimise the chance of detection after an attack was discovered the Ripper would have tended to attack later in the day the closer he was to home.'

With the time pressures Stuart Kind was under, which he later recognised as similar 'to those faced by a wartime bomber navigator', he was only able to do some rudimentary calculations that followed through the consequences of his assumptions. One set of calculations worked out the centre of gravity of the crime locations, doing this for different subsets of crimes in case they had erroneously linked crimes that were not by the same perpetrator. The other set of calculations considered the relationship between the locations and the time of day of the crime. Both these explorations gave similar results. He wrote:

'On 10 December I wrote a short monograph for my police colleagues in which I argued for the Ripper's base of action being in the Manningham/Shipley area of Bradford . . . On Friday 2 January 1981 the Ripper was arrested in Sheffield . . . It was then established that he, Peter William Sutcliffe, lived in the Heaton district of Bradford. Heaton lies midway between Manningham and Shipley.' Geographical Profiling had been born. But the Yorkshire Ripper was caught in the time-honoured way by two ordinary police officers on patrol, totally ignorant of Dr Kind's suggestions. They stopped a man because he was using number plates that did not relate to the vehicle he was driving. Later they became aware that he was responsible for more serious crimes than stolen number plates.

If Kind's ideas had played a more direct role in the investigation, as I was later so very fortunate that mine did in the detection of John Duffy, then his subsequent analysis of the weaknesses of the Yorkshire Ripper enquiry may have had more impact. He contributed to a major report that looked at what lessons could be learned from the mistakes in Yorkshire. Requested by William Whitelaw, the then Home Secretary, and prepared under the name of one of Her Majesty's Inspectors of Constabulary, Lawrence Byford, the report provided a detailed analysis of everything that went wrong over the five-year period that Sutcliffe was on his murderous travels. At the heart of the proposals from the Byford report was a recommendation with all the hallmarks of Stuart Kind on it: all police investigation teams should include a scientist who could help them to interrogate their data and challenge their assumptions as readily as police officers will interview and check out their suspects. In his autobiography, Kind summarised this idea elegantly: 'In the world of the air navigator, as in the worlds of the research scientist and the crime investigator, fact must modify theory and not vice versa.'

Sadly, though, the central message of the Byford report was either not understood or its implications were too challenging. From it the police took the need for more effective data management systems, especially computers, and began to draw upon the skills of crime analysts to make some sense of the patterns in the information they collect. But the crucial idea that Kind had offered was allowed to lie dormant. He showed how police data could be used to test systematic hypotheses and that these tests could be productively carried out on even fundamental attributes of crimes, such as the time and place at which they happened. It remained for others to bring this idea back to life.

THE YORKSHIRE RIPPER

The significance of Dr Kind's analyses, and indeed the opportunity he was given to carry them out, was due to the importance of the inquiry into the murders of the Yorkshire Ripper. Some murders, and more importantly their investigation, reverberate down through the busy corridors of police headquarters for many decades after the killer has been locked away for good – and few have been more closely examined than that of the Yorkshire Ripper. Small cogs in the police machinery, who happened to be in a crucial place at the right time, find such an unceasing demand to provide journalists with quotes, and documentary-makers with talking heads, that they have to hide away from the unwanted attention. Such a man is Sergeant Bob Ring, whose routine duties led him to identify the culprit the police had been seeking for over five years.

Post mortems more thorough than any carried out on the victims examined and re-examined what happened, where the investigation went wrong and where it eventually went right. Whole new developments in police training and computer systems emerged to make sure 'this will never happen again'; at least not in the way mistakes had happened that time.

What emerged in these quests to learn from history was that Peter Sutcliffe, the Yorkshire Ripper, could have been apprehended before his series of attacks and killings had got beyond the first few victims if the investigating officers had been able to make use of the sorts of techniques that Kind explored. A great deal of the investigation had been based on a tape recording purporting to have come from the killer. Unfortunately it was only after the special team reviewing the case, of which Dr Kind was a part, re-examined the information available, including a mathematical analysis that suggested the location of the offender's residence, that it became clear the tape was a hoax.

Before Dr Kind's results could be put to use the Yorkshire Ripper had been arrested. One January evening in 1981 in the red-light district of Sheffield, Sergeant Bob Ring was making a routine check of the number plate of a Rover car in which the driver was talking to a prostitute. To his surprise he found that the number plate was from a different make of car. Subsequent questioning of the driver revealed nothing; but Sergeant Ring remembered that before being taken in for questioning the man had gone to relieve himself. After returning there, Ring found a hammer and screwdriver that were later linked to the murders of the Yorkshire Ripper. The man was Peter Sutcliffe.

The power of Dr Kind's ideas was therefore forgotten. It was only when I was able to discover for myself a similar procedure five years later, that happened to be helpful in the investigation into the Railway Rapist,[3] that these ideas began to be of more interest to the police. I had not known of Dr Kind's work. It had not been published in the journals I normally look at. The *Journal of Navigation*[4] is not a publication that a social psychologist usually reads. More detailed information was also presented in Kind's book,[5] but this was published by a publisher so small that it can almost be regarded as a private publication. However, as soon as I came across this material I realised that Dr Kind had seen to the heart of a criminal's geography and that we could have been moving along these tracks rather earlier if we had all been in touch with each other.

To understand Dr Kind's approach and how he thought out a mathematical foundation for geographical profiling we need to understand the task his special team was faced with. They had been brought into an investigation that did not seem to be getting anywhere, after thirteen women had been killed, all apparently by the same man.

The murders and assaults were difficult for the police to investigate. To begin with they did not have enough forensic evidence to link the cases with confidence and so had to carry out a number of parallel inquiries. The spread of the offences across a wide swathe of the north-east of England moreover made it difficult for them to decide where to focus their attention.

Some of his victims were prostitutes working the streets of northern cities, including Leeds and Bradford, but they also included other girls and women. He attacked them with a hammer and a screwdriver, inflicting horrible injuries and thus earning the nickname the Yorkshire Ripper. Seven women survived to identify their attacker, but although the police had the culprit in their hands five times, they did not recognise him as the killer or arrest him, until Sergeant Ring decided to look more closely. Sutcliffe's name was also in the many police records that the different inquiries had collected, but before computerisation the police had no way of knowing how many times he had slipped into their net and out again.

Dr Kind,[6] in an attempt to find the killer's 'base of operations', made the simplifying assumption that throughout the series the Yorkshire Ripper 'had used the same starting point'. Beyond this he also assumed that the Ripper would have wanted to be able to return relatively quickly to his base once the crime had been committed. For reasons of speed and simplicity Dr Kind worked with 'crow-flight' distances, but he also offered the argument that 'road distances approximate to crow-flying distances the longer the journey involved'. My own work shows that there are also good psychological reasons for working with straight lines, because these capture the mental processes of relating locations in space rather better than actual routes do.[7]

Having determined that there must be a base and that it would be most efficient for the killer for this to be, on average, the same sort of distance from all the crime locations, Dr Kind sought to calculate the 'centre of gravity' of these locations. He described it as similar to determining the positioning for 'the warehouse for a network of supermarkets, or the fuel dump for a group of bomber airfields ... for minimum travel overall'.

Dr Kind did not explain why all the crimes were not at one spot very close to the criminal's base or clustered together in a small area to which the criminal had access. Presumably this was because he took for granted that the criminal was looking for opportune victims and would not return to an area where he might be recognised or where potential victims might be more alert.

He explains his calculations as being like putting pins in a map for each of the crime locations, then joining them all up with a taut piece of string. There is one point where another pin can be put within the existing pins that will require the minimum addition to the length of string. This is the 'centre of gravity' of the locations.

In Chapter 10 I described in some detail the arithmetic behind this idea. Kind's illustration of pieces of string around pins is another way of representing the same process. Indeed, before the advent of computers, pins and string were used in the design of buildings. If you wanted to put a crucial room, say an administrative centre, in the location where there would be the minimum travel distance for everyone who would want to go there, then you could treat rooms as pins and travel distance as lengths of string. The overall distance from every room to the crucial room would be the total length of the string. However, there is always one location that produces the minimum total travel distance for all concerned. A pin in this mathematically central location will not add to the overall distances. Put the room somewhere else than the centre of gravity and it adds further distance to the total that everyone has to walk. Of course, with the advent of computers pins and bits of string are no longer needed, but people still have to walk to the administrative centre if they want a good idea of what mood the boss is in. There is a limit to what is revealed over email.

In Kind's determination of the centre of gravity of the Yorkshire Ripper's crimes, as we have seen, it indicated a base somewhere in the Manningham/Shipley area of Bradford. Without knowledge of the elementary maths that Kind

6. THE YORKSHIRE RIPPER'S CRIMES

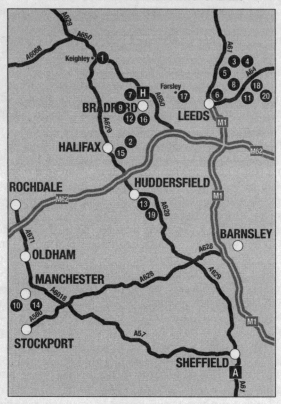

1. Anna Rogulskyj, 5.7.75. Attempted murder, Keighley

2. Olive Smelt, 15.8.75. Attempted murder, Halifax

3. Wilma McCann, 30.10.75. Murder, Chapeltown, Leeds

4. Emily Jackson, 20.1.76. Murder, Leeds

5. Marcella Claxton, 9.5.76. Murder, Leeds

6. Irene Richardson, 6.2.77. Murder, Leeds

7. Patricia Atkinson, 23.4.77. Murder, Bradford

8. Jayne McDonald, 25.6.77. Murder, Leeds

9. Maureen Long, 27.7.77. Attempted murder, Bradford

10. Jean Jordan, 1.10.77. Murder, Manchester

11. Marilyn Moore, 14.12.77. Attempted murder, Leeds

12. Yvonne Pearson, 21.1.78. Murder, Bradford

13. Helen Rytka, 31.1.78. Murder, Huddersfield

14. Vera Millward, 16.5.78. Murder, Manchester

15. Josephine Whitaker, 4.4.79. Murder, Halifax

16. Barbara Leach, 1.9.79. Murder, Bradford

17. Marguerite Walls, 18.8.80. Farsley

18. Upadhya Bandara, October '80. Attempted murder, Leeds

19. Theresa Sykes, 5.11.80. Attempted murder, Huddersfield

20. Jacqueline Hill, 17.11.80. Murder, Leeds

H = Sutcliffe's home location, 6 Garden Lane, Heaton

A = Place of arrest, Melbourne Avenue, Sheffield

---

applied, and the thinking behind their use, it does seem uncanny that Peter Sutcliffe lived in Heaton, midway between Manningham and Shipley.

Had the police had that information earlier, they might have rejected as a hoax the tape they had recieved taunting the investigation. The confidence of phonologists in locating the accent of the voice on the tape to Wearside in the north-east possibly persuaded detectives that they had a special clue as to the criminal's location. This led them to concentrate their attention a hundred miles away from where Sutcliffe lived.

Dr Kind also considered the time of day of the offences. He proposed that the offences committed later in the day would be closer to home. The argument was that 'the prospect of driving long distances on relatively unpopulated roads late at night, after carrying out an assault, would have doubtless been a factor in the choice of location of a victim'. This is certainly an interesting idea, but not one that has been followed up in subsequent studies as far as I know. Its usefulness would rather depend on the density of activity and the sorts of times of day that attacks took place. It may therefore turn out to be a hypothesis that is only relevant in very few cases.

Curiously, Dr Kind did not consider the sequence of the offences or whether that might influence the calculations. The Yorkshire Ripper's first attack was in July 1975 when he beat a young woman with a hammer in Keighley. Just a few weeks later he bludgeoned a middle-aged office cleaner in Halifax. Both survived but, in October, a 28-year-old mother of four was murdered in Leeds. These three murderous attacks were all a dozen miles from each other but they mark out a vicious triangle, which ultimately turned out to contain the culprit's home.

We may speculate why it is that the first three crimes did in fact pinpoint the offender's base. These attacks show the offender beginning to mark out his territory; but when there is a large police inquiry he needs to move away. Once he had started on his career of killing, the Yorkshire Ripper probably realised, like Jack the Ripper a century before, that he needed to keep away from the scenes of his earlier crimes. After his first three attacks, he thought he could escape detection in the west of Leeds and committed a further three offences there, but after those people were alert to the dangers and looked out for possible culprits. He therefore moved back to an area close to home, before returning to Leeds when anxieties had quietened down. But now he was committed to this vicious life and his crimes spread out even further, although all were still within reach of his home in Bradford. It was this idea of a developing crime series that was the basis of my calculations when a few years later I contributed to the Railway Rapist inquiry.

The pattern of the Yorkshire Ripper's movements makes it clear that he had access to a vehicle. He was also familiar with a number of cities, and had reasons to visit them. As Kind pointed out, the killer would have wanted some legitimate reason for being in any location if stopped by the police. It was just those reasons that had enabled him to avoid detection. If he had a vehicle, he probably also had work: something that would have taken him into these different cities. His visits there would not seem unusual. As it turned out, he was a truck driver. It may be thought of as hindsight, or the development and testing of hypotheses – either way, it is remarkable how much travelling offenders reveal about themselves from where they commit their crimes.

Although the crimes of 34-year-old Sutcliffe centred on his home in Bradford, they were widely dispersed across Yorkshire. This dispersal carries its own message. This was a criminal for whom travelling was a way of life and who had easy access to a mode of transport. He was convicted and sentenced to a minimum of thirty years in jail, but was later declared insane and is now at Broadmoor Special Hospital.

THE SPREAD OF CONTAGION

Dr Stuart Kind thought of the criminal's crime locations as resources he drew on, like fuel dumps. But over a century earlier people going to collect water for their daily use had revealed a different, and in some ways more appealing parallel to a criminal's actions. The criminal's mental map causes his crimes to spread like a malignant disease. So I was intrigued to discover that the source of an outbreak of cholera in Soho in 1854 was detected[8] by mapping the water pumps that drew water from the wells in the area and the locations of the victims. This was the first application of geographical profiling. It pinpointed the contaminated well and helped to stop the outbreak, just as pinpointing an active criminal stops the spread of his malignancy. When crimes are being mapped we are turning into pictures a complex process of interactions. It is the visualisation of all these events that shows their underlying theme.

John Snow was a remarkable doctor: one of the Queen's physicians by the age of 24, and much lauded for his many contributions to medicine. The studies he did to find the source of a cholera outbreak laid the foundations for present-day epidemiology. Possibly his special claim to fame, though, is that he is unusual in being a doctor who had a pub named after him, a sort of shrine to his memory. The pub is in London's Soho, close to the spot where Snow removed the pump handle in 1854, bringing to an end a cholera epidemic that had claimed at least 500 lives.

In the 1850s, as the teeming city became ever more crowded, nobody was sure where the killer disease lurked.

7. CHOLERA IN SOHO, 1853

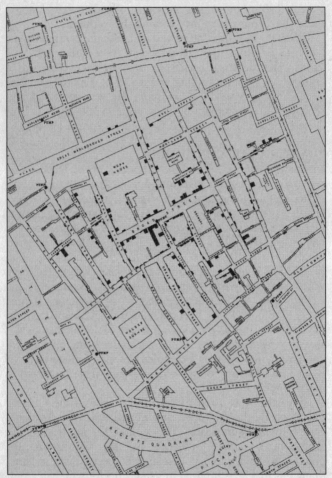

Site of pump/wells in Soho, 1853. Density indicates number of cholera victims

One suspect was the water supply. Dr John Snow took on the task of finding the culprit, like a medical Sherlock Holmes. But instead of looking at individual clues and talking to witnesses, he did something at once more sophisticated and simpler. He marked on a map the number of victims in each house where the disease had struck. On the same map he located the water pump/wells of the area. One well was clearly at the centre of gravity of the infected houses, at the corner of what was then Broad Street and Cambridge Street. Looking at the map Snow produced, that pump can be seen surrounded by the highest density of cases of cholera. No calculations were needed to see it as the prime suspect.

Putting the location of suspect wells on a map today seems an obvious thing to do, but in an era before the bacteria that cause cholera could be seen there was still a debate amongst experts as to whether it was borne by the air. Few suspected it could survive and be transmitted by water. By removing the pump handle Dr Snow tested his hypothesis in the most dramatic way. The fading away of the epidemic gave powerful support to the theory that cholera was carried by water. It also showed that the patterns of human actions, when represented on a map, open up the possibilities of a form of careful analysis that is not available by other means. We are learning that if one person is polluting his surroundings with dreadful crimes, the source of his actions can often be revealed on a map.

PREDATORY ANIMALS OR STREET TRADERS
Peter Sutcliffe was eventually diagnosed as being insane. There is therefore a tendency to think that his actions and those of other serial killers and rapists are random and illogical. It is thought that they are crazed and out of contact with reality. Psychiatrists are called upon to comment on their mental state and the media treats them as monsters, different from ordinary human beings. Our findings do not support this. *What* they do may be bizarre and beyond reason, but to escape detection and capture over and over again, there has to be an ordinary logic to *where* they commit their crimes.

The modern city is a haven for vicious criminals. They can remain anonymous, confuse the police with their mixture of crimes, and frighten their victims into silence. They are moving targets, one step ahead of the detectives searching for them. To avoid detection they have to follow some logic that will reduce the risks of detection and capture and enhance their ability to satisfy their appetites for crime.

There are analogies here to the actions of some predatory animals; revealed when their kills are mapped, when they maraud out to find vulnerable prey. This is not to say that they are acting as if they are animals, or that it is some animal instinct that drives them, but rather that when the simpler world of animals is considered then the elemental logic of survival that underlies the actions of serial killers and other criminals can be more clearly seen.

In order to minimise effort and maximise benefit most predatory animals will go to the nearest place in which they've previously had success. If the prey is too vigilant, or has moved on, they will range a little further, but not normally to areas they have no familiarity with. Studies of leopards,[9] for example, show that this behaviour creates a clear pattern of kills around their dens. In a roughly fifteen-kilometre square area, which is a typical range of a leopard on a game reserve, it will be found that most of the kills are concentrated in the middle of this area, with fewer kills as the animal strays further from its den. A simple yet profound spatial logic shapes the actions of animals and vicious criminals, as it does for all of us.

I am no more acting like an animal when I go to my local pub of a Friday night than a lion is acting like a weary professor when he goes to his regular watering hole after a few days hunting for prey. The analogies are amusing, but they should not be taken too far. It is the patterns of habit and the limiting of effort that I share with the lion, not any atavistic drive for survival.

There are other more productive parallels to the spatial patterns of criminals that can be drawn from the logic that shapes the actions of people engaged in legal activities. A particularly informative comparison is with the way street traders choose their pitches.[10]

They will go to a place where they think they will find customers. If they are reasonably successful they will stay in that place for a while, returning home when they think they have exhausted that particular market spot. The next day they will not return to the same pitch but to one as far away as possible from their first, while still being one they can get to in the same sort of journey time as the previous day. The idea is to have the widest range of new customers available, far from their previous audience. The next day they will move on again to try to catch a different market. Moving out each day to a different location, as far as possible from the last, but still in reach of home, is a logical process to find new customers. Eventually, of course, all possible pitches are exploited, so the street trader either returns to an earlier place or moves his whole operation elsewhere.

Superficially, if pinpointed on a map, the street trader's pattern will look not unlike the leopard's mapped kills. What they have in common, though, is not some innate, genetically ingrained hunting pattern. They are both operating to maximise their benefits with minimum effort. There is a logic to what they are doing. But only the trader has a reasoned framework, even if his actions seem to him to be so habitual that he is not fully aware of what he is doing. The trader's logic more closely parallels that of serial killers and rapists than does the leopard's.

The serial criminal is using his knowledge of where crimes are possible, where vulnerable victims can be found, to seek out opportunities to offend and escape. But he tempers his choice of locations with knowledge of what the risks of detection are, moving on to other places once he thinks he may have exploited local opportunities once too often to avoid detection. Like the leopard, there may often be a centre of gravity to his crimes that indicates his base of actions. But unlike the leopard, much more like a street trader, serial killers and rapists will be weighting their consideration of the opportunities any given location offers against the risks associated with that place. Many of these risks will be a consequence of the offender's earlier actions. The difficulty for police investigators is that often the only person who is fully aware of these risks and opportunities is the offender himself.

13. MENTAL MAPS OF CRIME

THE RAILWAY RAPIST

A couple of years after the arrest of Peter Sutcliffe, a series of rapes and murders started in London. Many of the victims were seized close to railway lines, sometimes by one offender, sometimes by two. With their delight in alliteration the press dubbed the series the work of the Railway Rapist.

By 1985 the police had linked more than forty rapes that might have been the work of the same people. These were tied in to two murders that took place on the opposite sides of London and had very similar features, in the way the victims had been bound and the attempts to burn evidence. It was at this stage, as with Dr Stuart Kind five years earlier, that I was asked to help. The police did not tell me of Dr Kind's earlier work. Indeed I suspect that none of the senior officers knew about it. In the canon of policing it had not directly helped catch anyone, so it fell out of view. Nor did they, as far as I have been able to establish, follow the detailed recommendations for the involvement of scientists in police investigations that had been central to the Byford Report[1] on the Yorkshire Ripper investigation.

What the police had drawn from that report, and the admitted failures of the Yorkshire Ripper inquiry, was the need for more effective management of police records through the use of computers. When I was called in there was therefore already a very full set of computer-based information.

One of the worst crimes involved a fifteen-year-old Dutch girl, Maartje Tamboezer, who they attacked near a railway station in Surrey as she cycled through woodland. The offenders dragged her for half a mile through the woods before raping and killing her. The investigation at the time suggested that an unknown man had been staking out the area for some days, looking for a vulnerable victim.

The Surrey police were investigating that crime. Detective Constable Rupert Heritage had been assigned to work with the flow of information through the investigation. Rupert and

I knew we had to look beyond the wood where Maartje had been found, and to examine all the crime locations.

Examination of the statements given by the victims suggested that the crimes had developed from opportunistic attacks, often carried out at the weekend, almost as a vicious form of recreation, on to much more planned actions, which usually took place during the week. The later attacks were more likely to have been reported as having only one attacker. The most recent crimes had been the murders, and the police informed me that they thought these were the work of one man. This all implied that one or both of the offenders had been developing through the series of crimes from casual assault, grabbing victims when they saw the possibility, through to careful consideration, finding situations in which they could commit their crimes and get away with them. The murders had happened most recently and were at the extremities of the crime area.

This case showed a person on a vicious journey, starting with unplanned, opportunistic rape and leading to planned, brutal murder. What if this mental journey was reflected in the killer's journeys to his crimes? This would mean that his early crimes grew out of his daily activities in the areas he knew best. I therefore asked Rupert to reorganise the map so that we could see if there was any chronological development to the crimes, year by year, showing the geographical progress of the assaults. The results that emerged changed my life.

The map showed a startling pattern moving outwards like a disease. It was only later that the criminals moved further afield, as they became more confident. The early rapes marked a vicious territory around North London, West Hampstead and Kilburn. One further murder had happened whilst we had been studying the material, so that by the time the map was completed the extremities were marked by a triangle of murders. It seemed obvious to me that the killer must have had a residence near the hub of criminal activities. I proposed that at least one of the offenders had been living within the few streets demarcated by the crimes that had taken place in 1982.

Only one of the many police suspects lived in this area: John Duffy. Close surveillance of him produced the evidence that the police needed to get a conviction in court. In 1987 Duffy was convicted of two murders and five rapes.

The police claimed the geographical and related analyses[2] I had carried out had been of enormous value in helping to catch the criminal. It was only later that I realised we had made a surprising rediscovery of the power of mapping rapes and murders, an idea first mooted by Kind. But over the fourteen years since I first looked at the map Rupert had prepared I have come to realise just how fortunate I was. The information we were working with was much more complete than is often the case. It also turned out that the assumptions I had made, and the conclusion I drew, were valid. Peter Sutcliffe left a similar trail on a larger scale, but many other series have somewhat different patterns to them.

The central assumption was that the rapists were setting out on a criminal journey that became ever more a focus of their lives. I thought they must be seeing themselves as outlaws of some kind, against society, turning accepted ways of life on their head, almost like iconic characters in fiction. At the time I had no way of checking out these possibilities. For many years Duffy claimed amnesia for the rapes and murders and would not talk about them.

Recently, though, apparently because of counselling he has had in prison, his memory has returned and he has admitted the crimes, implicating his erstwhile close friend David Mulcahy for many of the rapes and all the murders. There are still unanswered questions around these assertions, even though Mulcahy has now been convicted of the crimes. What we can now understand, though, is more of the unfolding inner narrative that I had assumed their criminal geography had represented.

The map I had originally worked with included all the possibly linked cases. The pattern of evolution of the crimes there was very evident. But when Mulcahy came to court a set of rapes was identified that had been carried out by two men, and eventually Duffy and Mulcahy were convicted of these. What is particularly striking, if these are put on a map with where Duffy and Mulcahy were living at the time, is that the offence locations spread out between their two residences, moving north away from the centre of London. The particular

8. DUFFY AND MULCAHY'S RAPE LOCATIONS

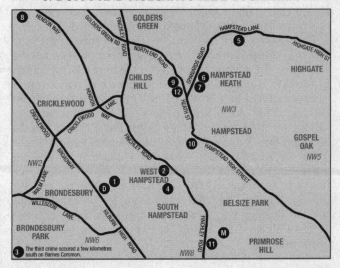

DATES OF RAPES

1. 21.10.82

2. 26.03.83

3. 20.01.84

4. 03.06.84

5. 08.07.84

6. 15.07.84

7. 15.07.84

8. 26.01.85

9. 30.01.85

10. 02.02.85

11. 02.03.85

12. 03.03.85

D = Duffy's Home

M = Mulcahy's Home

Note: Rape victims cannot be named for legal reasons.

influence that two offenders can have on each other is not always easy to disentangle. The map certainly shows the way in which their vicious actions could be combined.

The way that they had actually set about their journeys to rape was revealed in court when Duffy described his actions. This gave the unique possibility of testing out my earlier hypothesis. He said that he and Mulcahy had realised there were sometimes lone women leaving railway stations in the evening. They drove around in a car to various stations looking for these women. Many people had assumed that the offenders were travelling by train, so the label Railway Rapist turns out to have been somewhat misleading. It was the availability of victims that took them to railway stations, not the form of transport. 'We normally travelled by car. We called it hunting. Part of it was looking for a victim, finding her and tracking her. David had a tape of Michael Jackson's *Thriller*. We used to put that on and sing along to it as part of the build-up.'

They drove around with increasing excitement, but once they were aware that the police were looking for what the papers initially called the 'North London Rapists' they avoided that area, spreading their attacks to other parts of London and eventually to the Home Counties. This development reflected their increasing commitment to their violence, as the map had shown. 'To begin with it was in areas we knew well. We would plan it quite meticulously. We would have balaclavas and knives . . . We did it as a bit of a joke, a bit of a game. It added to the excitement . . . You get into the pattern of offending – it is very difficult to stop.'

DRAGNET

My work on other cases following the conviction of John Duffy led to my realising that, although some of the principles involved in the use of maps in that case were not going to work in all cases, there was much to be gained from careful analysis of criminals' activities across a map. In the case of Duffy and Mulcahy's crimes, as with John Snow's map a century earlier, the core of the infection could be seen clearly. In the Yorkshire Ripper case the dots on the map did not indicate the focus of activity quite so clearly and calculations were needed to determine the most likely origin of the crimes. It therefore began to dawn on me that we needed to start testing various mathematical approaches to finding the likely location of the offender. The centre of gravity calculations that Stuart Kind had used were only one way of thinking about the appropriate mathematics. He had also pointed out that the difficulty of being sure that all the crimes identified were really the work of one person required that various tests be run on the crime locations to see the effect of different configurations on any posited base.

In order to calculate various possibilities I realised that some form of computing procedure needed to be developed that would take the effort out of putting dots on maps and calculating by hand the likely location of an offender's base. I therefore employed a gifted computer programmer, mathematician and psychologist, Malcolm Huntley, to develop software that would allow us easily to input crime locations and then run various calculations on those locations to see which approach would be most productive. Somewhat whimsically I eventually called this software Dragnet.

Malcolm quickly understood the mathematical problem of calculating the centre of action of a series of points. He also realised that using a simple arithmetical calculation like finding the centre of gravity, as Kind had used, does give more weight to the crimes that are at some distance from the offender's home. For many years it had been known that criminals' journeys, like those of shoppers or even those of people seeking wives in societies with limited mobility,[3] tended to be less frequent the further away they were from their base. Many people had seen that this 'decay' in the amount of human activity from a fixed point was not unlike the fading of the power of gravity as one body moves away from another. Malcolm therefore used formulae derived from Newton's theory of gravity to calculate the likelihood of any location on the map being the offender's base.

Dragnet allowed us to do detailed studies of many solved cases in order to lay the groundwork for future applications. One of the most thorough explorations we were able to carry out was based on information about seventy US serial killers.[4] The software allowed us to test 570 different ways of calculating the area in which these offenders might be living. The most effective method only required a consideration of one-tenth of the total area defined by the crime locations. Over half of the offenders lived in an identified area that was just one-twentieth of the area circumscribed by the crimes. These extremely encouraging results showed that the findings of John Snow and Dr Stuart Kind, and the studies of leopards and street traders, were not curious accidents with little relevance to the general logic of criminal activity. They had opened the way to a new understanding of how offenders act on their world.

Dragnet was a research tool, developed for our studies. Some people working within the police who were at home with computers, such as Dan Helms, were keen to use it in their day-to-day work. It did not occur to me that this might be a process that could be given a catchy name and turned into a commercial product. We have always made it available for free to colleagues and charged just a small handling fee to others. The principles were so obviously part of an existing set of ideas that I assumed the research community would eventually embrace them and they would become part of forensic science.

However, shortly after I had contributed to the detection of John Duffy a Canadian police officer, Kim Rossmo, also started applying geographical analyses to locate serial killers. As is so often the case, it takes someone on the other side of the Atlantic to come up with a name for an activity that we in the UK have just seen as a process, not something that needs to be graced with a label. Rossmo started using the term 'geographic profiling'[5] to describe what he was doing and created a commercial software package that he managed to sell for tens of thousands of dollars to a few police forces.

MARAUDERS AND COMMUTERS

The success of any geographical profiling software currently relies on one basic factor. The offender's base must be within a region that can be defined by the locations of the crimes. If the base is outside that region then software that uses the crime locations for its calculations will not find the criminal's home. I realised this in my early studies of criminals' personal geographies. I found that anything between a half and three-quarters of the offenders studied did live in an area that could be defined by a circle whose diameter joined the two furthest crimes: the 'circle hypothesis'.[6]

I had never intended to imply that criminals' places of crime naturally formed a circular shape. A circle is just the simplest way to define the area of a set of points. My view was that if the base did not even sit inside this very crude definition of the crime zone then it was not of any value exploring any further the use of geography for detection. It was our discovery that very many criminals did have a base in this circle that encouraged me to see how much further we could take these ideas.

To be clear what we were talking about we needed a term to describe those offenders whose base was within the circle and so distinguish them from the others whose base was not. I came up with the term 'marauders' as a label for those in the circle. My idea was that these were people who, like old-time bandits, travelled out from their base to commit crimes and returned home afterwards, just as Peter Sutcliffe, Justin Porter and John Duffy had done.

The remainder, defined more by exclusion than inclusion, were apparently seeking out targets away from a base, possibly moving into an area to carry out a series of crimes then returning back to base. One of my students said they were a bit like commuters going to work, so the label 'commuter' stuck for this second group. As we shall see, it is not a very appropriate label in many cases. It is probably better to consider these criminals as travelling offenders who find opportunities for crimes as they move around; although surprisingly often the places they choose do have a special meaning for them, and their journeys are anything but random.

Another complication, which is obvious from any simple consideration of the geometry involved, is that such a direct definition from the geometry of the crimes will force many borderline cases into one camp or the other. For example, killers whose homes sit close to the circumference of the notional circle may be arbitrarily assigned to the 'commuter' or 'marauder' group depending on an accident of street layouts.

The spatial geometry of crimes is only part of the story the offender is developing. It deals with dots on a map that ignores major routes and land use patterns. It takes no account of the opportunities for crime, or the particular targets for which the criminal is searching. Most crucially of all there is no way of determining with complete confidence from the geometry of the crimes alone whether the offender is a 'commuter' or a 'marauder'. That assignment remains a hypothesis until the offender is caught and convicted and his residence at the time of the crimes determined.

MENTAL MAPS OF CRIMES

The route that has taken us to a consideration of the spatial behaviour of criminals has included bacteriology and epidemiology, models of gravity, animal hunting patterns, references to forensic science, navigation and of course the tools of geography. But at the heart of all these explorations is an offender thinking about where to commit his crimes. The closer we can get to these thought processes, the better we will be able to interpret that personal geography.

We need to understand how the home base for many criminals influences what they do and how their understanding of their domain around that base transforms their use of place and their finding of victims. The criminal's understanding of what is possible where is shaped by where he lives; and that in turn shapes where he will go and how he will get there.

One way of thinking about the criminal's understanding of his domain, or the understanding that any person has of an area, is to consider the person's internal representation of the places he uses. This bundle of knowledge, feelings, familiarity, habitual paths and half-forgotten experiences is often referred to as a 'mental map'[7] of an area: a person's unique geographical knowledge, often shaped by his distinguishing residential experience. This is not really a map like that which can be bought in a shop, but it will contain map-like information, which can be brought out for public view by asking people to draw a sketch map of an area. The errors and accuracies, dominant features and omissions of these sketch maps help us to see the idiosyncratic world in which the individual lives.

THE MALAGA RAPIST

One striking illustration of how the mental map of an offender shapes his crime locations was made available to me recently by some colleagues from Spain.[8] They had been asked to contribute to the search for a man who had committed at least 29 rapes in the central area of the city of Malaga on the southern Spanish coast. The victims had been found in two areas of attack. The earlier attacks were to the south of the Avenida de Andalucia, a major road that runs into the central city area, and the later ones to the north. Both areas of attack were about a kilometre in diameter. The puzzle for my colleagues was whether he lived within one of these areas or somewhere between the two.

The question this poses for a psychologist is why there would be two areas of activity. It suggests the possibility of two different bases – one, say, a workplace and the other a residence. There is another possibility, though. This is that his mental map somehow links these two areas together and that his main base is sited between these two areas.

Eventually the rapist made a mistake and approached a victim he had attacked before who recognised him. She noted his car licence-plate number and he was arrested. He was found to live between the two areas of his crimes.

The opportunity was then taken by my colleagues to carry out a thorough interview with the man, including asking him to draw a map of Malaga. He told them how he drove around looking for possible victims, then parked his car wherever he could. (He had collected many parking tickets along the way.) The locations he went to were therefore, to some extent, influenced by the one-way system around Malaga.

The map he drew also shows how he thought of the opportunities available to him. At the physical centre of the map he placed a cross for the house in which he had grown up. Not far from that was the place in which he was currently living, which marked the centre of the most detailed area of his sketch map. The streets he drew on his map fold around this mental centre.

The main Avenida de Andalucia that cuts through his two crime zones, and is a highly notable geographical feature of this section of Malaga, hardly figures at all. He rarely used this

9. THE MALAGA RAPIST'S SKETCH MAP

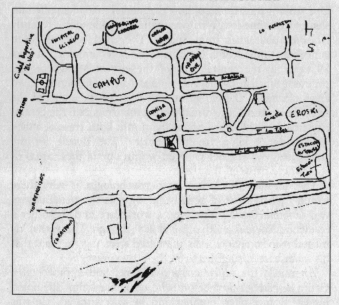

busy highway with its complex intersections, but preferred the roads that brought him into contact with the pavements of the town.

There are other illuminating differences between his sketch map and an actual map of Malaga that reveal something of his mental geography. At the right (east) side of his map he has drawn the main roads reasonably accurately. Plaza Cruz del Humilladero is very clearly marked with Passeo de Tilos and La Union running from it. This then connects to the west with Avenida de Juan XXIII, which runs north–south through the middle of his map. This area is quite accurate and even reasonably to scale. This is where his early rapes took place, providing the psychological density of his crimes.

But his scale becomes confused in the rest of his sketch. He links Juan XXIII closely to the university campus and sports ground, thereby pulling the area north of the Avenida de Andalucia into an inappropriately limited zone. His second area of assaults is hardly indicated at all. In his mind it is just a little area that he found his way into. This area is north of the main Avenida de Carlos Haya that runs straight into the city centre, parallel to the Avenida de Andalucia which is not given any detail on the sketch map at all.

He stretches his area of criminal activity out across the page instead of up and down. This suggests that his mental map, and presumably therefore his crimes, are shaped around his understanding of where Juan XXIII takes him. This is especially interesting because of his base in the middle of that road, with the city centre and its opportunities on the other side of it. These opportunities seem so significant to him that he draws them in to his anchor point. But they are also part of one overall area that is foreshortened in his mind by minimising the dominant highway on his mental map.

CORROBORATIVE OR INCEPTIVE

In discussing his particular contribution to the Yorkshire Ripper inquiry Dr Kind explained the change of relationship to the investigative process that his actions implied for police and scientists. He pointed out that most scientists preferred to keep at some distance from the police and their inquiries, wishing to comment objectively on the artefacts and samples put before them but avoiding being part of the hunt. Essentially they kept to the position of commenting on anything put before them. As Dr Kind put it, 'most scientific involvement in cases is corroborative rather than inceptive'.

These scientists always have an eye over their shoulder towards the evidence they may have to give in court and how they might defend that evidence. Psychology by its very nature is usually at the softer end of science. Hard and fast judgements of the type that can be given about DNA samples are a rare luxury for the student of human actions and experience. A valid opinion about a general trend is an achievement to be proud of. Perhaps paradoxically, therefore, psychologists may be of more use in helping to set up ways in which the police may search for suspects, rather than in telling them with confidence if they have the right person when he is caught.

If students of criminal behaviour wish to see psychology as a branch of geography, navigation, zoology or even epidemiology, I have no objections, provided that at the core of their assumptions is the understanding that we all build internal representations of our world, representations which are not entirely in accord with the way others may see that world. These are representations of who we are and the psychological journey on which we are engaged, and they are reflected in the places in which we choose to act.

14. STEALING SEX

THE VALUE OF LIBRARIES

In June 1996 a quietly spoken New Zealand police officer, Detective Inspector John Manning,[1] turned up in my office in Liverpool. The only contact I'd had with him before he arrived was to arrange that meeting, which he'd requested to discuss my research. It therefore came as something as a surprise when he told me how I had helped him catch a very dangerous criminal.

Manning explained that a violent rapist had been active for twelve years in the south Auckland area of the North Island of New Zealand. Even though over fifty assaults had been reported, the rapist had not been caught during prolonged investigations, which had lasted into the early 1990s. Then, as John Manning tells it, he heard about my work and my recently published book, *Criminal Shadows*. The bit I particularly liked in what he said was that he made it clear that the police do not waste scarce resources on speculative purchases. So he got a copy of *Criminal Shadows* out of the library. Manning's claim was that within three months of his reading the book, the rapist had been arrested and eventually pleaded guilty on 31 July 1995, to 129 charges. He was sentenced to 30 years in prison, with an order that he serve a minimum of 25. At the trial the judge, Justice Fisher, said: 'It is difficult to think of any person who has brought more pain and misery to so many people in New Zealand's history.'

THE PLAGUE OF RAPES

This pain and misery was concentrated in the poorer areas of New Zealand's largest city, Auckland, which has a population spreading out into its distant suburbs of over one million people, almost a third of the country's total population. Most of the suburbs of New Zealand consist of low wooden houses that are typically detached, in their own quarter-of-an-acre plot. Otara, the main area in which the offences took place, was a mixture of detached and semi-detached houses showing signs of the poverty of their residents, with unkempt gardens and little hint of the pride in personal identity that is typical of more affluent areas. This was an area with a reputation for being rough, with a high level of day-to-day crime.

The unmanaged trees and shrubs offered cover for a prowler to look through windows, silently and unseen, to find out the family activities and to ensure that those who remained in the house were weak enough for him to control. Many of the houses targeted were also near open spaces, close to schools, parks or footpaths ('walkways' as they are known in New Zealand), enabling the offender to discover vulnerable targets when wandering around the area, but also allowing a ready escape route into territory where he was less likely to be seen or followed. As Detective Sergeant Henwood, who eventually arrested the rapist, put it: 'I wouldn't mind a dollar for every murder or rape scene I have attended where a walkway is next to the address, or a school or park adjoins.'

The rapes and assaults from the mid 1980s onwards – that were pieced together by the police as all being the product of one man – were in the suburbs of Otara, Manurewa, Papatoetoe and Mangere, where low-paid labourers or unemployed single women lived with their children, often in dysfunctional families, with one parent or both frequently away from home at night. Such a situation creates many potential victims for a man looking for a young woman or child who is alone and who lacks easy access to others for help. Some of these areas do have more affluent enclaves, but the offender kept clear of these more protected localities, in which any sort of crime was more likely to generate a quick report to the police and heightened vigilance.

The attacker knew the lifestyle of the areas he was operating in; how little notice was taken of lone men wandering around. One fifteen-year-old saw a strange man staring through the window, but when she alerted others in her house, they told her to check for herself. Leaving the house and seeing nothing she returned, only to be grabbed and raped, her screams drowned out by the rain. She was then dragged to a nearby park, tied to a tree and raped again.

As is usually the case with serial crimes, the offender here had a sense that not only were there many vulnerable victims available, but that the physical layout and community life-styles of the area also helped him to continue to commit his assaults and get away with them. As the police were later to admit, the general level of crime in Otara during the '80s was such that all their efforts were focused on dealing with one challenge after another, a sort of policing by crisis that does not allow anyone what is seen as the 'luxury' of getting an overall perspective on what is happening, so that a general strategy for dealing with it can be developed. Serial offenders may not be consciously aware of this situation but they quickly get a feel for the opportunities for crime available in an area once they get away with the first few offences.

Many of the residents in these areas were Maori or Pacific Islanders. Some of the victims were family members of the ethnic gangs that can have a powerful influence in this area of New Zealand. This turned out to be helpful to the police investigation once there had been a sustained inquiry that excluded many people as suspects through blood samples. As Henwood explained: 'When we went blooding later most were more than happy to supply blood and be cleared, rather than risk the word getting out that he had refused and therefore get some summary justice on the street.'

It was possible to link the assaults to a common offender because his pattern of activity remained so consistent throughout his long reign of terror, often generating the sort of distinct modus operandi (MO) so beloved of detectives and fiction writers alike. Nearly all his assaults were indoors and, although he gained entry to houses by various means, he commonly took advantage of the fact that these cheap wooden buildings had been built twenty or more years earlier, and the wooden window frames had swollen over time so that they no longer locked properly. He was therefore able to pull open an upper window that was not fully shut and lean down to open the larger lower window through which he would enter the house. The layouts of these houses were all very similar, which allowed him to find his way quickly to the kitchen and grab a knife to take with him to the victim's bedroom.

His actions were clear from the earliest reported rapes:[2]

My friend left after TV closing time and, after going to the toilet, I went to my bedroom. I got undressed and sat on my bed and had a cigarette and after pulling across the drape, over the net one, went to bed.

The next thing I knew was when I woke up and the guy was beside my bed. My clock said 2.25. I asked him who he was. He said, 'Never you mind' and told me to lie down or he would hurt me badly. He said if I don't be quiet he would cut my throat and he would kill my sister. He put his hand on my mouth and face. I could feel the sharp bit of the knife against my throat.

When I tried to push his hand away and scream he said, 'Shut up and be quiet.' I tried to get up but he pushed me down and punched me in the face. He started trying to get my pants off and said, 'Get these damn things off or I'll kill you.' He held the knife tighter to my throat until I did. Then he raped me. The whole time he held the knife against my throat. He ejaculated and got straight off.

While he was doing his zip up I tried to get off and push him out of the way. He virtually threw me back. He said, 'Just stay there.' He said that about three times.

I ran into Dad's room and woke him up. Dad said I was dreaming and I said I wasn't and that it was true.

Dad got up and checked the house and when he got to the hallway he saw the back door was open. After Dad found the back door open he closed it and went upstairs to get changed and then called the police.

The trauma many of his victims had suffered destroyed their lives. Confident, outgoing young women became terrified of being in their homes alone. They had difficulty sustaining close relationships and became anxious and irritable. The wounds that many of them had received became constant reminders to themselves and their families of the attack. Some even emigrated and tried to start new lives overseas, still dogged by the emotional scars of their ordeals.

The ages[3] of his victims varied, although more than half were under the age of seventeen and many were only ten or eleven years old. He was not discouraged when some girls bravely fought back, kneeing him in the groin or cutting him across the face with a pocket-knife. Sometimes even if he was frightened away he would come back later to complete the assault. He tormented some victims by telling them he would be back, saying to one twelve-year-old (after kissing her on the cheek), 'Maybe I'll come and live with you.'

The consistency in his MO was maintained over all the offences, numbering more than sixty across the many years he went uncaught. In fact his MO was so consistent that when he eventually admitted to his crimes he had no difficulty in agreeing with his police interviewers as to which violent assaults he had committed and which ones in the same area he had not.

RECOGNISING THE SERIES

These crimes became the focus of attention of Sergeant Henwood, known by his colleagues as Chook, because of its simple association with his surname. He is one of those dedicated detectives for whom catching the bad guys gets close to an obsession, which he only manages to shed from time to time with a round of golf. He stands out in a crowd of police officers with his trademark short white hair, tanned complexion and an immaculate suit that would not be out of place on a London Metropolitan police officer. Athletically slim, he takes care of himself and eats healthily.

In February 1993 he investigated a rape in the Manurewa area of south Auckland, about five miles south of Otara. A twelve-year-old girl had woken up early one Saturday morning to find a hooded man standing by her bed. He then climbed on top of her and raped her. She was then taken into the hallway and raped again at knifepoint, the rapist threatening to kill her if she made any noise. The man had already tied up and sexually assaulted her mother, who had been sleeping in another room. Eventually he ran away when the mother shouted that her husband was returning. Quite perspicaciously, as it turned out, the twelve-year-old estimated the rapist's age as 37.

Chook, already an experienced detective, immediately set out to find other crimes that may have been committed by the same offender, because he figured that 'this offender didn't just wake up one morning and decide to be a stranger intruder rapist, tying up victims etc.' He recognised that here they had a man in the middle of a criminal career, not at the start of one. But before they could find any previous cases to link in, two more very similar offences occurred in Manurewa. So similar, in fact, that the detective who attended the report of the second attack telephoned Chook at home, saying, 'Our man has struck again.'

Chook assumed the rapist must have come from some other area, or prison, because there had been no similar rapes in Manurewa in recent months. He believed that the determination and sheer audacity of the attacks, and their strongly sexual focus, made it unlikely that they had been the work of a local man who had suddenly changed his criminal trade. He therefore broadened his search, and started to look closely at a number of unsolved rapes in Otara.

Whilst he was checking these out the forensic results came back, showing that four rapes in Manurewa had been the product of one man. This gave him a firm base on which to build a larger series. When forensic evidence from an Otara rape in 1990 came to light, they checked it out and found the offender had the same DNA. This greatly strengthened Chook's belief that he was uncovering a serial rapist who had been active for some time, and helped him to get a good grip on the offender's characteristic style of offending:

> He generally chose insecure housing where he knew young girls lived; he would place an object under a window and climb through. He generally took a knife from the kitchen, often as innocuous as a bread and butter knife, and used it to threaten his victims. If they resisted, he would punch them in the face, telling them to 'shut up, bitch'. Minimal foreplay was characteristic, followed by vaginal rape.

The man also took considerable care to avoid having his face seen. He moved around in the dark, covered his victims' faces, or wore some sort of hood to hide his face. Over all the years of his attacks very few victims ever got a clear view of him.

STEALING SEX

Although some of his victims were beaten unconscious, badly injured, and required hospital treatment for broken teeth or severe lacerations, it does not appear that he was ever close to killing his victims, unlike other serial rapists we have considered. He seemed only to use sufficient physical and verbal violence to control the victim and overcome resistance. There is no indication that he exhibited any extremely violent responses to resistance; there was no use of wantonly sadistic force to imply he got direct pleasure from inflicting pain or injury.

Another interesting aspect of these offences is that there was no indication that they got any more violent as they progressed. It is almost as if the offender avoided the sort of confrontation that could have led to murder. If fought off by the victim or a guardian, he would leave and occasionally return when his prey was more docile. He was prepared to watch and wait until friends had left, the household was asleep and there was little chance of being disturbed during the assault.

This was a man breaking into houses and stealing sex. He was not engaged in a vendetta to avenge a wrong, and nor did he see himself doomed by the fates to carry out his assaults. His victims were just vehicles for his lusts. Here was a man who found adventure in these repellent attacks. In these tree-lined suburbs he had found a hunting ground that proved ideal for him to spy on his prey and then pounce when she was at her most vulnerable.

In his search for a readily available target he had no need to move far from where he knew he could get away from the scenes of his crimes with ease. His adventure took him out to look for criminal opportunities as part of his daily activities, almost certainly 'marauding' out from a base to find his victims, fanning through an area that he must have known well.

After three initial offences known to have happened in Sandringham in central southern Auckland in 1983 and 1984, there was little sign of him until 1988, when he moved his attention to the denser suburb of Otara, a few miles to the south-east. Here he found he had rich pickings, and was able to offend every few weeks, committing more than twenty offences in Otara without the police getting anywhere near him. By 1993 this area had become less attractive to him and he moved. Seven attacks now took place in the suburb of Manurewa, a couple of miles south of Otara. His adventure seemed unstoppable and his confidence in his invincibility took him back to Otara for more rapes in 1994, before spreading out to the adjacent suburb of Papatoetoe, with the odd foray back to Manurewa.

THE USUAL METHODS

As these violent crimes reached public awareness and it became clear that particular suburbs were being targeted, some of the areas took on the feel of fortresses. But this awareness was far from universal, and often came only after the Auckland rapist had moved the focus of his attention. Many people, especially in the indigent areas where the pressures of daily life demanded more attention, went about their business oblivious to the fact that there was a predator at work; attempts by the police to counter this disinterest through the wide distribution of flyers in all Pacific Island languages and Maori, as well as English, seemed to be in vain.

The investigation was followed closely by press and TV, highlighting the weaknesses of the police investigation. The opposition spokesman for the police represented one of the hardest-hit areas in the country in parliament, and so complaints about police ineffectiveness became a topic of national political debate. In response the police inquiry took on an ever more fervent tone. On 30 August 1993 it became known as Operation Park. Detective Inspector John Manning was put in charge of it in April 1994.

For a year and a half the inquiry team followed standard investigative procedures, still used throughout the world in many investigations. They put plain-clothes police officers on the streets of the plagued areas to see if they could catch the offender either prowling, in the act of the offence or soon after. They interviewed local known sex offenders to determine their whereabouts at the times of the offences. House-to-house inquiries were made to determine if anything suspicious had happened. But all this produced, as Chook

Henwood later told me, was 'over 200 *Eastlight* folders of data including hundreds of suspects'. As it later turned out, the culprit's name was not in any of these folders.

GETTING A GRIP
As the inquiry started to run out of steam John Manning went to a course in Australia, where he heard in earnest for the first time about criminal profiling and my book *Criminal Shadows*. It may be the distance that New Zealanders feel from the rest of the world, or it may be the more scholarly turn of mind that the police have there, but they did not then do what many police forces would have done. They did not fly in an expert 'profiler' to do the thinking for them, or even send a copious file overseas for guidance. Instead they raided their local library and read everything they could on patterns of criminal behaviour and the development of 'profiles'. This had the enormous advantage of giving them what social scientists like to call 'ownership' of the process. Like enthusiastic students, who soon forget that they have learned at their professor's knee and play back ideas with the confidence of those who had the original thoughts themselves, Manning, Henwood and their colleagues became convinced enough from what they had read to alter the whole course of their investigations.

It says something for the simplicity and clarity of what they got hold of from their local library that they made a perfectly good job of formulating distinct ideas about the offender for whom they were searching. That alone puts a lie to the claims of Hollywood, and many of the 'expert profilers' who write their autobiographies, that there is some arcane knowledge and subtle skill to profiling that is only available to those with years of training and complex computer systems. As has often been said about psychology, if it is any good it tends to be given away. People with reasonable intelligence and diligence can rapidly absorb the ideas that emerge from the behavioural sciences and make effective use of them. These detectives quickly saw the almost self-evident possibilities for putting together a generalised description of the person they were looking for and using that as a way of generating suspects then filtering them to focus their inquiry.

In a couple of the later cases the offender, wearing gloves so that he did not leave fingerprints, had nonetheless left semen. In one case a victim had been punched in the mouth and her broken tooth had cut her assailant's hand. So they had small samples of his blood and semen from which to derive forensic evidence. But they had to get to the culprit first. Furthermore, DNA testing is extremely expensive and time-consuming, and there was no central record of convicted offenders' DNA. The investigating squad therefore needed to move cautiously and systematically through the possibilities.

They had some pointers to go on from victim statements; the offender was an athletic man of Maori or Pacific Island descent aged between 20 and 50, of slim to medium build, over 1.6 metres tall, with a local accent. His actions were also readily open to interpretation. He broke into houses at will and on some occasions he stole property. His stealing of sex seemed to be part of a pattern typical of some burglaries, rather than the property theft being an opportunity that emerged during the sexual assault.

This turned out to be a crucial point and was one of the first discoveries I remember making in our early work on rape.[4] There is a tendency for most people, especially police officers, to think of sexual crimes as a deviation all on their own, but whilst it is true that many criminals do not indulge in sexual offences, the reverse is not the case. Most sexual offenders have been involved in other forms of criminality, often including property crime. We found 80 per cent of rapists in one sample with a previous criminal history for theft or burglary. It would seem that many criminals, for whom crime is a sort of adventure, start their criminal journey with theft and other property-related crimes. A few of them find increasing excitement in taking sexual advantage of their victims, once they have penetrated the homes of these women. Some find this aspect of their exploits so satisfying that, if they are not caught and stopped, it begins to take centre stage in their minds and eventually becomes the dominant focus of their lives.

Following this line of thought the people in Operation Park realised that the attention they had given to known sex offenders had been unnecessarily limiting; they had to broaden their search parameters. The fact that the rapist wore gloves also supported the idea that his fingerprints were somewhere in the police files. Strangely, many criminals think in terms of avoiding being caught, rather than about the evidence that may be used to gain a conviction. So they will only avoid leaving fingerprints if they know the police already have their prints on file. If they are not on file they will often be less cautious. This meant that the rapist probably had a criminal conviction.

Because burglary is such a common route into a criminal career, broadening the range of people to be covered by the search net to this group greatly increased the number of possible suspects, so other indicators were needed to help limit the scale and cost of the investigation. The squad turned to the more speculative aspects of inferred offender character-istics. They made the assumption that rape comes quite late in the career of burglars who move in that direction, and that he would therefore have been at least 25 years old in 1994, when the systematic search started in earnest. With a nod in the direction of the early studies of male sexuality, which generated the most depressing finding in the history of behavioural sciences[5] – namely that male sexual activity declines rapidly from 35 years onwards – and the athletic build of the assailant, they assumed that the offender would be no older than 35.

Other rather more vague ideas were also culled from the often over-confident 'profiling' literature. One of these was that he was a 'power-reassurance' rapist,[6] although I have to confess that not only have I never really understood what that can mean and how it can ever be reliably determined from the information available to the police, but also I do not see how such a label can possibly help a police investigation.

Rather more helpful was the recognition by the detectives that this man's knowledge of the area went beyond casual contact. He seemed to know a lot about the lifestyle and detailed action patterns of his victims and their households. This must have meant he prowled the area, like many serial rapists do, seeking out opportunities then watching for the right time. For him it must have been a roller-coaster quest, in which the early excitement of seeking out possibilities gave way to the crucial struggle with the victim and the eventual satisfaction of overcoming that adversary. This required a frequent and regular presence in the area of his crimes, most easily afforded by living there or having a welcoming base or safe bolthole, as with the other criminals we have seen who moved out from their base to find their victims. This would mean that his crimes defined the area of his residence, providing the most powerful filter for narrowing down the field of suspects.

15. 'I'VE BEEN WAITING FOR YOU GUYS'

THE JOURNEY TO RAPE
The wide spread of assaults and rapes across a number of suburbs over a decade led the Operation Park team to realise that this was an offender who was probably moving around and that by 1995, when the inquiry moved into high gear, he might no longer be based in the localities of his offences. As Chook so poetically put it, 'We decided that as we were having trouble finding the offender at the present time we would look into the past and find him there, being that his past was set in concrete and that he could not change.'

Sergeant Henwood's reference to time travel shows the scientific stance Detective Inspector Manning and the team were taking. All science is time travel, especially scientific psychology, looking to the patterns of behaviour in the past in order to use those to predict the future. Operation Park was making a radical break with the tradition of policing, which is to look for clues in the here and now that will set up a trail that leads to the offender. This is the mainstay of detective stories, giving them their crossword-puzzle fascination. If only we can uncover the meaning of the bite marks on the walking stick, or why the victim's face was so brutally disfigured, then this will lead us to the villain. I think this is why detectives who become enamoured of popular psychology become particularly entranced by Freudian theory and its psychoanalytic paraphernalia. Freud himself was a fan of Sherlock Holmes and saw himself as a 'detective of the mind'.[1] He constantly searched for particular illustrations of what a given symbol might mean, as if that symbol were a clue that would lead to the perpetrator. It does not therefore require any real change in a police investigator's (or fiction writer's) mindset to look for the 'meaning' of violence against the face of the victim, or the reason why a body has been covered after a violent assault, or to follow any of the other rules of thumb that come out of popular attempts at 'offender profiling'.

10. THE SOUTH AUCKLAND RAPES

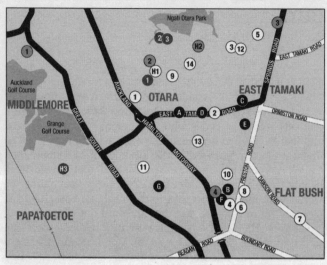

Offences committed from 3 bases:

H1 = Lappington Road, Otara

H2 = Parker Crescent, East Tamaki

H3 = Shirley Road, Papatoetoe

A–G offences committed from Lappington Road, after Thompson left address but when visiting his mother

Operation Park was, probably unwittingly, moving away from the idea that existing traces could be followed to provide the pathway to the rapist. They were coming round to the need to look for him using the general trends found in the geographical patterns and criminal history typical of many similar offenders. It was these trends that they hoped could be used to filter out the innocent men, leaving them with their culprit. The strongest pattern they had related to the density of crimes in south Auckland. The offender had to live in that area. This established, they set about narrowing down the haystacks they had to search to find their needle.

They decided that they were first going to identify every possible suspect then winnow that list down, using criteria (or 'probes' as they liked to call them, by analogy with biological tests that distinguish blood types) drawn from the inferred geographical and criminal history as well as the physical descriptions they had of the offender. Interestingly their fishing expedition, as we have seen with so many police investigations, started with a broad sweep that was slowly narrowed down, rather like Polynesian islanders encircling the area of a bay with their nets and moving in until their quarry has nowhere else to jump but into their arms. Moving outwards from the most likely area was, presumably, considered too risky because the rapist had swum unseen through their surveillance before.

The grouping of attacks that could be most confidently linked together by the offender's actions was in Otara in the late 1980s. Investigators therefore set out to find all those Maoris/Pacific Islanders who had lived in Otara and had burglary convictions from the mid 1980s to the 1990s. This would be much easier to do now than it was ten years ago; although even with today's computer systems there can still be many difficulties. In 1995 computer data-handling systems were not widely available, so retired police officers were initially brought in to go through arrest sheets for the period. This is a hugely labour intensive and very slow process, as well as being open to many human errors.

The team then realised that there were centralised records of every person charged with any offence in New Zealand. Those records had been in place since 1976 when the New Zealand police started their process of computerisation. But this was a huge national record that would take months to search, and was little more than a computerised card file with few search facilities. So a contracted computer programmer built the first police database, specifically so that the national files could be searched.

There are always problems with computer searches of databases. In effect they are like having the search carried out by an exceptionally quick idiot. The search parameters have to be very precisely defined and anyone who does not fit them exactly will be missed. So, once again, the police searched from the general to the particular. They identified every Maori and Pacific Islander between the ages of 20 and 50 who had been charged with any offence since 1976 and had appeared in court, in a broad swathe of the top of the North Island. The database spewed out over 150,000 people who fitted these parameters: rather too many to do blood tests on.

Ever more refined probes were therefore used to generate subsets of likely suspects. These started with the assumption that a triangle surrounding 34 residential streets in Otara held particular significance for the rapist, both because of the many crimes he had committed in that area in 1988 and also because he had returned there to commit crimes in 1993 and 1994. Therefore the spotlight was turned on people living in that triangle in the mid 1980s. Added to this crucial residential focus were the other criteria drawn from the initial 'profile', i.e: Maori, aged between 25–35 years old, with burglary and/or sexual convictions, of the height and build described by the victims. The 88 people thrown up by this search were identified and asked to give blood samples. None of them was the culprit, so the search was broadened to cover Pacific Islanders as well. The offender was not one of the 66 people subsequently checked.

Undaunted by these initial failures, and still confident that their system would eventually lead them to their man, they broadened the search further. The third probe removed any upper age limit, and any limits due to build, and extended the criminal convictions to cover drugs and offensive behaviour, assaults on children and women and theft. This produced a list of 227 people who once more had to be traced, identified and have their blood type checked. If that was the same as the offender's then a further (more expensive) DNA test was carried out. This search drew a blank as well.

Nearly 400 people had now been carefully checked out, covering most of the people known to have criminal records who lived in an area of less than ten square kilometres. Yet the offender had to have a local presence. He had committed many offences in this area, usually in the early hours of the morning, and had not been picked up by any patrols or sighted on his way back from an offence. He had to have a base in the area, but where was he? Had they perhaps defined the area too narrowly? The fourth probe increased the size of the search area to cover 52 streets around the Otara triangle.

People of any height or build who had committed any offences were considered, but they were still limited to Maori or Pacific Islanders over 25 years old. The database found 508 people fitting these criteria, and adding some more to take account of people who had been charged during the months of the inquiry brought the number up to 532. None of them was the rapist.

Now the whole of Otara was included in the search. An additional 804 Maoris and Pacific Islanders over the age of 25 with criminal charges were identified, bringing the total to 1,717 people. One of these was on the list because he had been charged with driving whilst disqualified, hardly an offence that would immediately make you think about serial rape over more than a decade. He was 36 years old, so had been missed out of the earliest probes, with their upper age limit of 35. It turned out that he had lived in a couple of places within the crucial Otara triangle over the years of the rapes, and his parents lived in the area, but when charged with the driving and other offences the addresses he had given were never in that area of Otara.

This was Joseph Thompson. When he was contacted for a blood sample he was just a routine call in the hundreds the police were still making. They became a little suspicious when he told them that he was a Jehovah's Witness and therefore unable to give blood. They convinced him that instead he should provide a saliva sample. When he did not turn up to do this, apparently off work sick, police suspicions grew. He was traced and, although he had tried to impair the test by smoking directly beforehand, the saliva test turned the case around.

By mid-June 1995, the results of the oral swab were showing initial indicators that Thompson's DNA was similar to that of the offender. He was therefore put under covert surveillance for a month. He was observed getting close to attacking twice before he was disturbed. The DNA test eventually showed that Thompson was the man the police had been seeking for so long.

At 7.15 a.m. on Saturday 15 July 1995 Detective Sergeant Henwood and his colleague Detective Sergeant Simpson went to arrest him, supported by four police cars and a police dog.

Thompson opened the door to them and said, 'I've been waiting for you guys. It had to come, I know that.' He even expressed some surprise that it had taken the police so long to find him, but expressed relief that his exploits had now come to a close: 'I want to clear it up. The day had to come, I know.' He had a wash, got his turquoise and navy parka, put on his baseball cap and spent the following two days being interviewed.

During 18 hours of interviews he admitted to 129 charges, of which 61 were sexual offences, making probably the largest number of guilty pleas in any Commonwealth country. Thompson was sentenced to 30 years in prison with a recommendation that he serve a minimum of 25 years.

THE MOVING NEEDLE

The problems of finding Thompson illustrate only too well how far geographical profiling relies upon good police records for its success. Finding the needle in a haystack of hundreds of possible suspects is much more difficult when the needle moves around and police records do not keep up with those movements. The police searched for the Otara rapist through their database using the address offenders had given at the time of their arrests. So although Thompson lived in at least two different addresses in Otara while committing these rapes and many burglaries, the crimes he was charged with that had Otara addresses recorded were for resisting arrest and driving whilst disqualified. These charges had been excluded from the early probes.

It was also later discovered that his mother and father lived in the Otara area, and he had lived there as an adolescent. But even though he had spent a while in the custody of a boys' home around that time for theft and burglary, this did not result in a recorded charge. Police records are usually collected for administrative and legal purposes. It is necessary to know where an offender is living so that court orders and other clerical details can be handled. Sometimes the information is collected to add to general statistics on numbers and types of offences, but it is still rare to collect information about suspects and known offenders with a view to its potential value in future investigations. There are, of course, civil liberty implications for tracking the whereabouts of people before they commit their crimes (as the recent film *Minority Report* explored so dramatically) but there is no doubt that, as Chook put it, 'Relying on addresses at time of being charged can sometimes hurt our investigation.'

The other administrative difficulty the police have in such a growing, sprawling inquiry is keeping a clear focus on their priorities and assumptions. Henwood had linked over forty cases together beyond the Manurewa rapes he had first become aware of. He had assumed the rapist was not from that area and was more likely to have a base in Otara, where the majority of offences had happened. Yet when the police did a house-to-house canvas looking for reports of suspicious activity or possible suspects, they focused this on Manurewa, because that was where the rapes that had initiated the linked inquiry had taken place. This focus was also partly influenced by reports of the directions in which the offender had been running, although (like Barry George in London) Thompson had usually run in the opposite direction to his home, aware that he might have been followed, looping back home across main roads. He even made a point of going through gardens with dogs, thinking this would put tracker dogs off the scent, even though the police never managed to track his route at all.

Thompson had missed the early probes because he was 36 years old, although ironically the 12-year-old victim who had first brought the series to police notice had estimated her assailant's age as 37, a rather more accurate estimate than that made in the initial police profile. He had moved two or so miles west to Papatoetoe, just across the motorway from Otara, after some of the initial rapes, and so his current address was not on the lists used in later probes examining possible offenders in the Otara area. He was even missed by a day in one specific trawl for suspects amongst known burglars. The time frame was set at six months on either side of the date of a target rape. He came into police records in that area one day after the cut-off date.

'IT HAD TO COME, I KNOW THAT'
After he was arrested Joe Thompson admitted, with a remarkably accurate memory, 5 abductions, 61 rapes, 17

physical assaults, 29 burglaries, and 6 counts of entering a building with intent to commit a crime, carried out over a 12-year period. It later emerged that in total he had committed twice as many sexual offences over the years, including at least 30 incidents of incest. In total the police have 234 crimes recorded against his name.

In the two days following the arrest Detective Sergeants Henwood and Simpson interviewed Joe intensively. This drew to a conclusion after eighteen hours, on Sunday evening at 8.00 p.m., when Thompson and his two interviewers had agreed on the catalogue of violence he had inflicted. Finally, with a commendable desire to try to understand what had led Joe along his journey of violence and depravity, Simpson invited Joe 'to give some explanation or some reason why all this came about and why it continued over all the years'. In the unexpectedly friendly atmosphere that can creep into such concentrated interplay between police and criminal, Simpson offered the floor to Joe with the words, 'So now's your opportunity, mate'.

What followed is one of the most remarkable explanations for a life of sexual assault I have ever come across. Still wearing the baseball cap and parka he had put on when arrested, Thompson sat with his head down, talking more to himself than to his two interviewers and the watching camera. Although he had had no preparation for this, and as far as anyone could tell he had never discussed his years of offending with anyone else, he had clearly been thinking for a long time about himself and what he had done to others. There unfolded a fluent, unbroken narrative of what others had done to him and how he had lived within a milieu of ill-treatment. At one level his account is a textbook picture of abuse which, having been visited upon him, he then somehow felt impelled to pass on to others. But we can also read it more closely to reveal how he had created a picture of himself as a victim whose appetites were out of control, even though he claimed no satisfaction from his deeds.

His opening response was to recall his earliest memory. Most of us have one or two strong memories from the age of four or five, perhaps of a birthday party or a trip to the zoo. For Joe it was like this: 'I remember one time, I was only three or four, my older sister she got me down on the floor and tried to get me to put my penis in her . . . almost any time our parents weren't there my female cousins would come round, I was four or five and they were five or six and the same thing would happen . . .'

He defines himself in terms of the sexual activity that others drew him into. The truth of the matter, not often recognised, is that young children are curious about many things, including sex. They often play secret exploratory games of the 'I'll show you mine if you show me yours' kind. These games are usually innocent and tinged with the knowledge that they are naughty, and are soon replaced by an awareness of what is acceptable and discreet. But Thompson saw these as self-defining experiences that had not been curtailed by a maturing awareness of the appropriate constraints on sensual gratification. He felt his early licence had been engendered by an environment in which childish indulgence had held full sway because there had been no adult control. He followed up these early memories with the explanation that 'my parents always used to be away on the beer . . . with no parents' supervision and all that'. He let his voice trail away, implying no further elaboration was necessary because this said it all. However, a little later, when he had thought more about it, he did elaborate: 'I'm sure I wasn't born like that. In our family we had no discipline. We had no authority or anything really, the whole lot of us we were just let loose to do what we wanted whenever we wanted. It's not only been going on for ten years, with me it's been going on my whole life.'

He warmed to this theme, suggesting that lack of adult supervision was only part of the story. He saw his family as generating an atmosphere in which sexual abuse and exploitation were commonplace:

Even my own mother I know, there were times my grandfather was trying to sleep with her . . . my sister was abused by her people for her to do that to me . . . My parents used to bring their friends over. This guy used to sleep with me and he used to rape me every night. Now and then he used to give me money and then I started accepting that. The abuse was just part of my normal family routine . . . My whole family has a history of abuse. My own half-sister told me that my father raped her and the daughter she has now is his. I know for a fact that my father has interfered with my sisters.

He sees himself as a victim of circumstance caught in a circle of sexual abuse and exploitation, and hints that he knew no better; his self-image is similar to that of Bram Stoker's vampire, who turns everyone he bites into another vampire. He just did what others had done to him, and was encouraged as well by what he saw others around him doing. There was no way out, other than being caught by the police:

When we first came to Auckland I myself started doing these things to other people. I done it to my nieces. On one occasion I even done it to my own daughter.

A vicious circle that just goes round and round and round and I was part of that circle. It had to come to this to break the circle. If you'd never taken that swab it just may never have stopped. It would just keep going round and round.

He talks himself into this role in which he subtly implies the fault is not really his, but rather a product of his environment. Yet he is still careful to hold back recognition of the true depths of his depravity. In passing, as an apparent indication of his total honesty, he says, 'On one occasion I even done it to my own daughter.' With the two detectives listening quietly, remarkably restrained, with not a hint of approval or disapproval at the debauchery being softly described, he shares his recognition of how low he has sunk – 'even done it'. That adverb 'even' shows he thinks this act is unexpected of a person like him, who is not really inherently bad. But he is careful to make clear that he is not totally dissolute, by slipping in that it was 'On one occasion'; a most unlikely rarity given how prolific his other crimes were.

The limits of his confession are also clear when you remember how he frightened his victims, tied some of them up and abducted a number of them. His cycle of offending was fuelled by more than unthinking habit, as becomes clear when he reflects on what else might have stopped him if the police had not got to him: 'I may have been caught by someone at one of the scenes and I may have been killed or something like that.'

Never does he comment on his victims and how their reactions might have changed his. He never thinks he might have hurt them. His only concern is that he might have been killed. This was an adventure that he continued because he could get away with it. He had been destroying people's lives and causing fear across a wide swathe of Auckland, yet he sums it up by saying, 'This is the worst thing that I've ever done.' Over two hundred crimes were a 'thing', the way he says it, suggesting that at least he had not murdered.

His father was later convicted of many incest offences and sentenced to a long time in prison. Yet there was no indication that his brother, for example, although convicted of burglary, had ever sexually abused others in his family or outside. Without mentioning this Joe seems to sense that the lack of constraints, and his family's abusive habits, are not the whole answer. He goes on to say, 'I guess that's part of the reason, it's not the whole reason, I accept a lot of the blame myself. I'm grown up, I should be able to tell what's right and wrong.'

He had been a grown man when his first recorded assaults occurred. In his mid-twenties he climbed into houses and raped ten- and twelve-year-old girls. There is therefore a powerful need for him to recognise that the domestic brutality of his earliest years could only be part of the story. But his insight into the conditions that supported his activities seems paper-thin. He just sees himself as having an unusual appetite:

You become conditioned to those kind of things then it's one of the reasons why I get this urge inside of me [he gets more animated] that's been there since I was a little kid, it's just like being hungry for a feed. When you get hungry for a feed you go in the kitchen and you get a feed. I get this urge, I don't even know if it's sex, whether it's to have somebody in my arms, whether it's hate, I don't understand, myself. I know that all of these things play a big part of it.

Joe was one of twelve children in a family that had little stability. He was farmed out to live with various relatives from the age of ten, and stayed with his grandfather for a while when his parents separated. He was sent back to his mother after a year or so and she just put him and his brother in a taxi off to his father, who was not in. So the boys spent some time in the care of social welfare. This was to be the first in the series of increasingly long periods of time that he spent in one institution or another.

These institutions undoubtedly gave him the only stability in his life as well, perhaps, as a feeling of significance. His schooling had been very patchy but, as is clear from his thoughtful and articulate confession, he is not unintelligent and in the appropriate setting, where he knows the boundaries, he is quite comfortable, as has been shown in his settled life in prison since his arrest.

He could certainly not maintain a settled family existence. For although he had two children by a woman he lived with for some time, she left him. She could simply no longer tolerate being beaten by a man whose drunkenness and frequent contact with the law made her life a hell.

The pattern of emotional deprivation and abuse that Joe Thompson experienced as he was growing up is a common background for violent criminals, especially those who go on to abuse others. It is rare, though, to see as clearly as we do in his confession the emotional turmoil this background generates. In Thompson's case he had moved beyond anger or simple gratification. As he says, 'I don't even know if it's sex, whether it's to have somebody in my arms, whether it's hate, I don't understand, myself.'

He lacks any emotional focus to his life. There is a bundle of conflicting feelings that do not really make any sense to him. He creates a meaning for his rapes of vulnerable girls and young women, describing them in terms of responding to an urge. That urge is the only anchor that gives his inner world stability. In his confession he struggles to get beyond this need to satisfy this hunger, yet he is unaware of the immaturity of his control of his appetites. How many people see hunger as simply as he does: 'When you get hungry for a feed you go in the kitchen and you get a feed'? There is here no social process to eating, and no time frame of when it is appropriate; his hunger is more like that of a newborn baby or an untrained animal, getting 'a feed'.

He tries to get beyond his construction of himself as simply driven by his unfettered desires when he goes on to say, 'At the end of the day it's all come back on me. I know that hasn't been the full reason why I couldn't stop doing these things. I could've probably sought help.'

But he drifts back into seeing himself as not really being in control of his actions. He pictures himself as an organism that has been programmed to behave in a particular way with no free will at all, returning to the need to satisfy his appetites: 'I'm so conditioned. Like I was saying earlier if you want a feed you go in the kitchen and get a feed. With me I have this urge to go out, this compulsion to go out and do these things, probably while I'm out there doing them I can't stop doing them. I can't get anybody to stop me from doing them.'

He claims that he is aware of the wrong he is doing when he says, 'I feel remorse and guilt,' but there is no reference to why he is guilty, no comment on what his victims suffer. What he calls 'remorse and guilt' is really his own lack of satisfaction in what he gets out of the assault: 'I feel like shit afterwards.' He does not seem to understand that it is the whole process of searching out his victims that gives him the excitement. All he is aware of is that: '. . . suddenly I'll get this urge again . . . and I push aside all that guilt and that and I do it again. I do these things, I'm sort of hungry inside, but what makes it worse is after I've done those things I'm even worse inside.'

There is a hunger, as he says, although it is not clear exactly what the appetite is for. He sees it as sexual gratification, which he is unable to get with an adult woman (although some of his victims were adult women). He then comes up with another explanation for his particular interest in assaulting girls:

You know the physical abuse that I've been through has had a physical effect on me. I'm incapable of satisfying any adult woman because of the abuse that I've suffered . . . I caught a lot of diseases from the people I was abused by . . . it's made me unfunctionable. My only way of getting sexual satisfaction, or gratification or whatever you call it is with a young woman, and even though I say that I've never ever been satisfied.

Here he offers the curious theory that he has caught a disease that makes him sexually dysfunctional with older women. What is more plausible is that his preoccupation with his immediate sexual urges is so focused on non-reciprocated gratification, where he could control his victims readily, that he quickly learned that girls and young women offered ready targets. His excitement in the quest and conquest of these victims dissipated once the act was over, but picked up again once he started to think of future possibilities.

John Banks, the former New Zealand minister of police and now mayor of Auckland, got some way to understanding what had given rise to Joe Thompson's decade of offending when he commented: 'It goes right back to the family . . . They have many fathers, sometimes several mothers; they are taken from pillar to post . . . They are like savage dogs, if you tied a dog to a tree and if everyone who passed it was to kick it, when it was let loose it would bite everything in sight.'

But while this appropriately emphasises the external life circumstances that created the processes that led Thompson to offend, it does not connect directly with what those processes actually were. His statement misses the significance that the 'urge', which Thompson is aware of, gives to his life. The minister of police makes the same mistake as Joe does in thinking that the rapes and abductions are just a thoughtless reaction to life's turmoil. Listening carefully to his confession it is clear that Thompson found excitement, meaning and even purpose in prowling around Otara and other suburbs. Once the act itself was over he felt unsatisfied, but the prospect of the adventure of finding another victim soon replaced that feeling. The hours that he spent wandering the area looking for possible victims and planning his escapade became his life story. It was what his life was about. The opportunities provided by the layout and residents' lifestyles of the suburbs in which he operated fostered his search for an adventure he could be part of.

GEOGRAPHICAL PROFILING

Joseph Thompson had started his attacks opportunistically, when visiting a friend in Mount Eden, a few miles north-west of the Otara area where Thompson had spent his formative years. He was 25 years old when he noticed an attractive 21-year-old woman living next door to his friend. Whilst his friend was away he broke into her home and hid until he was sure that she was sleeping, then raped her at knifepoint after cutting the telephone cord. It was to be almost ten years before this assault was linked to others in Otara and Manurewa. In that time he became a skilled housebreaker and rapist.

The detailed information available on the crimes committed by Joseph Thompson, especially on their locations, allows us – with the privilege of hindsight – to examine how he developed from climbing into a friend's neighbour's house and waiting for his target to go to sleep before he attacked her, to using the suburbs as his hiding place and waiting and watching on the street, which was an extension of his secret concealment.

Just think of a man, no longer a youth, staying quietly in a strange house for some hours, patiently biding his time until his victim was defenceless. The power he must have felt during that wait. The time he had to speculate on what he would do with his victim. For this man, who saw himself as having an urge that he had a right to satisfy, these generated an excitement that gave him a purpose. When later he was wandering around the familiar streets of Otara he would have found the same excitement in anticipation. He saw opportunities all around him and he could move freely through the area, in part because of the open, shrub-covered land that flanked the creek running down through the eastern edge of the suburb. The quest he was on to find victims produced his particular, personal spatial geometry.

Like the urban guerrilla that he was – except his targets were sexual, not political – he marauded out from his base, searching for opportunities then planning his assault. What kept his base hidden for so long was that it was the centre of his area of opportunity and familiarity, rather than where he was living when he declared his address to the police for his motoring offences. This mental base in Lappington Road, Otara, is at the centre of gravity for the majority of his crimes – those that were committed in Otara.

The first offence he was known to have committed in Otara was less than a mile, a twenty-minute walk, south-west of Lappington Road. For his next targets he did not return to this area but moved a similar distance north-east of Lappington Road. Having marked the western and eastern limits of his domain he now moved south a little further. With these first few rapes, in three different locations around Lappington Road, he marked off a rough triangle that defined his dominant domain of operation, an area determined in part by its proximity to his mental heartland. It was also defined by some natural and man-made barriers. The Auckland–Hamilton motorway acted as the main western boundary and the creek as the eastern one. To the north Ngati Otara Park provided a limit, and to the south the more affluent suburbs were initially less attractive to him, although he did eventually make forays there.

Again and again he found victims in one of the corners of this area. Usually he left a time interval of a few months before returning to any area in which he had successfully carried out an assault, criss-crossing his domain at will. None of the twenty or so offences he is known to have committed in this area were less than half a mile from his house in Lappington Road. He was not going to risk being recognised by neighbours, but of course that left a hole in the offence locations on the map, a hole that sat in the middle of a dense area of his crimes.

Chook Henwood had first become aware of a serial rapist from the offender's crimes in other areas. By the time the full picture had been built up of the extensive series of offences, he was known to have raped in other areas as well. This meant that, understandably, many house-to-house inquiries and searches of police records took place in areas beyond Otara, many miles away from Lappington Road.

LEARNING FROM CRIMINALS

The difficulty in locating Joseph Thompson had a big impact
on the New Zealand police. Their success in using systematic
procedures for finding him gave them impetus to develop
their procedures further, much as the weaknesses of the
Yorkshire Ripper inquiry lead to soul-searching amongst UK
police and the conviction of John Duffy opened up an era of
profiling in the UK. The successful application of these
procedures in a subsequent case in New Zealand led to the
setting up of a Criminal Profiling Squad that Detective
Sergeant Henwood is now in charge of.

He identified a number of difficulties in finding Thompson
that he has since struggled to overcome. One is that searching
through police records on the basis of prior criminal offences
is a hit-and-miss affair. The crucial information may simply
not be in the police system because the offender has never
been caught for related matters. As Chook pointed out:
'Thompson walked the streets three to four times a week from
before he was fourteen years old until his arrest by us at the
age of 36. During all these walks he was peeping and peering
and prowling around houses and yet he has no convictions or
even charges for any of these offences.'

Prolific offenders are rarely specialists in a specific type of
crime. They live deviant lifestyles that involve the sort of mix
that characterised Thompson – violence against his wife,
drunken fights, car theft and driving whilst disqualified – as
well as the crimes that eventually earned him a 30-year prison
sentence: incest, rape and abduction. There may be some
loose theme to their offending, whether against property or
against people,[2] and some are certainly less versatile in their
offending than others, but the labels that the law assigns to
crimes do not map with any precision onto the important
behavioural distinctions that separate one form of criminality
from another.

The locations in which an offender commits crimes can be
more clearly revealing of his characteristics, although that is
certainly not always the case. But even then, reading these
characteristics to find the culprit is fraught with difficulties.
Although Thompson had lived in a number of places in Otara
over a twenty-year period the police had no record of that

until after his arrest. Whether a different sort of search, not through police records but rather by using the density of his offences in Otara as a centre of attention, would have led more directly to him is a moot point. Looking back on Operation Park is a useful exercise in time travel, but can only give a hint of what is possible for the future.

16. A PATH OF VIOLENCE AND TERROR

In the late 1980s Scotland Yard's publicity machine had been boasting about my contribution to a number of serial rape and murder investigations. This had alerted John House,[1] when he was still a police constable in the city of St John's on the easternmost edge of Canada, to the possibility of making use of behavioural science to help his investigation into a number of very violent sexual assaults. John is one of those polite, self-effacing detectives who have nothing of the heroic arrogance that fictional detectives are required to portray. His reflective nature is shown by his educated interest in old lithographs and his collection of antique coins. It was this studious approach that eventually enabled him to catch a very dangerous man and get him locked up, probably forever.

He got in touch with me to see how I could assist, a couple of thousand miles away on the other side of the Atlantic. John described to me how painstaking detective work had uncovered a series of brutal rapes and vicious assaults. The judge later called these 'a path of violence and terror over the span of four and a half years'. I was able to shed some light on the form that path took, which strengthened the Royal Newfoundland Constabulary (RNC) investigation, but it was the intelligent resolve of John House and his colleagues, helped out – as so often in police work – by some strokes of luck, that led to the identification and conviction of Garrett Young.

The violent course this criminal followed illustrates a pattern found in many serial murders. It was not the places from which he abducted his victims that were significant, because the locations at which vulnerable victims were available were limited. It was the sites of his assaults, the places to which he took his victims in order to carry out his attacks, that told the story of his journey into ever more brutal crime, and helped to confirm that he was the culprit for whom the police were searching.

In 1990 John House had been working as a police constable with the Criminal Investigation Division in St John's, the major city of Newfoundland, when he came across files on three missing young women. Careful reading of the files indicated that at least one of the women had possibly last been seen when she got into a car driven by a man, who was likely to have been cruising the downtown area where street prostitutes were known to ply their trade. House was concerned that this woman, and possibly others, had been murdered; but he was working in the drug section at the time and could not follow up his concerns directly.

Crimes and criminals do not stick faithfully to the administrative units in which their files are held, so an alert detective must use every opportunity to follow up his suspicions. Anxious to know what had happened to the missing young women, John got the chance, provided by a drug raid downtown, to find out if there was anything more to the disappearances. The man arrested in the raid was taken into custody for a lengthy conversation. As John put it, 'He was a pleasant enough fellow, and was more than willing to be helpful given the difficult circumstances he found himself in.' John eventually 'moved the conversation' to the man's girlfriend TF whom, it transpired, worked sometimes as a street prostitute in downtown St John's. Constable House asked if the man's girlfriend had ever been assaulted by her clients. When John got a positive answer he sought out the girlfriend and got the full story.

When John and I met a few years later he explained the situation to me in the formal way of police officers who have bitter experience of being cross-examined, and are aware of the risks of being tripped up by a clever attorney if they do not express themselves clearly and with caution: 'The crimes came to light when I interviewed a young woman who was working as a prostitute and she indicated to me a particularly violent assault against her.'

DOUBLE JEOPARDY

Prostitutes all over the world, especially those who ply their trade on the streets, live in double jeopardy. There is always the risk of attack every time they get into a car with a punter.

Some men who use street prostitutes may be annoyed with themselves for giving in to their urges, and take it out on the women. Others regard the women as so undeserving of any respect that they will seek to control and abuse them, trying to avoid paying for their services. Then there are a few who delight in hurting the women, heightening their own sexual arousal from the sadistic pleasure. Virtually every street prostitute has experienced violence at one time or another.[2]

The second jeopardy comes from their fear of reporting this violence to the police. In most cities some aspect or other of prostitution is illegal, so the women fear their complaint will open them up to prosecution. But it is not the fine that usually results from prosecution that is their major concern. Women who work the streets often regard such fines as a form of tax. What stops them reporting attacks are their experiences of having their grievances dismissed or even ridiculed. It is the confused and hypocritical attitude that many communities have towards prostitution that makes any violence prostitutes suffer especially difficult to investigate. Their vulnerable lifestyle and the many anonymous men with whom the women come into contact open up a huge range of possible suspects in any crime against them, but also make for great difficulty in identifying the perpetrators. Yet the police are often pressured by the public to get rid of street prostitution, so that any attempt to make the women less vulnerable can be treated with derision by local politicians.

The laws that make prostitution illegal push prostitutes even further into the murky shadows of our cities, where they have no protection from assault and abuse, except the safeguards that they can make for themselves – the choice of punter they go with and the locations in which they do their business. These women survive through the rapid assessment of any man who approaches them, refusing to get into a car if he gives off the wrong vibes, unless they are desperate for the money he offers. Most importantly these women know that they are at their most vulnerable when in the process of providing a service. They therefore choose locations to do business that allow quick escape and are close to help if either should prove necessary. But these are weak defences, easily breached, creating a feeding ground for violent men who want to take advantage of the women's vulnerability to indulge their own vicious excesses.

John House understood that such violence does not limit itself to street prostitutes. Men who have experience of assaulting such vulnerable women may become proficient in getting away with their brutal acts, and develop a taste for them, taking them to other areas and victims where they cannot be so easily ignored. If there were a man attacking women, whoever they were, he needed to be apprehended as quickly as possible, but this required gaining the confidence of women who had become used to hiding their lifestyles with their scars.

It requires a determined police officer to overcome the fear of the police of the women themselves, and the often dismissive attitudes of his colleagues, some of whom do not recognise that the women who sell sex on the streets deserve the protection of the law like any other citizens. When Constable House got to talk to TF he learned that the attack was not the result of a squabble over payment, or anger about the services rendered, which just might have made it a one-off tussle between a particular client and a particular street-girl:

One night at the end of October 1989 TF was standing on the sidewalk opposite the courthouse, Duckworth Street, St John's for the purpose of soliciting. It was after 10:30 p.m. She was picked up by a man driving a red Tempo or Topaz. They were to drive to a secluded location. She became apprehensive when the driver disregarded her stated wish to go only to a familiar location and repeatedly indicated that he wouldn't hurt her. Their route and destination were unknown to her. They drove to the outskirts of the city and up a dirt road off a dead-end street, through a power-line clearing to a secluded location in the woods beyond.

Following consensual sexual intercourse the man violently assaulted her without provocation or warning. She was hauled from the car by her hair, swung round and punched in the face two or three times, resulting in cuts to her nose and lip. She was then thrown on the ground and kicked in the ribs. Throughout this period the man was shouting obscenities. He demanded money and was handed $140, including the $100 he had just given her. Her assailant, who was still holding her hair, smashed her face into the trunk of the car and threw her into the bushes threatening to kill her if she moved. He then drove away.

She eventually made her way back to the paved dead-end street and knocked at the door of the nearest house that was lit, exhibiting cuts and bruises to her face, which was bloodied, and having bruises to her legs.

The woman who answered the door offered to call the police but TF declined, fearing trouble because she was soliciting. The woman and one of her daughters drove her home, where TF told her boyfriend what had happened. No complaint was made or statement given to the police until she was approached by Constable House in March 1990.[3]

ST JOHN'S

This attack seemed unusual for St John's, a place that does not have a great deal of violent crime. When I visited John House, some years after the investigation had been completed, he took me to the scenes of some of the crimes. Being there made it even clearer to me that the offender's knowledge of his surroundings was one of the weapons he used in his assaults.

The small communities sheltering in weather-beaten corners of Newfoundland became famous when featured in the film *The Shipping News*. This showed long cold winters and balmy, sea-soaked summers, capturing the bleak mood of this vast, mostly empty island, only a little smaller than England, stuck in the middle of the Atlantic just off the coast of Canada. What that film avoided illustrating, though, was St John's, the capital of the province and the only city of any size on the island. Its vibrancy contrasts with the wilderness that is the rest of Newfoundland. It has a population of just under 200,000, which is the focus of activity for the whole province, and houses all the major services.

The city centre itself is very small, stretched out as a ten-minute walk along the quay that surrounds the long, narrow inlet of St John's Harbour, which has long given this isolated island its significance. Buildings above a few storeys high are very rare, as befits a province with so much undeveloped land. Sprawling out from the city stretch the suburbs of small detached wooden houses, past lakes which freeze solid during the winter months and on into the wilderness. In a twenty-minute drive from downtown you can get to many secluded places. But this is the oldest city in North America. Most paths are well trodden and houses have been built wherever ready access is feasible. It therefore takes considerable local knowledge to locate hidden places where accidental discovery is unlikely.

As would be expected for a small city in the midst of a wilderness there is not much serious crime. Most of it is petty theft, indulged in by unemployed, bored youths, rather than the violence or gangs that plague inner-city areas in the US. I witnessed a not unusual example of such petty crime when I was visiting. A young man wandered into the dining room of our hotel, took a bottle of wine and ran out the door. The lack of security in the hotel, and the chutzpah of the young man, speak volumes about the gentility of St John's. In many countries such a criminal would risk being shot.

Within this context of low-level crime and the focus of street prostitution in a limited area of downtown it was not too difficult for the local police to find out the names of all the street prostitutes. There were no more than a dozen providing services to this small city. They plied their trade along the only main street near the clubs, which are as animated as any that much larger cities could boast. Their clients are the usual mix of businessmen and labourers that use prostitutes in any city across the world. We discovered that the appetite for such services is still great when we set about filming a woman we had asked to be on the street, briefly, for a television documentary. Before the camera could be set up cars were stopping to ask her if she were available for business.

A SERIAL MURDERER IN THE MAKING

The calculated brutality of the assault on TF led John House to believe that this was not a one-off attack. And there was also the predetermined use by the assailant of a particular location. The attacker knew where he was going before the young woman got into his car. He knew how to get to a location where he would not be disturbed, while still being close enough to get to quickly with his frightened victim. It was moreover not a location that was known to the city's street prostitutes. His victim had no idea where she was going. This also marked the assailant out, revealing his mental processes in his physical actions. He had a distinct knowledge of secluded spots that could be accessed by car. This accorded with the likelihood that he had thought about this abduction, going through its possibilities in his mind as he drove around.

There are other aspects of the abduction and assault that throw light on the perpetrator. One is his reassurance in the car that he would not hurt the woman. How did that comment emerge if he were not aware of the possibility of inflicting pain? And what does it tell us about his prior contact with women, that rather than just telling her to be quiet or remaining silent, he sought to reassure her, as misleading as this was? The most likely explanation is that this was a man who had had longer-term relationships with women in the past, which might have turned violent, and he had got into the habit of reassuring those women as a way of keeping them under his control.

The second aspect, of particular interest because of its help in locating this offender, is to ask how he had come across this 'dirt road off a dead-end street, through a power-line clearing' that gave access to a secluded location in the woods, on 'the outskirts of the city'. This must have been a consequence of his familiarity with the area. But was this familiarity a product of him living close to that particular area, having some work that had taken him there, or could it have been a chance discovery with no particular psychological significance? If the location had been carefully selected beforehand it implied an offender who had been thinking long and hard about the possibilities for such a crime. That would make him of great potential danger. How far might his inner journey take him? Would he plan what he needed to do to carry out crimes so that his victims would never be able to identify him? If this were an almost casual, one-off crime he might be less dangerous at the moment, but if not, would he become more dangerous now he had got away with that assault? To answer these questions John House needed to find out if there were any related attacks.

So, as John House put it, 'I started canvassing a number of prostitutes on the street.' This rather underplays the difficulty of a young police constable in gaining the trust of these women. He had to track some of them to their houses and, when first approached, they would not even open the door to him. Perhaps this is unsurprising considering that the men they have most contact with are those who wish only to use them for atavistic satisfaction.

In the small city of St John's, though, word of violence gets around; this was fortunate for the investigation because the RNC files would not easily have led Constable House to appropriate related cases. He would have had to search through hundreds of thousands of files. Computerisation was just beginning to come in but, as would be the case even today, relevant cases may have been recorded as violent crimes, theft or sex-related crimes. The case histories may have included details of the sexual assaults, or focused solely on the violence. Police officers may have got all the details from the victims, or just those that the victims thought acceptable to mention without getting themselves into trouble. The full picture was only going to emerge by searching beyond the police records. John tracked down various police officers who had been part of an earlier major crimes unit and learnt from them of cases that may have been linked. Open-plan offices also played a role in helping John to find out about related assaults. On one occasion a former investigator overheard John talking on the telephone and recalled a similar case in 1985.

John also realised that the main hospital medical records collected in relation to police investigations might be easier to study than the thousands of police records. So he looked through the Family Practice Unit files that could have recorded medical examinations of any victims of crime. In one afternoon this led him to two more cases, one from 1986 and another from 1987. He also found that the medics kept samples from cases longer than the police did, giving rise to the rather unorthodox procedure of obtaining a search warrant for the hospital laboratory so that he could seize the exhibit he needed. This turned out to provide crucial DNA which later helped convict the offender.

These inquiries built up a picture of frequent violent attacks on a number of different women stretching back to 1985. Three had been working as street prostitutes. Others had been vulnerable because they had been drunk and alone in the downtown nightclub district where the prostitutes operated. A dozen different assaults were identified that were all likely to have been the work of one man. As John put it in his disturbingly hygienic way, 'Some of the victims received lacerations around their face and other parts of their bodies as a result of the beatings that they took. The level of violence could have ended in the death of the victims.'

Here was a serial murderer in the making.

He picked up women who were out on their own late at night. In some cases the women got into the car willingly, thinking they were providing their usual services. In one case the victim was not a prostitute, but accepted a lift because the man seemed pleasant enough and had a couple with him in the car. It was only after the couple got out and he drove on, keeping her in the car with threats, that she realised the danger she had embraced. In another case the victim had difficulty speaking, because of brain damage she had suffered from an attack by another man many years earlier. She was forced into the car at knifepoint. After she had been assaulted and thrown out of the car, she struggled back to the main hospital in the early hours of the morning, but owing to her difficulty in communicating the security guard turned her away.

The victims were vulnerable in many different ways. Their assailant had found a time and place where he could prey on such victims at will. The geographical patterns of where he took his victims combined with the details of his actions to show just how thoroughly his behaviour was planned and how his danger to women grew.

The women were abducted from the central downtown area. They were raped, beaten and left for dead. The rarity of such crimes in this small city, the similarity in the description of the assailant given by the victims, and his characteristic pattern of behaviour – picking the women up in his car then taking them to isolated spots where he assaulted them – also made it extremely unlikely that more than one person could be active over the same time period in the same area. The descriptions of the offender and the consistent method of the assaults convinced John House that 'we had a serial rapist operating here in downtown St John's. It was an individual that we really needed to identify and have dealt with . . .'

A LUCKY BREAK?

The rapist thought that he was immune from detection or prosecution; that the women he attacked could not be helped by any law. After close questioning TF remembered that she had seen her assailant some weeks after the assault, when she had returned to her perilous street trade. Oblivious to any sense of guilt he recognised her as he drove past, taunting her by sounding his car horn and waving. But she was more alert than he realised and made a note of his car number plate. Furnished with this Constable House determined it belonged to a red car driven by a man fitting the description more than one victim had given. Did the police now have a firm fix on this dangerous man?

On TV or in crime fiction that would have been all that was needed to bring the case to a conclusion, but in real life such a clue is only the start of intensive police work. The woman could have picked the car licence number out of the air or be trying to frame an innocent man. They needed firm evidence.

The owner of the red car came under close police scrutiny. His whereabouts on the date of the offence that the prostitute had given was carefully checked. He had a cast-iron alibi. He had definitely been at work at that time.

TF had been taken to a place in the woods near transmission lines, so John House and his police colleagues set out to see if they could locate the area. He took her to all the places he could identify that might have been where she had been assaulted. The first place they went to was unfamiliar. But when two other police officers then took her to the Thorburn Road area she immediately recognised it as the scene of the attack. This enabled her to identify a house nearby as the one whose residents had been so kind to her. They all remembered having been woken at 4.00 a.m. by the victim and how distraught and scared she had been, her face bleeding and swollen, her clothes covered with dirt and blood, but how reluctant she had been to go to the police or a hospital.

The daughter of the house regularly kept a careful diary. She had recorded this incident with its precise date. This showed that the victim had been confused by the trauma of that early morning and so had not given the correct date for when she had been abducted and attacked. The suspect's alibi was not so strong for the actual date of the offence, so the police felt they might be after the right culprit after all.

TF helped the police to build up a photofit of the man, one not unlike the man on whom their attention was now focusing. The police had DNA but the culprit could always claim that he had left his bodily secretions in some legitimate way. The police needed further evidence that would help them to present a strong case to court.

Careful analysis of the reports of the abductions showed that the offender typically picked his victims up at night in a very limited area of downtown St John's. They set up a classic 'decoy' operation. A female police officer posed as a prostitute on the street. On two occasions Garrett Young tried to lure her into his car. Now they had a reason to arrest him. One by one, his victims identified Garrett Young as their attacker.

But even this was limited evidence, reliant on the word of street prostitutes and other vulnerable victims, one of whom could only be interviewed using a sign-language translator. The police needed to strengthen their case further by any means available.

John House had heard of my work and thought it would help his case if I could come up with anything. So he sent me a remarkably thorough dossier that detailed the actions and locations of all the attacks. These told the unfolding story of all the aspects of the case. The footprints on the map helped to show what was going on in the offender's head.

17. TRAVELLING OFFENDER

LOCATING THE OFFENDER

In order to make sense of the patterns within the dossier, I drew upon some principles that were beginning to emerge within our work. A criminal searching for special targets may find them away from his usual haunts. The police therefore need to be careful not to assume that every crime series occurs around the offender's home. There are also a number of significant locations for any violent crime. In this case the locations where the victims were first contacted was different from those where the offences took place. In addition, there were two further important aspects of this offender's geography. One was the route he took to his crimes. What did that tell us about his knowledge and experience? The second was the rather more complex process of examining the sequence in which he made use of different locations. The targets of his crimes – the women of the street – and where they were found, told us something of the offender's psychological characteristics. The locations to which the victims were taken – and the order in which these locations were used – illuminated the mental map that shaped his predatory world.

The particular nature of St John's and its surroundings helped shape the significance of the locations and actions of the offender. There are very few places in St John's where women can be found on the streets who are willing to get into a stranger's car: all of them are situated just a few paces along a couple of downtown streets near the main harbour. Any men interested in finding street prostitutes would know this small area; many others would knowingly pass through it. So the locations where the victims were first contacted told us little about the offender's local knowledge, other than what he shared with other residents. They did, however, show that this was a man very familiar with the ways of street prostitutes. The regularity with which he would approach women in that area not only provided a key to his habits, which was of use to detectives in deciding to set up a decoy, but also told us that here was a man who had come to believe that the use of prostitutes picked up from the street was an acceptable routine. Just as the women who work the streets become hardened to the men who use them, it seems likely that men who frequently use women in this way are also likely to become inured to their humanity and treat them as objects.

Of even more significance was the location to which he took his victims. As I've seen so many times, although the violence of killers and rapists may itself be difficult to understand and appear senseless, the determination to carry out an assault and get away with it without detection often has a very obvious logic. It is a logic that is shaped by the offender's own familiarity with the area in which he is acting and his understanding of what goes on in that area. In the dense, well-populated centre of St John's the offender would have known that it was difficult for him to carry out any sort of attack without drawing attention to himself. He would also have worked out that this low-rise city was of the scale that encouraged walking, with few alleys to hide in; so if he released or disposed of his victim near to where he had accosted them the police would quickly be alerted. This would mean that unless he had a bolthole very near to where he made contact with his victims he would be at risk of detection before he could get away.

Offenders know they are most at risk when they are in the throes of their crimes and immediately afterwards. If they are abducting a victim they know they can reduce that risk by going to a location at which they will not be noticed or disturbed and from which they can get away unnoticed, preferably to a nearby safe haven such as their home.

A map of St John's shows that the downtown area, which lies alongside the harbour, is on the eastern coast of the island. The only major routes away from downtown are to the south, north and west. So to understand the behavioural patterns revealed by the location of the offences we needed to see which of the possibilities the criminal was using. To do this the actual sequence of offences was important. This is often difficult to establish. Either because victims do not remember accurately the dates of incidents that took place months or even years earlier, or because the police record the offences in the sequence in which they become aware of them, rather than in the sequence in which they happened. There is also always the possibility that some offences have gone unreported, creating an unknown gap in the sequence. But John House had been thorough. We were reasonably confident that the ten offences he presented us with covered all the significant crimes we should be considering, in the order we needed to examine them.

This enabled us to read the offender's thought processes in the map of his offences. In order to rape these young women and exert violent control over them he knew he needed to get them away from the city centre as quickly as possible. But after the first couple of assaults, he realised that once he had got rid of them he needed to get off the road as quickly as possible, just in case they were found before he got back to the safety of his house. He had to think it through. Where could he take them which would be isolated enough for them to be alone and yet still allow him to get back to his house quickly? Whether this was a conscious plan, or just the developing habit learned through what he knew and had got away with, was not important. What was crucial was that he was acting out a pattern of activity that allowed him to assault these women frequently and without detection. This, though, was an unfolding process of malevolence. If he had kept going to the same places with the women he had abducted, he could have been noticed or word could have been passed amongst them that would have made them more suspicious. The map of his crimes therefore told us how he developed his criminal tactics as his experience and confidence grew.

The first known assault happened sometime around the middle of 1985. Having picked up his victim, LH, who was then several months pregnant, and agreed a price for fellatio, he drove up to Signal Hill. This spot, just a few minutes' drive north-east of downtown, is probably the most famous landmark in Newfoundland, being the place from which Marconi first transmitted radio waves across the Atlantic. When LH insisted on payment first he became angry with her and hit her in the stomach and face with his fist. She managed to escape from the car and get back to town, seeing her assailant drive past as he returned on the same route.

A few months later, the second victim was taken further away from the city. He was not going to risk the danger of being seen with her, or of her seeing his escape route. This time he took the young woman, to whom he had offered an apparently friendly lift, as far west from the city as he could reasonably get in a ten-to-fifteen-minute drive. He finally stopped at a deserted wharf at St Philips, at the end of Thorburn Road, the main east-west route out from St John's. He left the woman there after he had violently raped her.

The dominance of Thorburn Road became even clearer with the third assault, less than a year later. This time he found a deserted area off that main road, halfway between his first two assaults. He was now declaring his geographical and behavioural repertoire with some clarity. Later offences strengthened the significance of Thorburn Road still further. He took the fourth victim far west to St Philips once again, and the fifth young woman was attacked close to where he had beaten the third, just off Thorburn Road. The sixth location was again to the west, near St Philips.

He never committed two sequential offences at the same location. This is a pattern I have often seen in the cautious offender.[1] No matter how secluded the location of the crime there is always a risk in returning there. Yet the location has proven its worth to the criminal in the past, so there is a tendency for the serial criminal to return to it when he feels any risk has cooled. The seventh offence was the attack on TF, the victim who had first enabled John House to realise just what a dangerous criminal he was looking for. The power-line clearing she was taken to was once more at the centre of Thorburn Road, near the locations of the third and fifth offences.

By now the serial rapist had demonstrated the extent of his geographical range. The choice of locations, and the dominant axis he was using, can clearly be seen on a map to run west and east along Thorburn Road. But we can see more than that if we consider the actual locations. To the east they were well-known and often passed, even by casual visitors. To the west he parked on a jetty that was easy to find. But in the centre of his domain he used hidden turnings that led off to openings in the woods that were not places anyone would stumble on casually.

After the seventh abduction and rape his self-confidence seemed to grow. He returned to Signal Hill with his eighth victim, and subsequent victims were taken a short distance out of town on the way to Thorburn. As the geography was taking shape so too was the violence. The viciousness shown in the punching of his first known victim, LH, had escalated so that by the time of his seventh assault, on TF, his actions were extremely brutal and not far from murder.

The geographical pattern of offences showed the psychological processes that were at the heart of his actions. He left his greatest distance between his first and second crimes, as though he feared he could be caught by returning to the first location. Then he continued to travel to and fro along the road, criss-crossing in a way that is similar to that of the attacker in Las Vegas. But this predator had already found his prey, and was instead looking for places where he could avoid being caught as he attacked.

One crime location in particular – an area he used on possibly as many as five occasions – showed a considerable local knowledge. This is the one halfway towards St Philips. He would drive up to a dirt road that goes off to the left out of St John's. The road is not at all apparent as you drive past. It is tucked in between trees to the side of a house a little way beyond a convenience store. Once in there and through the lines of high fir trees another track suddenly takes off to the right, opening out in a secluded, extended clearing in the woods. On a cold winter's day when I visited it, the snow covering between the trees, stretching as far as the eye could see, gave the scene an eerie, silent beauty. For the victims, though, the quiet isolation, invisible to any passing cars and with no lighting anywhere, must have contributed to the horror of their experiences; each had been assaulted with a knife, dragged from the vehicle and punched and kicked repeatedly, then abandoned.

There was space here to turn his car around quickly, drive back onto Thorburn Road and be swiftly lost from view. From the offender's point of view it was a choice location. This all added up to a man who lived close to this clearing, and used Thorburn Road regularly. This clearing had a central role in his mental map of possible locations for assaults.

Not far from that clearing was a vehicle-wrecker's yard, on Thorburn Road. Looking at the map that John had sent in England, the wrecker's yard was indicated as a point of reference. It was a readily identifiable focus to the offence locations, so that was the main feature to which I drew John's attention as being near the residential base of the offender. The patterns of behaviour were consistent with the offender having had a long-standing relationship with a woman, making it even possible that he was married and living with his wife near the wrecker's yard. Furthermore, this was a man attacking his way into a criminal lifestyle. His only fear seemed to be of being caught during the assaults. His choice of locations was primed to help him carry out those assaults and escape. But he did not disguise himself or worry about leaving other forensic traces. That suggested he was not 'known to the police' through a prior criminal history.

When Constable House got this report it added greatly to his confidence that he had the right man and enabled him to understand further the dangerousness of the person he was looking for. As he said to me:

> Certainly one of the main points was your predictions on the residential location. That was quite remarkable in terms of how close it was to his current base; the auto-wrecker location you indicated was just several hundred metres from his actual base. That reinforced to us that we were looking at the right suspect.

MORE ACCURATE THAN A SCUD MISSILE
From a desk in England we had been able to send a report across the Atlantic that pointed to a residential location that was right on target. Many military missiles are not as accurate. Garrett Young was another very violent young man whom the police had difficulty in locating, even though his violent assaults took place in a sparsely populated area of Newfoundland. My analysis was done entirely on my desk in England yet the report that reached John House described exactly the location where the offender lived.

Garrett Young lived with his family a little way up a lane on the opposite side of Thorburn Road and just up the hill from the wrecker's yard, close to where the main cluster of attacks had been. He had also lived just off Thorburn Road further into St John's a few years earlier, when he had been married.

He worked mainly in menial roles for his parents, who owned cafés in St John's. In 1993, when he was thirty-six years old, he was convicted of brutally attacking eight women. He is suspected of many more assaults over nearly a decade of terror.

Under Canadian law, the court can impose an indeterminate sentence on a prolific and especially dangerous criminal. But to do this they have to demonstrate that he has a consistent pattern of behaviour that goes beyond his actual known crimes and therefore makes him habitually dangerous. The geographical pattern of Young's crimes showed that he had developed such a vicious and perilous habit.

Garrett Young is not the most vicious, violent or inherently evil criminal I have ever come across. He is a mere novice in sadism when compared with many of the murderers in this book. The development in his violent actions, supported by his use of the hidden places of which he had such ready knowledge and easy access, shows he was moving inexorably towards ever more violent acts. It could not have been long before he would have killed a victim and buried her in the power-line clearing. The three missing women who had started John House on his quest may have suffered that fate, if not at the hands of Garrett Young then at the hands of some other criminal that police investigators had not tracked down so assiduously.

EXPERT TESTIMONY
How did Garrett Young get to the point where he was declared such a dangerous criminal that he was given an indeterminate sentence? He does not seem to have come from a particularly violent background or an especially dysfunctional family; he worked in cafés owned by his parents. At the time of his arrest he was living in a comfortable detached house in its own plot of land on the outskirts of St John's. He owned a number of different vehicles, so he was hardly destitute.

When the prosecution applied for Young to be declared so dangerous that he should serve an indeterminate sentence, under Canadian law it was necessary for at least two psychiatrists to assess him and report to the court. Here you might have thought that we would get to the inner secrets of this man, whom the judge had characterised as having exhibited such 'violence and rage, wreaking injury and terror upon his victims, giving substantial grounds for concluding . . . Mr Young poses a real and serious threat to the life, safety and well-being of others.'

One expert, Dr Flemming, was brought in from Ontario, where he was Psychiatrist-in-Chief of the city's maximum-security psychiatric unit. He reported to the court that Young's actions displayed evidence of:

> . . . the presence of a sexual deviation or paraphilia in which sadistic features are present. This basically means that Mr Young is likely an individual who achieves his highest level of sexual interest or arousal in situations involving aggressive, intimidating or assaultive behaviour. That is, it is likely that he not only does not feel remorse or regret for his actions in these circumstances, but actually seeks out situations to create specific opportunities.
>
> If Mr Young does commit further offences they will likely be very similar to those already under consideration, that is, involving at least the same level of violence and possibly carried out with even more care and planning than in the past.

By contrast, Dr Lahdha, a psychiatrist from St John's who had spent nine hours with Young trying to find out what made him tick – and who had talked to his grandparents, mother and former wife – came to the conclusion that Young's acts of violence 'were short in duration and did not occur during the act of intercourse and thereby lacked the more purposeful and vicious nature which one would expect from a sexual sadist'. He also concluded that, 'the offence history did not show the escalation and violence which one would anticipate in sexual sadism'.

Both these opinions owe more to discussions in the quietude of the consulting room, where offenders talk about their experiences – typically with a view to exonerating themselves – than to the realities of sexual activity in the hidden places of our cities. When being questioned by the police Young had said that he did not believe a prostitute could be sexually assaulted. Sadly, many men may hold this view, regarding with disdain the women who work the streets, agreeing with Young's comment to the police that, 'I can't see anything wrong with having sex with a prostitute and then taking them out in the country and dragging them out of the car and leaving them.'

This is practically a textbook quote for a particular class of men who attack women. In their remarkably thorough book on sex offenders the team from Indiana's famous Institute of Sex Research[2] put it like this:

the double-standard variety [are] males [who] divide females into good females whom one treats with some respect and bad females who are not entitled to consideration if they become obstinate. While one would not ordinarily think of maltreating a good girl, any girl one can pick up easily has in essence agreed to coitus and can legitimately be forced to keep her promise.

These views certainly come out of a macho environment in which the only distinction is between paragons and whores. But Young indicated that he had gone beyond that when, in denying he had assaulted one of the victims he was shown a photograph of, he blurted out, 'No, I didn't. I wanted to – I wanted to rip her head clear off her shoulders.'

What the psychiatrists disagreed upon may be regarded as their particular specialist knowledge, with which they attempt to assign criminals to diagnoses as if the offenders were suffering from medical diseases. The disagreement between Drs Flemming and Lahdha just shows what little strength there is to these categories. What they agreed upon was what Young's victims, and his ex-wife, could have told them without the need for hours of assessment. This was a man unable to form relationships with women of any depth or sincerity. As Ms Fiander, the social worker who gave expert evidence to the court, put it in the stilted language typical of that profession the world over: 'Assessment carried out does indicate some male batterer characteristics specific to use of physical hitting when in a relationship, resolving problems through the use of control rather than communication, suppression of feelings and traditional male role identification.'

THE PATH TO TERROR

Fortunately, though, the great majority of men who have 'traditional male role identification' do not abduct women, beat them close to death and abandon them in the woods. The chances are that Young had not intended to do this so early in his offence career. It was his personal discovery that he could find places where he could carry out these assaults which opened up an inner narrative in which it was acceptable to 'have sex with a prostitute, take them out in the country, drag them out of the car and leave them'.

The sad irony is that Garrett Young the serial rapist, who was not a serial killer only because of the robustness of his victims, was created by a society that puts fear into women who sell sex on the streets. Because their trade is illegal and brushed aside in most considerations of crime it became a school in which Young could learn the possibilities, and for him the pleasures, of violence. His knowledge and malicious use of his surroundings added further to his own personal narrative. Illegal prostitution destroyed Garrett Young as much as he shattered the lives of so many women.

John House was so impressed with the psychological input he had received that he convinced the RNC he should be allowed to spend a year in England studying with me. He turned out, unsurprisingly, to be an excellent student, setting up a Behavioural Science Unit in St John's on his return from study.

THE A55 MURDERS

The open spaces of Newfoundland have many similarities to North Wales. Wales can claim a bit 'more altitude', as American visitors have it, and the Welsh countryside has a much higher density, and indeed history, of population. Therefore it is perhaps not surprising that similar geographical patterns can be found in the extremely rare case of the serial killings that took place in these gently rolling hills in the 1990s.

A notable feature of the area of North Wales below its coastline, filled with caravan parks and small towns dedicated to providing passing tourists with bed and breakfast, is Clocaenog Forest. This stretches for many miles across the hills below the Denbigh Moors. Its dense spread was extended considerably after the First World War when the surrounding sheep farms could no longer be supported because so many of the young shepherds had been killed in the trenches. Today it is a secluded forest in a quiet area. Its peace is only broken by occasional motorbike or car rallies. The views out between the closely packed trees are of gently rolling hills that are still some of the most undeveloped parts of Britain, even though they are little more than an hour's drive from the centre of the busy cities of Liverpool and Manchester.

When I mentioned to some colleagues who lived not far away on the North Wales coast that I was planning to live in this area they delighted in telling me 'Clocaenog Forest is where our local serial killers leave the bodies'. It was easy to believe the deserted, dark forest would be the ideal location to dispose of evidence, but the notion that a serial killer could emerge unnoticed from this peaceful community, where public meetings get heated about nothing more threatening than on which hummock to plant celebratory daffodils, was difficult to accept. Yet just before Christmas Day in 1995 the decomposed remains of a 25-year-old man were found near one of the less trodden paths of Clocaenog Forest. The man, identified as Edward Carthy, had been viciously and repeatedly stabbed to death.

The body might not have been found for a long time if it had not been for the fact that a few days earlier Peter Moore, a cinema manager living on the North Wales coast about fifteen miles away, had confessed to that murder and three others. Moore described to the police in chilling detail how at around 1.00 a.m. he had driven Carthy in his transit van to Clocaenog Forest in order to kill him. He stopped the van in a lay-by and got out with Carthy, showing him a combat knife before stabbing him with it in the stomach.

In court Moore showed how clearly he remembered his actions and how little emotion surrounded his brutality. He remembered Carthy trying to stumble away from the attack but dropping where he stood and told the court, 'I think altogether I stabbed him four times.' Trying to hide the body in the trees he found it difficult to move the dead weight, so he 'drove off into the woods, across a very muddy junction to a point where the trees were a little bit thicker ... I just dragged him into the wood and left him'. Once the frantic stage of the killing was over Moore realised he could not quite remember his route into the forest and got lost, until he was eventually able to get back onto the main roads and drive home. Moore's callous confidence in being able to avoid detection was shown by his returning to the forest the following night, apparently to take the keys that Carthy carried in a leather thong, but he could not find the body.

Moore described in court how he had met Carthy at a bar in Liverpool. Carthy had invited him to go back to his house in Birkenhead for sex. But when Moore got through the tunnel separating Liverpool from Birkenhead, instead of driving straight on he turned south, heading for the forest. Carthy, known to be a drug addict, had realised that his life was in danger and tried to grab the steering wheel and then jump out of the moving van. He was too drunk, or drugged, confused and scared, to do more than make the car career across the road before Moore leaned over and shut the door, taking his victim on the further forty-minute drive to his death.

To call Peter Moore bizarre would be an understatement. He dressed in black to carry out his killings and enjoyed dominating and hurting others during sex. By his own admission he had violently attacked at least forty people beyond the four he was known to have killed. As bizarre as his sexual activity was, his murder locations were coldly calculated. They drew on his knowledge of the area from his travels as the manager of a local chain of small independent cinemas. This took him along the roads of Flint and Denbighshire where he was able to find his victims.

Moore was a travelling killer who killed four men and attacked many others along the A55 in North Wales. He moved ever further away from his home base and the locations of his cinemas as he grew in confidence and out of the necessity to evade capture. Eventually he became so confident in his invulnerability that he was able to talk his way through a police cordon set up to catch him.

The map of his crimes reveals, as with other travelling killers, that his home on the North Wales coast was still at the heart of his murders. One body was found near Holyhead at the easternmost end of the A55 coast road in September: a 56-year-old man, who had been killed and his body mutilated with a knife.

A second body was found towards the end of November on Anglesey, along the A55 but just over ten miles away from where the first body was left. Then, in mid-December, a third body was found on a beach halfway between Liverpool and Anglesey. Just before Christmas, Carthy's body was found in Clocaenog forest, having been killed in early October.

Like many determined serial murderers, Moore sought his victims far away from his home so that he would not draw attention to the area in which he was living. To begin with he kept away from both his home and the previous locations of his crimes, where people might be alert or the police might be looking. But it is just this care that creates a hole in the map of murders. A Dragnet analysis working with the five known locations of the criminal, including an abduction site, points to an area around Rhyl on the north coast of Wales.

Not long after the fourth body was found another man was attacked on the same beach. He managed to escape and reported the assault to the police, leading to the arrest of Peter Moore. Moore lived just where Dragnet would have predicted, in a four-bedroom house near Rhyl on the North Wales Coast.

A VIOLENT QUEST
He told the police that he had got the idea for attacking a local lorry driver from the Clint Eastwood film *Dirty Harry*. Whatever the truth of that, it shows how he had created a plot for himself to act out: a daredevil escapade, driven by his own

appetites. He saw himself on a quest much as Garrett Young did, overcoming adversity on the way.

This seems to be typical of these journeying criminals. Their victims are a means of expression, providing an opportunity for them to act out the sadistic roles they are driving themselves to play. In their inside-out lives the society around them is meaningless – only their own actions make any sense to them. But these are actions that require the unwilling, coerced participation of others. This takes them on a hunt for possible victims, a hunt tied in to their knowledge and experience of their surroundings, as they move around from their home base. They are not on the same journey as the killers we will be turning to next, whose victims are to them mere commodities and whose journeys take over their lives. The travelling killers we have been looking at are set on a path of violence and terror, but are still not at the furthest depths of depravity that human beings can reach.

MOVING TARGETS

So offend to make offence a skill
Shakespeare, Henry IV part 1

Serial murderers are not only at the extreme of a criminal continuum in terms of violence and brutality they are also at the extreme of a mobility continuum, travelling far greater distances than other types of offender.
Lundrigan, S. and Canter, D. (2001) 'A Multivariate Analysis of Serial Murderers' Disposal Site Location Choice', Journal of Environmental Psychology, 21, pp. 423–432

. . . the stage of the perilous journey and the preliminary minor adventures; the crucial struggle, usually some kind of battle in which either the hero or his foe, or both must die; and the exaltation of the hero . . .
Northrop Frye (1957) Anatomy of Criticism, Princeton University Press, p. 187

18. *VICTIMES DE PEDOPHILIE*

THE UNNOTICED HOUSE[1]

Charleroi is an old city in the centre of Belgium. It was the heart of Belgium's heavy industry in the nineteenth century, surrounded by steelworks, although the town itself was untouched by industrialisation. With the decline of manufacturing it has become a rather tense place. With fights in the streets and a tawdry red-light district just round the corner from the main square, it has become Belgium's crime capital: just the place for the country's most notorious serial murderer of children to set up home.

A short ride from the centre of Charleroi, in the Marcinelle area, there is a small plaque fixed to the railings on Rue de Philippeville. The railings protect a goods yard next to a railway line. The rumble of a nearby motorway flyover can be heard in the distance. On the pavement below the plaque is a small grave-like area, overflowing with weeds. This is a quiet, barely noticed memorial. The plaque reads '*En mémoire de tous les enfants victimes de pédophilie – le 30-3-1997*', whispering of the nightmare of child abduction, abuse and murder. It traces this horror to paedophilia, but that is far from being the whole story. The inscription neglects the larger picture that is told by the locations of related crimes all over Belgium. Children died in dreadful circumstances because of avarice and incompetence, victims to the deadly aspirations of a small-time car thief who had also been convicted for raping young girls. He thought he had found a way to take advantage of weaknesses in Belgium's law enforcement and make himself rich by exploiting the sexual deviance of others.

Paedophilia is defined as a predilection for sexual intercourse with young children. The very idea of this is so abhorrent to most people that those who have such preferences are outcasts. They must keep their desires secret, sharing them only with others who are similarly disposed. The myth has therefore grown up that because they cannot satisfy their lusts in any open way all those with such perverted sexualities are just waiting for the opportunity to abduct and molest an unsuspecting child. Yet, as in other areas of human deviance, there are many ways in which paedophiles can feed their distorted appetites without being the active agents of violent assaults.[2]

Although paedophiles need to search out secret opportunities to sexually exploit children, they are no more liable to abduct a child than a man who makes use of prostitutes is likely to become a pimp, or a drug addict is to set up a drug supply network. Of course the demand side of the equation is what drives the trade in human misery, but it is often people who do not use the goods and services they provide who turn solitary acts of abuse into a deadly trade.

The sexual abuse of children is repugnant. When it happens we have to help the victims in every way possible, and punish the perpetrator whilst trying to see if there is any way that person can be guided to a more acceptable lifestyle. But the full power of our anger and censure should be saved for the smaller group of individuals who extend their depraved desires to trade in the exploitation of youngsters. If such people, for whom the term 'evil' is appropriate, can spread their actions around a country, giving no clear geographical focus that would map onto police administrative units, they can go undetected for months and years. The havoc they can wreak by playing on police incompetence can subvert a nation.

Across the street from the plaque is the house in which at least six young girls were held captive. Some were killed, others allowed to starve to death; miraculously two survived. It is a run-down terraced house in an anonymous area of a small city; a place people might drive past as a short cut to somewhere else; where people would only stay because they had no choice and neighbours would know little of each other, spending their time indoors or away from the grey streets.

All cities generate such insignificant locations: on the edge of industrial estates; on the wrong side of perimeter roads; in semi-derelict inner-city areas, or near railway goods yards. It is these ordinary, anonymous places which sexual predators recognise as virtually invisible to people passing through.

They can spot instantly how to turn these zones into black holes, voids into which their victims just disappear.

MISSING CHILDREN

One warm summer's day on 24 June 1995, two pretty eight-year-old girls, Melissa Russo and Julie Lejeune, were playing in the fields near their homes in Grâce-Hollogne, a suburb of Liège in the east of Belgium. They wandered onto a nearby bridge over a busy road and were seen waving at the cars rushing along the carriageway below. Then the two girls were not seen any more. There was neither trace nor sign of them nor where they had gone; no clues at all. They were not lone teenagers who had run out of their house during a row, never to be seen again. Nor were they youngsters who might have wandered to a dangerous quarry or river. This lack of anything to mark the disappearance of two young children was itself an indication that this was an unusual event that might well have been managed by someone who was known to the police.

An obvious suspect was Marc Dutroux. He had, quite remarkably, been released four years earlier after serving seven years of a thirteen-year sentence for raping five girls. As part of a general plan, the Justice Minister, Melchior Wathelet, had encouraged the early release of many sex offenders.

The sentence Dutroux was given provides pointers to the Belgian justice ministry's attitudes to the sexual exploitation of children. The sentence was certainly much shorter than he would have got in many countries, but even more significant is the ease with which he was allowed out. He was able to convince the psychiatrists and other judicial officials that five separate acts of child rape were part of some passing aberration that he had put behind him.

In understanding the actions of the legal professionals at this stage, and later, we must remember that not all cultures regard sexual activity between adults and children with the same abhorrence. As reported in the most definitive study ever carried out of sex offenders:[3] 'Among some pre-literate societies a sexual relationship between an adult and a child evokes only a mildly negative reaction. The relationship may be considered somewhat ludicrous or it may be considered evidence that the adult is too socially inept or unattractive to obtain an adult partner.'

The question reverberates, throughout the unfolding story of disappearing children in Belgium, of whether there were, and indeed are, limited sections of the Belgian establishment that have attitudes similar to these pre-literate societies. Of course, the vast majority of Belgians were horrified by these disappearances and the Belgian police were keen to find the girls and whoever had abducted them.

Finding the girls and their abductor would be a feather in the cap of any law-enforcement agency. But that was part of the problem. The prospect of a significant success brought to the surface the rivalries between the many different factions[4] within the Belgian police. There is a local police force for every town and every city, and they deal with local crime, theft, assaults and burglary. They are quite separate from the nationally organised *gendarmerie*, which is mostly used for keeping order in the streets when there are public demonstrations, riots and the like. Yet despite that focus on public order, part of the *gendarmerie*, known as the BSR, is concerned with organised crime. This had a local division in every large city. Apart from that, there was still another police agency, the judicial police (PJ), which also tackled organised crime, and which also had sections in every big city. There was constant competition between the BSR and the PJ. Because of the nature of the disappearance it fell to the PJ to search for Julie and Melissa; but the BSR wanted this prize for themselves.

The BSR, therefore, put Dutroux under covert surveillance in secret, without informing any other police agencies. They wanted to capture him and triumph over the PJ. So in August 1995, Dutroux's terraced house on Rue de Phillipeville in Charleroi, 80 kilometres from Liège, was furtively observed. But these observations only took place in the daytime and nothing of significance was seen.

Two months after the girls went missing, early in the morning of 22 August 1995, two young women disappeared from Ostende, a resort town on the sandy north coast of Belgium. Seventeen-year-old An Marchal and her eighteen-year-old friend Eefje Lambrecks had been on a camping trip, holidaying without their families for the first time. They had gone to a seaside show and vanished on their way home. The distance of 200 kilometres between the two abduction sites, Ostende and Liège, and the difference in the ages of the victims was taken by the Belgian police to indicate that the abductions were not related. But as a matter of routine, with no urgency, Belgium's national police, the *gendarmerie*, indicated that Dutroux was one of the people they wanted to talk to. The BSR were still observing his Charleroi house, but did not see him return with the teenagers.

In December 1995 Dutroux was sentenced to four months' imprisonment for car theft. The BSR still thought that there might be evidence relating to Julie and Melissa's disappearance in Rue de Phillipeville. They therefore took the opportunity, whilst he was in prison, to search his house on two separate occasions in December. They still kept this secret from other police investigators, including the magistrate in Liège who was now leading an investigation into the missing girls. The searches found nothing. They had heard children crying, but assumed it was children playing in the street. Dutroux served his sentence and was released in March 1996.

On 28 May 1996, thirteen-year-old Sabine Dardenne did not come home from school. No trace of her could be found. She lived in Kain, near Tournay, 80 kilometres west of Charleville and close to the French border. In response to this disappearance the activity of the small local police force in this Belgian backwater was marked by its lassitude.

There was growing national concern about the totally unexplained disappearance of these girls. It was becoming clear that the police investigations were not going to help bring this trauma to a close. It was therefore the greatest good fortune when two months later there were witnesses to a further abduction. On 9 August another girl, fourteen-year-old Laetitia Delhez, was standing outside a sports centre after a swim in the small town of Bertrix, 130 kilometres south of Charleroi. A man she did not know approached her to ask a question. As she answered, another man grabbed her throat to silence her screams and bundled her into a white van.

Following this up in house-to-house inquiries the police found a student who remembered part of a white van's licence plate, because it was the same as his sister's birthday. A nun had noticed the van's defective exhaust system. The police computer search found the owner of the van: 39-year-old unemployed electrician Marc Dutroux, a married man and father of three small children. He was arrested on 13 August 1996.

After two days in custody, Dutroux told police where he was holding Sabine and Laetitia. He had constructed concrete dungeons in the basement of his house, and had hidden the access point behind a metal cabinet that police had never bothered to move during their various searches.

When the police returned to Rue de Philippeville, armed with the knowledge provided by Dutroux, the television cameras were waiting. They were able to film a poignant, tearful meeting when the young teenagers Sabine and Laetitia were reunited with their parents. Sabine had been held for 79 days.

Although he was unemployed, it transpired that Dutroux owned at least six properties across Belgium. One was a small two-storey house in the sleepy village of Sars-la-Buissière – about 20 kilometres south-west of Charleroi. The house, surrounded by a large garden, faces onto the village square. Backing onto fields that are not overlooked by any buildings, it was another location carefully chosen by Dutroux for its nameless nonentity. The house is just a few paces from the only bar around, which is by default the social centre of this small community – the sort of place where locals kiss friends on the cheek, then shake hands with each other and any passing visitor before settling down to a drink and gossip. They are used to people wandering through, and city folk with country residences they use only rarely.

In the back garden of this house, four metres underground, the police found the bodies of Julie and Melissa, who had been abducted from Liège over a year earlier. Buried with them was an accomplice of Dutroux's, 44-year-old Bernard Weinstein. He had died whilst buried alive. Here again, Dutroux was building underground dungeons where he planned to keep girls.

After his arrest in 1996, Dutroux initially told the police that Weinstein had been given the task of feeding the girls while Dutroux was in prison for car theft. But it was clear that Weinstein had already been buried alive in the garden before Dutroux went to prison. Dutroux then said that Weinstein had killed An and Eefje and had wanted to do the same to Julie and Melissa. So, he claimed, he had killed Weinstein to protect the two eight-year-olds. It seems more likely that, horrified by what was happening, Weinstein threatened to expose Dutroux to save himself, but Dutroux killed him first.

In response to police questioning, Dutroux now said that he had asked his wife, Michelle Martin, a schoolteacher, to feed the children. Her story was that she had been afraid to go into the dungeon and so had never fed the girls. When Dutroux got out of prison in March 1996, he found the girls starving to death. One died within a few hours, the other after four days.

The casual disregard for human life and any sort of trust between people that this episode illustrates is difficult to comprehend. Dutroux was clearly intelligent, occasionally charming, and had gained a tradesman's skills. He was married to a primary-school teacher. She had known that Julie and Melissa were locked in the basement of one of their houses, but claimed she had been too scared to feed them. How could this person, who spent her working days with young children, not bring herself to inform the authorities that two eight-year-old girls were starving to death in a makeshift dungeon? Dutroux passed through a civilised society without raising enough concerns to be kept in prison, even after a series of assaults on young girls. He and his wife allowed two young girls, hardly different in age from their own children, to be kept incarcerated for over a year.

An and Eefje were not found for several weeks. Their bodies were finally found on 3 September 1996, buried under concrete next to a shed at a house in Jumet, 5 kilometres north of Charleroi; Weinstein had lived there for three years, and had frequently been visited by Dutroux.

Also recorded around Belgium were as many as eleven abductions and several murders of children that may have been the actions of Dutroux or his accomplices. Whether other girls were moved through such incarceration by Dutroux and on to other fates is difficult to establish.

A NATIONAL CHALLENGE

By spreading himself across the country Dutroux successfully delayed any recognition that here was a series of related crimes. He understood all too well that in Belgium the disappearance of a child would soon be forgotten. Like Fred West before him, Dutroux knew the weaknesses of his local police. They both knew that they could make their victims invisible, and their own actions would be hidden in the lairs they had constructed for themselves. Fred West took advantage of the unintelligent policing of a small rural force. Dutroux took advantage of the incompetence of a small country's police. In both cases there are inevitably suspicions of corruption.

There is a phenomenon in psychology known as the 'just world belief'. This is one of the many simple-minded ideas in social psychology[5] that are drawn on to help students summarise the essence of complex attitudes. In a nutshell it is a belief that the world is essentially logical and just; that people get what they deserve and deserve what they get. Ideas such as illness being in some way or other caused by the patient is one of the consequences of this belief. Using another vocabulary it is the view that there are no cock-ups, just conspiracies.

When used in relation to crime it is the assumption that a person gets away with many crimes over a long period of time either because they have some sort of evil genius or because they collude with the police in some way. Police investigators certainly harbour a parallel view. If a criminal remains uncaught following an intense search there is often the assumption that he must be a police officer. Ineffective, incompetent policing is not the first explanation that people reach for.

What these notions oversimplify is that inept investigations pave the way for various forms of corruption. These run from the corruption of assuming some citizens are less worthy of help from the law than others, through to turning a blind eye to criminal activities for personal gain and on to outright involvement in offences themselves. The evidence of the geographical distribution of Dutroux's crimes, and the breath-taking mistakes made by the Belgian police, do suggest that all these different levels of corruption were involved.

As the full details of the investigation into Dutroux came to light, the full depths of the ineptitude of the police emerged. Dutroux's own mother had tipped off the police that he was planning kidnaps, yet this known sex offender was not put under careful surveillance. When on two occasions the house where Julie and Melissa were being held was searched, this was done in such a desultory manner that the underground cells were not found. During their first search the police seized a video that Dutroux had made, but they did not watch it for a year. It was of Dutroux carrying out building work on his house. Another cassette was a recording of a television documentary on the disappearance of Julie and Melissa. On the side was written 'Perdu de vue, Julie et Milissa. – Marc'.

It was not only the lowly police officers who took their inquiries less seriously than might have been expected. The more senior levels of Belgian law enforcement were equally casual. A magistrate responsible for the investigation did not remember to tell her replacement about missing children when moving on from the post, later claiming 'it slipped her mind'.

The details of the information fed to the police are, with hindsight, such clear predictors of what was to come that very serious questions have to be raised about why they were ignored. As early as 1993 an informant had told police that Dutroux had offered him money to kidnap children. There is little that the police could do at the time to act on this information, but why was it not sitting in his file – already thick with details of car theft and related offences, as well as child abuse – when his house was first searched so that the search could be resolute? By 1995 the same informant had told police that Dutroux was building underground cells which he planned to use to imprison children. What does it take for a modern police force to find hidden rooms? Especially when neighbours had complained about building noises, and Dutroux himself, again like West before him, had told them he was refurbishing his house? Why were Dutroux's other houses not examined closely? Why was the very possession of so many houses by a lowly electrician not examined? What about the people in the bar at Sars-la-Buissière? Why were they not closely questioned about their visitor and his activities?

As the case against Dutroux and the incompetence and possible corrupt involvement of the authorities became ever more public, these questions were being asked in every house in Belgium. In October 1996, not long after the bodies of the four girls had been uncovered, the largest demonstration in Belgium since World War Two took place. A third of a million people took to the streets of Brussels, many dressed in white – a symbol of the victims' innocence. They carried banners with the somewhat prolix slogan: 'The world is a dangerous place to live in not because of the people who do evil things, but because of the people who know about it but do nothing to stop it.' A general strike developed spontaneously with all the makings of a revolution to overthrow a corrupt government. But the murdered girls' families called for calm and asked people to protest 'with dignity'.

All over the country people walked away from work to show their disgust. In Liège, firemen and women directed their fire-hoses at the city court building, demonstrating the clean-up they felt was needed within the judicial system. Train drivers went on strike in some regions, causing cities to come to a standstill. People called for a national inquiry; some called for a return to the death penalty. Even the Belgian monarchy became involved when King Albert called for major reforms in the political and judicial systems.

An inquiry was set up. A report was published six months later, in April 1997, agreeing with the conclusions that the public had already reached: the girls might have been alive today if the police had not made so many mistakes. The police were accused of negligence, amateurism and incompetence and found guilty of ignoring informant information at key stages of the investigation, of mistreating the families of the victims and of failing to share vital intelligence. A number of officials were found to be responsible for the girls' deaths. However, the inquiry rejected allegations that Dutroux was actually protected by senior police. It did make the insightful comment, though, that the investigation was so poorly conducted that, in effect, Dutroux had enjoyed 'indirect protection'. The political significance of all this was not lost on the inquiry. It reported that the investigation had been so badly handled that it had 'put at risk the state of law'.

A response to mass protests in Brussels has international significance. This city is, after all, the administrative capital of Europe. Here are housed European ministries and the thousands of Eurocrats who keep the wheels of the European Union creaking along. If the country that hosts the management of Europe cannot deal with such a frightening series of crimes, then it raises questions about the judicial health of Europe as a whole. This was not lost on the European Parliament, which searched for a scapegoat and called for the resignation of the Belgian Justice Minister, Melchior Wathelet, for sanctioning the early release of Dutroux from his thirteen-year prison sentence for raping five girls. Later on Wathelet was promoted to become a judge at the European court.

19. A DESTRUCTIVE GEOGRAPHY

The catalogue of errors at all levels of the Dutroux investigation became ever more clear as the details unfolded. But at the heart of these blunders was a man able to use the very geography of Belgium to take advantage of the bungling all around him. How did Dutroux weave such a seductive web?

Dutroux, like all the serial killers and rapists we have looked at, learned his destructive trade as he progressed from one crime to the next. He became aware of the possibilities when he got away with a large number of car thefts and rapes of young girls before a brief respite in prison. The spread of his houses and crimes showed that he was concocting a story about himself, developing a personal narrative as an old-style brigand who was operating outside of and beyond the law. In the various interviews he gave, and other reports that leaked out, it became clear that he thought he could destabilise the country, as he so nearly did.

He had deliberately and consciously gone to the four corners of a country that is still divided by religious and cultural rifts. There were six abductions in the north of Belgium, north of Brussels, which have never been directly proven to be linked to Dutroux; certainly none of his known kidnappings took girls from this area. Was this a testing out, or the work of accomplices based in that area?

The first two young girls he was known to have taken were snatched in Liège, an ancient French-speaking city in the east of Belgium, not far from the Dutch and German borders. Despite the decline of its long-established coal-mining industry this is still a busy city with nearly 200,000 inhabitants.

The second two were taken almost as far away as it is possible to get within this small country, in the north-west seaside town of Ostende. This Flemish-speaking town, best known as a long-standing holiday resort, the erstwhile summer haunt of European aristocracy, hardly inhabits the same mental map as Liège.

The fifth victim was taken on her way home from school in the small city of Kain, to the west of the country by the French border. With its fine Romanesque cathedral and lively manufacturing industry, this is a confident place, the oldest settlement in Belgium. The local police and inhabitants would not have thought of themselves as subject to the same decadence as the Flemish resort 80 kilometres north.

For the fourth abduction, the sixth child was grabbed and pushed into a van in the small town of Bertrix, in the heavily forested and sparsely populated Ardenne hills 130 kilometres south of Charleroi. In choosing a place with around 8,000 residents, Dutroux may not have appreciated that his actions were more likely to be noted and acted upon. His objective was doubtless to operate in a place that was so different again from anywhere else he had been that the links to his other offences would not be made, and the local population would be less alert. Fortunately he severely miscalculated.

The locations he chose and the sequence of those locations have two strong characteristics that we have found in many serial criminals, whether burglars, arsonists, rapists or killers. Although the distances between the various abduction locations run into tens of kilometres, two hundred at the extreme, it is notable that, as with Porter in Las Vegas, Young in Newfoundland and many other offenders who operate over very different scales, Dutroux's house in Rue de Phillipeville in Charelroi is at the heart of the area described by his crimes. Here is a man plotting out a whole country as his criminal territory.

The second aspect of this sequence, which directly parallels the sequence of murder locations of Jack the Ripper (although those were at a walking scale rather than the driving scale of Dutroux), is the trend for each place to be more or less as far as possible from the previous one.[1] Certainly there is no indication that Dutroux or his accomplices returned close to places where they may have been spotted earlier. This is planning to avoid unnecessary risk.

The wide distribution of offences also accords well with him having access to vehicles. His trade in stolen cars provided him with that access and the confidence to know he could drive such cars without fear. There are even indications that he used them for abductions.

The mental map revealed by the differences between these locations, the distances between them, the sequence in which they were selected, and the way they pin out the four corners of Belgium – all at some distance from Charleroi – is a mental map that speaks of a criminal who is taking on a country. It reveals an arrogant, self-assured psychological journey towards a ruthless criminal end. The criminal journey, spread around the map of Belgium, showed Dutroux's ambitions. The details became apparent when his associates started talking to the police.

AN EVIL BUSINESS

His aim was to make pornographic films for the European market, using kidnapped little girls. If anyone still thinks that downloading child pornography off the web is a benign perversion they should visit Sars-la-Buissière and read the plaintive notices below the photographs of young children fixed to the metal fence surrounding the derelict house, a few steps down from the bar. Thirteen-year-old Sabine had been told by Dutroux that she must learn to like 'sex things'.

He anticipated a great income in making these films, which can fetch between 20,000 and 40,000 dollars in France and Germany. Six hundred such films were actually found in Dutroux's Charleroi house. Police believe he was also planning a long-distance prostitution trafficking network, importing girls from Slovakia using the contacts he had in place for trading in stolen cars.

Whether Dutroux was the prime mover or just one of the lieutenants may eventually emerge when all the criminal proceedings against him are completed. What is clear is that the careful distribution of abductions spread across the four corners of Belgium provides a picture of a criminal empire in the making.

TESTING STAGES

The sequence of abductions and their spread shows a developing plan of action, but when some other crimes that are likely to have been related are also considered, the full force of the malevolence that was driving them is revealed even more starkly. There were a number of other attempts at

11. MARC DUTROUX'S ABDUCTIONS AND ATTEMTPED ABDUCTIONS

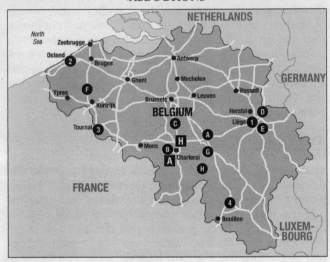

H = Dutroux's home just outside Charleroi and Weinstein's house at Jumet

A = Rue de Philippeville 128, Sars-la-Buissière

Abductions

1. Julie Lejeune and Melissa Russo, 24.6.95, abducted from Grâce-Hollogne (suburb of Liège)

2. An Marchal and Eefje Lambreks, 23.8.95, abducted from Ostende

3. Sabine Dardenne, 28.5.96, abducted from Kain

4. Laetitia Delhez, 9.8.96 abducted from Bertrix

Attempted abductions

A. Natacha, April 1992, Jambes

B. Aurelie, May/June 1995 and Melissa, October 1995, Gerpinnes

C. Thyfene, June 1995, Spy

D. Lindsay and Stephanie, May/June 1995, Jupile

E. Vanessa and Dikana, 24.6.95, Ougree

F. Sylvia, June 1995, Kortrijk

G. Samantha, April/May 1996, Dave

H. Tiffany, 31.7.96, Profondville

abductions in the years before Julie and Melissa were taken from Liège which only came to light later; the police were then able to find a link.

Of particular note is that these attempted abductions first took place in small towns around Charleroi. They define a circle within which all three of Dutroux's bases sat: his home just outside Charleroi, his house in Sars-la-Buissière and Weinstein's house in Jumet. The abductions then moved to the area around Liège. Had the crimes closer to his home proved less successful, more risky, and less productive from his point of view? Certainly they define the circle of disappearances as a black hole even more clearly than those that Fred West committed. They also show an early set of crimes closer to the criminal's base, as was so significant in fathoming John Duffy's home, and clearly present in Peter Sutcliffe's activities.

Two abductions were attempted near Liège in June just before Julie and Melissa were snatched. This shows what a determined effort Dutroux and his associates were making to get hold of girls for their horrific trade. Once they had been successful in this area they then started to spread out to the corners of Belgium.

THE PSYCHOPATH CLICHÉ
Psychiatric labels are usually more valuable as terms of abuse than in helping to understand people. They pigeonhole the complex variety of human beings and give an air of confident precision to what is inevitably a very personal judgement. But the evil business that Dutroux was building required a textbook psychopath: a smooth charmer who would happily kill for personal gain. Or, to put it in more formal language, a person 'high on the interpersonal dimension of selfish, callous and remorseless use of others'. Such people combine 'superficial charm with a grandiose sense of self-worth, pathological lying and deception, lack of sincerity, remorse, emotional depth, or empathy, and sexual promiscuity'.[2] This describes Dutroux uncomfortably well.

He was a handsome man with dark hair and a thick moustache (like so many of the killers and rapists in this book!). That he was clearly attractive was shown on his frequent visits to the small quiet town of Topolcany in west Slovakia. Masquerading as a tyre businessman, this child abductor and murderer was readily welcomed into the homes of families, and would take the young daughters to the disco. One girl remembered him as amiable, funny and polite. She said of Dutroux, 'Most young girls of thirteen and fourteen were crazy about him. He would dance with them until they were completely exhausted.' The head of Slovakian Interpol pointed out that 'Dutroux made friendships with ease and won many people's trust.' Similarly in Belgium, the public prosecutor described Dutroux as 'very intelligent . . . very seductive.'

He even thought he could convince his victims that he was helping them. Sabine recounted, 'I read my exercise books which remained in my satchel and I wrote to my parents describing my days.' Dutroux hid Sabine's letters to her parents under the carpet and faked replies from her mother telling the thirteen-year-old that her parents did not want her back. Sabine said:

> He tried to pass himself off as a kind person who had saved my life. Apparently I was going to get myself killed or be caught by someone else. Someone more senior, the boss who wanted money from my parents. But apparently they did not have enough money or did not want to pay. I wondered what I had done to my parents for them to withhold the money . . . he told me he would hand me over to some gang or other and that the person that he'd give me to would torture me and kill me after making me suffer.

The depth of this ability to convince others of his trustworthiness was revealed after he had been arrested. On 23 April 1998 Dutroux overpowered two armed policemen in Neufchâteau Courthouse. He had been allowed out of prison, with two guards, to examine files relevant to his upcoming trial. (Why were files not brought to him, as happens in most countries?) He talked the guards into undoing his handcuffs so he could read the papers and escaped with one of their guns.

He hijacked a passing car then, showing his intelligent understanding of the habits of the police, swapped it for another to throw them off the trail. He managed to stay on the run for three hours before police tracked him down, 10 kilometres south-west of Neufchâteau in woods in Saint Medard, on the way to Luxembourg. Dutroux's car had got stuck in the mud, so he had abandoned it and set out on foot. Although heavily armed police, guided by a surveillance helicopter, were looking for him, he was recaptured by a forester doing a routine inspection of the woods.

This mixture of suave talking and impulsive, grandiose action captures his belief in himself as a man beyond the law; a person whose excessive confidence in his own significance overcame any shred of feeling for others. He even had the audacity to take the state to court in February 2001 to complain about the conditions in which he was being held in prison. Dutroux, whose specially constructed cell is markedly larger than the small cages he constructed for his victims, asserted that the state should be fined for holding him in solitary confinement for too long; conducting too many body searches and interrupting his sleep.

CORRUPT NETWORKS

The ineptitude of the police still raises big questions in Belgium. How much was this a product of Dutroux's evil genius: his convincing manner whenever approached by the authorities; his careful selection of locations and the sequence in which he went to them; and the effort he put into building hidden dungeons in houses where, even if questions were asked, there would be no serious attempt to answer them? And how much was it due to a much larger network of corruption and even active involvement by the authorities in his crimes?

Parents of the victims claim that what has come to light is just a small part of a wider network, possibly covered up because senior politicians and police were part of it. It is easy for the authorities to dismiss their claims as products of their own trauma and the inevitable, but totally inappropriate, guilt they feel for the loss of their loved ones. But when a Belgian senator, Anne-Marie Lizin, raises serious doubts about the complicity of officials, perhaps we have to take it more seriously. She said, 'It's a question of stupidity, incompetence and corruption . . . Dutroux must be a friend of somebody important . . . Stupidity can't be the only explanation.'

Dutroux certainly was part of a network of accomplices. The question is how far it spread into the law-enforcement agencies and other powerful groups. In such an atmosphere petty criminals can play on general paranoia to imply their own significance, and it is difficult to know if they are telling the truth or not. For example, Jean Michel Nihoul, who was a businessman and estate agent, is alleged to have been the leader of what the Belgians now call the 'gang-Dutroux'. It is emerging that this gang was dealing in weapons, drugs and cars and was also planning to traffic in prostitutes between Belgium and Slovakia. At one stage Nihoul confidently stated that he would not end up in court because the information he had on important people would bring down the government and indeed the whole state of Belgium. Yet he has now been accused of taking part in the abduction of Laetitia and other related crimes.

Dutroux himself has talked of 'the network' – a far wider organisation of child-sex abusers. In January 2002 he reportedly told an undercover journalist, 'I was in regular contact with people belonging to the network. But the justice system doesn't want to investigate this lead.' Is this the psychopathic charmer once more trying to imply that his intentions are honourable but nobody will take him seriously? Or is he, unusually, telling the truth?

The Belgian authorities have searched for an abusive network with tentacles within the seats of power with much the same determination that they searched Dutroux's house. They have found nothing and therefore claim that Dutroux was an 'isolated pervert'. No attention seems to be given to the fact that this 'isolated pervert' was married to a primary-school teacher and admits to having buried alive a man he had been working with for many years. He built dungeons to hold young girls in one of his houses, and was building more cells in two other houses. He carefully chose his abduction sites to be many kilometres from each other, spread out across Belgium. These are not the actions of an obsessed 'pervert' merely acting out some depraved fantasy. They are part of a larger plan that drew on others and required considerable time, energy and money to complete. But as Belgium still awaits the trial of its most notorious criminal, questions remain unanswered. Indications that point to an evil domain that extends far beyond the man who now inhabits cell 801 of Arlon prison stubbornly demand attention:

- Somebody paid Dutroux large sums of money following each of the kidnappings. No answers have so far emerged about who this was.
- Nihoul has confessed to organising an orgy attended by police officers, a number of government officers, and even a former European commissioner at a Belgian castle.
- A close relationship between Investigating Judge Van Espen and two people accused of being in the network was unearthed by a journalist.
- There have been the unexplained deaths of up to twenty supposed witnesses to the alleged larger network and state corruption. In one case Bruno Tagliaferro, a scrap merchant from Charleroi who had some evidence relating to the car in which Julie and Melissa had been abducted, died suddenly of an apparent heart attack. But his wife, who did not believe this explanation, arranged for the body to be exhumed and samples sent to the USA for tests. These showed Bruno had been poisoned. Not long after this came to light, Mrs Tagliaferro was herself found dead on a smouldering mattress in her house. This was recorded officially as a suicide.
- One witness who has come forwards, Regina Louf, claims that twenty years ago a family friend took her away to be abused at sex parties. She alleges that judges, one of the most prominent politicians of the time and a prominent Belgian banker all took part in these. The authorities have dismissed her as mad. As Louf says, 'In Belgium, if you're a potential witness you're either dead or, like me, "mad".'[3]

A SORDID CHAIN

As the debates swirl around Belgium and on into the European Union, it is easy to forget that the man at the centre of this storm scoured the extremes of his country to find helpless young girls. He brought them back to put in metal cages in makeshift dungeons just a couple of paces wide, containing a mattress and little else. The girls were kept naked (Dutroux claims this was to stop them escaping). They were fed through the bars. He had a plan to use these girls as merchandise in his horrific business.

Although the lair that Dutroux created, as a black hole which would not be noticed in the shabby backwaters that he inhabited, has many parallels to Fred West's house in Cromwell Street, there are important differences. These are reflected as much in the differences between their predatory maps as in their own accounts of themselves.

West saw himself as the loving father, killing himself when his black hole imploded. Dutroux, by contrast, was not kidnapping girls purely for his own uncontrollable desires. The map of his activities – abduction locations, houses and places of residence – provides a graphic image of how, centred in Marcinelle, he aimed to build a vicious empire as a crucial link in the chain that makes up an evil industry.

20. FINDING A TRAVELLING KILLER

Catching those extremely rare serial killers who travel great distances to commit their crimes has always proven to be extremely difficult. It usually requires a stroke of good luck, a quick-witted member of the public, or an alert police officer carrying out routine duties. It is not uncommon for senior investigating officers to admit that they are unlikely to catch the man unless he is caught in the act in a subsequent crime. This is precisely how one of Britain's most sought-for killers was eventually apprehended.

A string of abductions and murders of young girls across Britain in the 1980s had become the focus of a major inquiry; costing millions of pounds, it had given rise to the creation of a dedicated computer database. But although police collected details on 187,186 people, many of whom were possible suspects, and 220,470 vehicles, having interviewed 59,481 people,[1] the man finally convicted was not in the system. His capture was the result of the quickwittedness of a watchful neighbour and the rapid response of the local police.

On a warm summer's day in July 1990 in the village of Stow, in the quiet Scottish countryside a few miles north of the border with England, David Herkes was working in his garden. He noticed a blue Transit van stopping and then saw his neighbour's six-year-old daughter being bundled into it, before it was driven off at speed. He quickly told her parents, who immediately informed the police. They moved with speed to locate the van. Even then, it was partly good luck that police cars were close enough to set up roadblocks swiftly.[2]

A further stroke of good fortune was that the offender decided to retrace his route. When the blue van returned through the village, Herkes pointed it out to police officers. One jumped into the road, bringing the van to a swerving stop. The girl's father found his daughter, hooded, gagged and bound within a sleeping bag, in the back of the van, close to suffocation.

This brought 41-year-old Robert Black's depraved career to an end. He had killed at least three children, including Caroline Hogg, who was only five, and ten-year-old Susan Maxwell, and was known to have abducted two others. He had almost certainly been carrying out serious sexual offences against young girls, and probably other murders, for over a quarter of a century.

Black's criminal career shows just how difficult it can be for the police to link cases to a common offender when they have no forensic evidence to aid them. Beyond the problem of linking the cases there is the even greater difficulty of finding the killer. Sixteen different police forces across the United Kingdom had met to review nineteen unsolved murders of children in which no associate of the child seemed to be implicated. A joint inquiry had been established in July 1981 into two murders which, although committed fifty miles apart on either side of the Scottish/English border, were so similar that the same offender was assumed to be responsible. The importance the authorities assigned to this inquiry was demonstrated by the appointment of a Deputy Chief Constable, Hector Clark, to oversee it.

This was the first major British inquiry to be established after the search for the Yorkshire Ripper. That inquiry had sent shock waves through the British police because it had taken them so long to catch Peter Sutcliffe, who avoided police detection despite having been interviewed as a possible suspect by different police officers, unbeknownst to each other, on a number of different occasions. The police belief was that the problem with large investigations was one of data management. If only they could computerise the great amount of information that is collected as part of such investigations the computer could do the thinking for them.

The idea is seductively simple. If the same person is drawn to police attention by different routes, so that his name crops up a number of times in searches through the database, then he has to be a serious suspect. This is like panning for gold. There is a great deal of dross that has to be put through the panning process, but if it is shaken about in the appropriate way the gleaming nugget will be spotted. The problem with this approach is that there has to be some gold in the earth that you are searching through, and you have to have the skill to spot it when it emerges. If the special metal is rare where you are looking, as will always be the case when looking for serious offenders, then you will have to put one hell of a lot of dross through your apparatus before you strike lucky.

It was not until July 1990 that the computer system was eventually ready for operational use. Even then Black's name was not in it until after he had been arrested in Stow. Many of the names in the system were there because of previous sexual assaults on children. The inquiry team had excluded his name because his previous sexual offences had been considered so minor that it was thought unlikely he would progress to abduction and murder. He did have a criminal record for indecency. A Scottish court in 1967, when he was just out of his teens, had thought his three counts of indecent assault serious enough to sentence him to one year in borstal. This had been after a history of lewd and violent activity, most of which had not been reported or resulted in a criminal record. The national sex-offenders' register today, and the police monitoring of people with even the most limited sexual offences, are a direct result of perceived weaknesses in the records held in the late 1980s. The current procedure, that assigns all people convicted of any form of sexual offence to a register, is a consequence of the belief by the police and the public that an all-embracing computerised record would inhibit the actions of predatory sexual offenders and facilitate their detection. Whilst these processes have certainly had the desired effect in many cases, they just as certainly have not prevented all violent sexually-related crimes, or always led to a speedy identification of the offender.

Even with modern computers and huge lists of known offenders, police investigators still have two significant challenges when they become aware of a number of serious crimes that may or may not be linked. One is to be confident that the crimes really are the work of the same person. The second is finding the suspect in the huge lists of possible suspects that the computer throws up.

THE LINKING PROBLEM
Hector Clark had initially been put in charge of a joint investigation into two murders, those of Susan Maxwell in

1982 and Caroline Hogg in 1981. The similarities, in that they were both wearing colourful summer clothes and abducted on hot July days near main roads which were established long-distance drivers' routes in the Scottish borders, were taken to indicate that they shared the same killer. When Sarah Harper was abducted on a dank March evening in Morley in the north of England in 1986, Clark was less convinced it was the same offender.

The multiplication of factors that are actually related is an aspect of criminal activity that frequently confuses people; a confusion that can be dangerous when those people are leading police investigations. The two apparently different features of the summer dresses and the hot July days were taken as two pointers that should be considered separately, thereby adding weight to the murders being linked; but they also reduced the likelihood, on two distinct characteristics, that the March abduction was linked. But would anyone expect young girls to wear the same clothes in a warm July as in a wet March? Was this distinction really just the distinction of the time of year? If it was assumed the offender was travelling, what would limit him to the summer months?

One distinction of Sarah's abduction was that Morley was not obviously on any main transit routes. It therefore seemed likely that it was someone in that neighbourhood who was responsible. As we have seen, a high proportion of offenders who attack apparent strangers are people who are local to the crime scene. It remains the single most challenging aspect of any inquiry to determine if the offender commuted or travelled to the crime location or was a local, possibly marauding out from his base to find his victims. The key to resolving this may well lie in having a functionally complete set of information about all possibly linked crimes. This enables investigators to make sense of the geographical pattern and determine from that what sort of predatory journey the offender is taking.

In the case of Susan, Caroline and Sarah, the bodies had all been found within about 25 miles of each other, which is remarkably close when the nearly 200 miles between their abduction sites is considered. This area became known to the police as the 'Midland Triangle', clearly a reference to the

'Bermuda Triangle' where many unexplained disappearances of boats and planes are reported to have occurred.

All three girls had been grabbed and kidnapped in places where others might have seen what was happening. This is a risky activity for an offender, quite different from lurking down an isolated country path waiting for a possible victim to pass by. The distressing forensic evidence showed that all three girls had been sexually assaulted in similar ways.

When it was determined, in 1987, that the three murders should be treated as quite possibly linked, the newly established computer system with the optimistic name of HOLMES was brought into play. The name of this system was doubtless determined before the acronym it describes was worked out (Home Office Major Inquiry System). The name was surely meant to imply that at last the police had computer intelligence on their side. It was an era when many people believed the science fiction world of thinking computers was close at hand. Expert systems, that could make decisions better than human beings, were thought to be about to blossom into science fact.

As a psychologist involved in some of those early discussions I was always convinced the computer scientists were overselling the possibilities, for less than altruistic reasons. Politicians and senior management were only too ready to take the cybernetic experts at their word because it showed how readily they were embracing the new possibilities. Naming the Home Office system after the most famous detective of all time was an elementary way of implying that it would solve crimes that the police had been unable to crack before. Hector Clark seemed to have faith in the new technology sorting out problems that mere mortals struggled with. He was quoted as saying the £500,000 machine would be used 'to determine whether or not the girls were killed by one man'.

The task the police faced went beyond the three girls whose bodies had been found. Over the course of twenty years a number of young girls had disappeared and in many cases their bodies had not been found. These abductions and murders had happened all over the country. In 1969 one twelve-year-old disappeared while riding her bike near her home in Cromer, Norfolk. Three years later, another young girl was never seen again after leaving her home near Scunthorpe. This was over 100 miles north of Cromer. Throughout the 1970s and into the 1980s young girls went missing; many of them have never been found. The locations of their disappearances ranged from Devon in the south-west to the Scottish borders. Investigators puzzled over whether these were isolated, unrelated incidents. But even if they accepted the possibility that the bodies of abducted young girls might all be the result of the crimes of one offender, they still had the problem of determining if they were acts of a random, predatory killer roaming at will wherever he thought he could find a vulnerable victim, or someone with a plan and pattern to his actions.

In 1990, three years after the HOLMES system was announced, it did eventually have enough data to be of some use, but it did not have the capability to link crimes. Over a decade on, the latest version of HOLMES still does not have that capability. There are other even more vaunted systems in North America, with less inviting names such as ViCAP and ViCLAS. Whatever is claimed for these systems, they do not make a decision as to which crimes are linked. They are all very fast indexing databases. An operative can request the computer to find all the records that share a number of characteristics: all the blue vans that were stopped, and were driven by men on their own, during the working day. These records can then be examined to see if they share other similarities that support the view of some important link between these incidents. The crucial point is that a human operative has to decide the parameters on which to search and then has to make a decision about the results that are generated. If crucial information is not in the system, or cannot be found because of how it was recorded (the van was specified as green, not blue) then the search can miss key links.

It had become clear to the police officers pulling all the information together on the various possibly linked abductions and murders that they needed a computerised database that went beyond the information solely available to three murder inquiries. Therefore, in parallel with the development of HOLMES as a nationally supported resource, the Derbyshire police started to create an even more ambitious system with the particularly optimistic acronym of CATCHEM (Centralised Analytical Team Collating Homicide Expertise and Management).

This remains one of the most powerful frameworks for a crime database anywhere in the world. It brings together all the information on child homicide that is available. It started with the intention of going back ten years, but now goes back to the 1960s. It has huge potential both in helping to solve crimes and as a research resource for understanding murder. Sadly, it is not available to the research community, so no advantage has been taken of the in-depth benefits that could be gleaned from this mass of information. It has moreover always been 'owned' by Derbyshire Police, and run and managed by two or three very capable and dedicated individuals. Detective Inspector Chuck Burton was awarded an OBE in recognition of the service he had given in maintaining and using CATCHEM. A further limitation is the constraint of recording solely offences against children. Violent men are not all as specialised as that.

The crucial innovation of CATCHEM was to record not just information from the existing inquiry but information from other solved cases and other inquiries. But this makes the search for links even more demanding. The person searching the system has to work out the most productive way of pulling out cases that may belong to a common offender. This is no trivial task. If highly frequent characteristics of crimes are the search criteria, such as the victim being taken against her will, then a very large number of cases will be generated, with the subsequent task of checking each individually to see if it is likely to be linked to any others. If a very specific 'signature' characteristic, such as a unique form of mutilation, is the basis of the search then it may not link in cases where, for example, the offender was disturbed before he had the opportunity to perform the act.

I have supervised three-year doctorates, and together with other colleagues have been provided with government funds, to study the problem of how crimes can be connected to each other when there is no hard forensic evidence to prove the link. All that these studies have shown is that linking crimes together is an extremely difficult task. What is clear, though, is that the more systematic information there is available about each crime, the more likely the informed crime analyst is to be able to spot links.[3]

FINDING THE CULPRIT

The second challenge for those using police computer systems is to find the offender among the many suspects that may be suggested in various searches. Increasingly this is where the myth of 'offender profiling' rears its head. Some filter needs to be used when rummaging around in the database that will narrow down the range of possible suspects to those that are most worthy of close attention. These filters, though, are often fairly obvious to those with some experience of criminals. Hector Clark told reporters that he thought the killer he was looking for was 'probably a man between 25 and 45 who travels a lot in Britain and possibly abroad, and has previous convictions of a similar nature involving female children'. Quite accurate as it turned out, except that the system, even when eventually up and running, would not at that stage have regarded Black's earlier offences as 'of a similar nature'.

Various examinations of people who abduct or kill children reveal[4] that in three-quarters of the cases the offender does have a previous conviction. But what is also important is that in 14 per cent of cases with no convictions there is still information in police criminal intelligence indicating the person has come to police attention under suspicious circumstances. This means that in 86 per cent of solved child-abduction cases, which is almost all of them, the name of the culprit is sitting somewhere within police records, if only it could be found.

The interesting point that is clear from the cases reviewed in other chapters as well as other examinations of serial killers[5] is that the offences of which they had been convicted were not necessarily violent crimes. Often they were the more common crimes of theft, fraud or burglary. Those killers who indicate a sexual interest in children will be more likely to have a history of crimes against the person and of sexual offences. But these will often be relatively minor offences. This poses a huge problem for investigation teams because of the vast number of individuals that need to be eliminated before the culprit surfaces.

Finding a travelling killer in the vast amount of information that a major inquiry collates may therefore be aided if those involved are able to build up some mental picture of the person they are looking for. This can give life to the arid numbers and endless computer records they are searching through, offering a more human, dynamic quality to the consideration of what is on the computer screens. If the picture is looked at in the right way then it may also help detectives to determine the most appropriate strategies for their investigations. Panning for gold is not the only way to find nuggets in the earth.

TRAVELLING TO KILL

Robert Black was that extremely unusual serial killer who travelled widely, and his journeys reflected his personal story. Susan Maxwell was abducted from Northumberland and her body found south, in Staffordshire, two weeks later. Caroline Hogg was snatched from a playground in Edinburgh, and her body too was also left far south of the abduction site, in a lay-by in Leicestershire. Sarah Harper was taken from near Leeds and left dead further south as well, in the River Trent near Nottingham.

The consideration of all the information in the CATCHEM database threw some light on this pattern of abduction and body disposal.[6] Very young children are usually frightened into submission and will travel further with somebody without putting up a fight than an older victim. If a victim is, say, sixteen it is found that the distances travelled are very much shorter. The people most aware of these issues are the abductors themselves. They learn from their early 'mistakes' and 'successes' which victims they can take great distances with relative ease.

Analysis of the details within the CATCHEM database showed that these abductions were the only ones of all the cases ever recorded in which the child victims had been transported over 80 miles. The offender was taking them from one country to another – from Scotland to England. The first

12. ABDUCTIONS AND MURDER SITES OF ROBERT BLACK

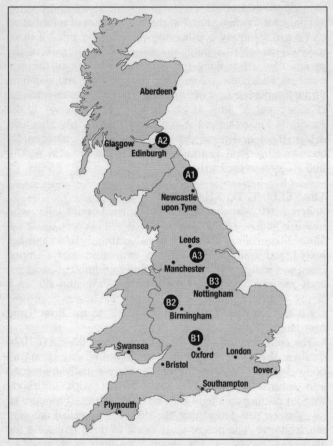

1. A1, B1, July 1982 – Susan Maxwell abducted from Cornhill on Tweed. Body found in a ditch next to a lay-by on the A518 at Loxley.

2. A2, B2, July 1983 – Caroline Hogg abducted from Portobello. Body found in a lay-by at Twycross near to the A444.

3. A3, B3, March 1986 – Sarah Harper abducted from Morley, Leeds. Body found in River Trent. Was left near Junction 24 of the M1 when still alive.

murder had a distance of 296 miles between abduction and disposal site, the second murder 108 miles and the third murder about 84 miles. These are all significantly large distances. No crimes out of those reviewed over a period of 26 years prior to Black being taken to court had distances so large; even when the database was extended to cover 40 years no other cases were found.

TRAVELLING TO DELIVER

The uniqueness of the pattern of abductions and body-disposal locations was of great value in getting Black convicted. It added weight to the evidence that he was responsible for all these crimes. He had admitted his guilt in the abduction in Stow; he could hardly challenge it. But he refused to admit to the other abductions. The police therefore had to put a case together that would provide circumstantial evidence. In doing this they enabled us to understand more about Black's criminal journey and to lay the foundations for future investigations, as well as even more effective use of emerging computer systems.

Poster Despatch and Storage (PDS) had employed Robert Black for many years as a delivery-van driver when he lived in London. These deliveries took him all over the country. Even though he had had many minor accidents that had cost them a great deal in insurance premiums, he was fortunate that changes in management kept him employed. Part of the reason was that, unmarried and with no ties, he was willing to go on the longer runs that other employees were more reluctant to do.

There is no public account of how the many small car accidents had occurred. Black had been slightly above average at school, so he was not intellectually impaired, or ever under great pressure to deliver. Indeed he seems to have liked the job because it enabled him to be his own time-keeper and manage his routes as he wished.

It is worth speculating that it was his becoming distracted in seeking out possible victims that had given rise to these minor accidents. The Malaga Rapist we considered in Chapter 13 had no previous criminal record but many car-parking violations. He got these because as soon as he saw a possible victim he would park where he was, whether it was illegal or not. In another study,[7] it was found that about a quarter of the cars parked illegally across a city were of some interest to the police for more serious crimes. People who ignore the mores of civil society are not likely to limit their actions to one narrow area of criminality.

There is no centralised record of parking violations. The records held by PDS seemed a much more likely source of circumstantial evidence. However, like many companies, PDS did not keep the records of day-to-day actions for very long; but they did keep their wages book. Different lengths of journey attracted different payments, so the police were able to determine from the amount he had been paid the times when he was doing longer journeys to Scotland and the north of England. These fitted the timings of the abductions near the Scottish border.

In order to narrow down the time frame within which he might have been travelling near the abduction locations the police looked at the use Black had made of PDS's fuel credit card. It took thousands of hours of police time to go through these paper records, then to trace people who had bought petrol before and after so that the timing could be verified. This revealed the chilling prospect that he had refuelled before and after snatching Susan Maxwell. He must have pulled into a petrol station with her trussed up in his van. The police were also able to establish that near the day he had taken Caroline Hogg he had been delivering posters close to where she had disappeared.

TRAVEL PLANS

There is a tendency in discussions of serial killers and rapists to regard them as some form of animal. Clearly their actions are off the end of the scale for any decent human being. It is also tempting to use implicit animal metaphors like predator, or even raptor. The only value of this cross-reference to the animal kingdom is to draw attention to the economic logic in their actions. Animals are constructed, by evolutionary processes, to have an efficient relationship between the effort they expend and the benefits they accrue, the main benefit being food. For criminals the process is much more complex, demanding much more abstract thought and the weighing-up of many different factors. For although television documentaries and the more publicity-minded students of animal behaviour will find brutish analogies with a criminal reducing risk or seeking out targets, these parallels limit our understanding of offenders' actions rather than enhance them.

It is more appropriate to look for parallels in other areas of human activity. If we establish the different ways in which wars may be conducted, the different strategies people use to search for a place to live or a place to work, or even the mundane task of the travelling salesman planning his route, we will gain access to the mental processes that people draw upon, and these will have very real parallels with the location decisions of criminals.

Robert Black was a travelling delivery-man, but he was also using his travels as an opportunity to seek out possible victims, grab them and escape. There are many parallels in his criminal activities with those of a travelling salesman. The latter have to optimise their journeys to minimise their effort, but they will optimise them around the opportunities for sales. So although there will be some dominant route that will eventually take them back to their base, this route will be modified to open up sales potential. Once the likely customers have been exhausted in a given place, the travelling salesman will not return there for some time, until new prospects emerge.

In the case of a criminal looking for victims, the dominant route will be adjusted to take in places where he thinks victims may be found. Black explained to his work-mates that he preferred the back roads instead of the fast motorways. He later admitted to the professionals who interviewed him after his conviction that this gave him the opportunity to locate young girls in spots where he would not be observed. When a location appeared threatening or unproductive he moved on. But if he found possible victims in more promising locations, he would return to them.

Both the locations of the abductions, and the sites where the hapless victims' bodies were left, stretched across a large section of Britain. However, they were certainly not random. It is striking that all the crimes occurred along an axis that is dominated by a major route. They show someone for whom the eastern route up and down Britain was his territory. The crime locations do suggest an efficient journey, like that made by a delivery-man or a travelling salesman, making many calls whilst keeping the overall journey as short as possible. London is at one end; Scotland at the other. Might there be something that pulled him at either end? But he left his victims' bodies in the Midlands, where he felt confident enough to finish his awful work. This was not a casual, passing traveller, but a person with some knowledge or involvement in this area too.

Black was born in Scotland and lived in various places around Edinburgh and Glasgow before moving to London where he took up the job of delivery-van driver. He often travelled north at the weekends to stay in Scotland.

What gave him the focus in the Midlands and took him off the motorway route through the area? He had befriended the Rayson family, having met them in a pub in London, and took up residence in their attic room. Their son John set up home in Leicestershire in the centre of the 'Midlands triangle' where the three girls' bodies were found. Black often stopped there when he was on his travels. So here was a man with his route up and down the country mapped out, with even the halfway stop-over explained; the route of a travelling delivery-man, or of a travelling killer.

Many other unsolved crimes that Black may have committed are on the same delivery route up and down the country, and across to the south-west.

THE VAN AS BASE

Black's criminal journey reveals a man whose base was not his home but his means of transport, his delivery van. He kept various objects in it that he could use while he was masturbating to thoughts about touching young girls. He admitted in interviews with the police[8] after his arrest that he would get into the back of the van at night and dress himself in girls' clothes, such as swimming costumes, whilst masturbating. He also kept the tape and sleeping bag he used to bind and restrain his victims there, as well as sex toys, bondage equipment and a mattress. He was always ready to act on an opportunity if it emerged, constantly on the lookout for the best moment to pounce.

As with the Washington snipers, the greatest difficulty of finding this killer was that he was literally a moving target. Psychologically, though, his van was his fixed base. He lived in the attic of the Rayson family home and although he was able to keep his collections of child pornography there, the family had no truck with his sexual predilections, the Rayson boys telling him he was a pervert. The van was therefore his safe zone; the place where he could act out his deviant thoughts.

The van also gave him feelings of freedom to roam at will looking for the thrills he craved. Each victim was another episode in a quest that had become a vile adventure by the time he was seventeen. He had convinced a seven-year-old girl he approached in the park to come and 'see some kittens' with him. The girl had gone with him to a deserted building.

After his conviction in 1994, Black gave unique interviews to a criminal researcher, Ray Wyre, admitting to some crimes and giving clues which linked him to others. Remembering that event from a quarter of a century earlier, Black told Wyre: 'I took her inside and held her down on the ground with my hand round her throat ... I must have half-strangled her or something because she was unconscious.' He then sexually abused her, leaving her without worrying whether she was alive or dead. She was later found dazed on the street, crying and bleeding.

The psychiatrist who examined him when this assault came to court said that this was an isolated event, highly unlikely to recur, so he was let off with a formal warning. But Robert Black had learned a lot from this experience. He had learned how easily he could escape punishment for these crimes. He had learned what excited him to ejaculation. Most crucially he had learned the value of an enclosed place away from the eyes of others in which he could abuse a child at will. His van became the moveable equivalent of that first deserted building.

He became aware of the possibilities that travel gave him. By moving his locus of activity around he could search for opportunities, picking and choosing as he wished. He made it clear to Wyre that his choice of holiday destination was partly determined by his sexual interest in children: 'Initially it was Denmark and Holland. At the time of my arrest I was saving for a trip to Bangkok, Thailand; countries which had liberal pornography laws, especially. Access to child pornography was also a deciding factor.'

He was in France when three girls were killed there. He was in Germany when one girl was killed. He was in Belfast when other girls were killed. This was a man who was so aware of the possibilities offered by geographical mobility that he planned his crimes internationally. It seems likely a van was his main weapon in committing all these crimes.

OBJECTS OF EXCITEMENT

Black's comments to Ray Wyre illustrate yet again how little regard such criminals have for their victims. When asked how he could treat a young girl the way he had done, Black answered, 'I wasn't thinking about her at all . . . like, you know, what she must be feeling.' He regarded the death of these girls as 'a pure accident'.

The travelling criminal has little opportunity for developing any role for his victims in the narrative he is living out. They are objects that are managed to feed his desires. Each victim becomes the temporary focus for his depravity, like items to be collected in a quest, and is then disposed of once they have been used. The travelling offender sees himself as an adventurer, taking an active role that will take him to the next episode in the destructive drama he is writing himself into. He sees no end to his activities unless his actions are brought to an abrupt stop.

The killer who abducted eleven-year-old Susan Maxwell from a country lane in July 1982 put a point on the map, and prompted a police investigation that involved six police forces and cost twelve million pounds. Yet it still took the police eleven years to track the culprit down. In that time he killed at least two more young girls. Geographical analyses that the police have carried out show he may well have killed more. He evaded detection for many years because he had a job delivering all over the country, finding vulnerable victims wherever he could on his travels. If the police had been able to search the sorts of records available today they would have been helped by being able to find who had been travelling through those places at those times, before the trail had gone too cold to find sufficient evidence.

In the future, instead of the laborious task of panning through huge mounds of information to find the important lumps that will identify the killer, investigators may be able to use the different strategy of hooking onto the key pieces of information that will lead them to the killer. They may be able to follow the scent, so that they do not have to wait for the criminal to make a mistake that will identify him – to wait for another death to appear on their map.

21. BODILY VIOLATIONS

We have been concentrating on the most obvious aspect of murder and rape. The aspect that is not always given the attention it deserves: *where* the crime happens. But there is one other feature that cannot be ignored, that gives added depth to our understanding of the crime: *how* it happens. In particular, we should consider the rather gruesome but important details of the way the victim is dealt with: *what* is done to her body.[1]

These variations in the offender's physical interactions with the victim do tend to map onto the geographical patterns of their crimes, often for quite simple reasons. If some sort of relationship, however bizarre, is to be developed with the victim, and there is likely to be a great deal of bodily abuse, then the offender needs to find the opportunity for extended contact. These will be the focused killers, most notably West and Dahmer. At the other extreme are offenders who have minimal contact with their victims: the Washington snipers and even in his disturbed way Robert Black. Their victims mean nothing to them at all, so they can journey at will hunting for any opportunity. Between these two extremes are many of our 'marauding' criminals, who travel out from their base and back again to find a means of acting out their disdain.

These considerations take us into the heart of the dark actions that are rape and murder. They draw attention to the different ways in which people and their bodies can be violated. In doing so they tell us something of what it means to be human, and the difficulty we all have in both distinguishing and separating person and body.

THE COLOUR OF MURDER

In Raymond Chandler's *The Long Goodbye*[2] the plot revolves around a private detective, Philip Marlowe, being unconvinced that the violent murder with which the story opens could have been perpetrated by the central suspect. Marlowe is convinced that the suspect adored the victim too much to assault her in this way. The vicious, disfiguring actions revealed at the murder scene did not 'add up'. They were at variance with what was known about the suspect and the role the victim had in his life. Real-life examples are often more horrific but reveal similar processes: as, for example, when the mutilation of sex organs is clearly part of an act of jealousy, or the single shot to the head shows a psychological distance from the victim. As so often happens, fiction writers appreciated the significance of such matters long before detectives, and in their wake psychologists, began to examine these subjects systematically.

Many murderers have similar characteristics. Not only are they likely to be men, but the great majority are in their early twenties. They come from disturbed, dysfunctional family backgrounds with some prior criminal experience, although not necessarily for crimes of violence.[3] These features that murderers tend to have in common can be seen as contributing to their limited portfolio of ways of dealing with other people. Their dysfunctional backgrounds mean that they have difficulty in feeling and knowing what it means to be a person, and especially in seeing the world from another's point of view. They see the cause of their frustration, anger or jealousy, or the opportunity to slake their greed, as encapsulated in the object of another being. They want to remove or destroy that entity; and this is the only way they can relate to the individual they see as causing their reactions. Murderers therefore provide a rather exaggerated illustration of the consequences of confusing the person and their body, violating the body through acts of aggression as a product of this confusion.

Yet there are many different ways in which a murder can be carried out; different styles which are likely to relate to differences between the murderers themselves. The vicious rage that leads to violent mutilation is likely to be a product of anger with the victim in which the act of murder is what drives the killer on. The American sociologist Jack Katz[4] identified this as 'righteous slaughter'. Few of the killers we have been considering have this rage because it tends to grow out of a long-standing relationship with the victim. It is the most common basis of murder. In contrast the murderer for financial gain that William Bolitho identified in his popular 1920s book *Murder for Profit*[5] has the end result clearly in mind as he goes about his devious plan to poison, or kill in some other way, thus distancing himself from his victim. The people we have been considering, with the exception of Marc Dutroux, are those extremely rare examples who kill and rape people they do not know, in the main, with little reason other than to satisfy their lusts.

These variations in murder, and other forms of bodily violation, illuminate the confusions surrounding the relationships between the person and the body. These confusions are not limited to serial killers. They are now at the heart of many debates about the influence that contemporary science may give us over our bodies. Attempts to reduce so much of the complexity of being people to the processes of physics and biology also challenge the rich notions we have of the relationships between self and body. Variations in the chosen modes of killing people might be thought of as the colours that distinguish one dark crime from another. These colours are reflections of many other differences that can be found in the struggle to make sense of being human.

BEYOND THE ANIMAL

The recognition that murder, and the all too often related violent crime of rape, grow out of a confusion of person and body drives a stake through the pretensions of animal behaviourists, biologists and the baying plethora of neuroscientists and physiologists who want to explain away human violence by reducing it to a chemical or physical cause that is embedded in a person's brain structure, hormones and genetic make-up. Of course our biology and evolutionary ancestry provide a backdrop to our thoughts, feelings and actions. But as all the violent men we have looked at have taught us, there are so many profoundly human processes – choice, contemplation etc. – involved in all their activities that to claim the central and primary cause is purely biological is ludicrous.

There will always be dramatic individual examples that can be drawn on to defend a generality. Charles Whitman, who, uncharacteristically, killed his wife and mother and then sixteen other people with guns including rifles and a shotgun from the University of Texas clock tower, was found to have a brain tumour in the area of the brain that relates to emotional response. Whitman had been to a psychiatrist seeking help for the way he was feeling, yet still took his rifle to kill. Would a different psychiatrist have changed the way he was going to act? How was it that he had a rifle and ammunition, and that this was his chosen way of acting out his feelings? What history did he have that enabled him to determine how effective he could be with a rifle up a 307-foot tower? Most importantly, how many other people diagnosed with such tumours do not take a rifle and kill strangers? How many such people have no access to a rifle at all?

Recently scientists, keen to claim ownership of human experience, have declared that the previous estimate of a 95 per cent overlap between human genetic make-up and the make-up of our nearest primate relatives is a gross underestimate. The figure is nearer to 99 per cent. They therefore declare that human beings should not be regarded as a different species from these primates. What unmitigated nonsense this is. Surely, until such a time as one of our primate cousins publishes a paper on the topic, we should come to the conclusion that these genetic comparisons show the opposite of what is claimed. If there is such an overlap in the genome with such huge differences in the nature of the animal it must show rather that the genes are largely irrelevant to what makes us human. They may be germane to considering certain aspects of biology or anatomy, but they are immaterial when deliberating on what it means to be a person.

The various shades and hues of murder throw further light on being human, because they are not solely products of the offender's practical considerations. The use of a knife or a rope, slow poison or an illegal firearm derives from the offender's lifestyle and way of seeing the world. The choice of method is a consequence of the meaning of his victim, as much as the ready availability of a particular weapon, or the overt demands of the task at hand.

The activities surrounding the choice of method for despatching the victim grow out of the killer's inner journey, taking us beyond the murderous act itself to a consideration of the way the body is dealt with after death: for instance whether it is hidden or covered. The type of interaction that may have occurred before death, such as whether the attack was sudden and unexpected or grew out of an argument, also provides important signifiers of the mood and tone of the killing. They may indicate what the victim meant to the offender: the role that the victim played in the killer's life.

As Bolitho wrote in 1926 about murderers, 'They very commonly construct for themselves a life-romance, a personal myth in which they are the maltreated hero, which secret is the key of their battle against despair.' In other words the victim takes on a significance in the offender's self-constructed life story that is reflected in the way the body of the victim is violated.

Therefore, beyond the twists it can give to the plot of a thriller, or the assistance to a police investigation, the significance of the variations in violent physical assault raises questions about crucial psychological processes. It draws our attention to the fact that different ways of assaulting the body imply different ways of relating to the person whose body it is. The psychological examination of violations of the body is therefore an important, if somewhat unusual, gateway to considering the fundamental nature of the relationship between the person and the body, and what makes us human.

THE RANGE OF VIOLATIONS

The problematic nature of violations of the human body, and the profound questions those problems raise, can be illustrated further from something I noticed near the Royal Courts of Justice on The Strand in London. In a telephone kiosk outside the courts it was difficult to avoid becoming aware that Tara and her colleagues were advertising their services by means of blu-tacked postcards. What was especially interesting about Tara was that she was willing, presumably for a fee, to be spanked. By contrast one of her colleagues, who preferred the more anonymous sobriquet Severe Mistress, was charging for the service of humiliating, binding and torturing her clients. I suspected that this latter service was rather more expensive than Tara's because of the higher overheads. Severe Mistress boasted a 'fully equipped dungeon'.

The irony of these services being on offer so close to one of the highest courts in the land is that, nowadays, those courts would never countenance spanking as fit punishment for any felony. Neither would they ever endorse humiliation or torture as an appropriate redress for even the most serious of crimes. This irony reflects the changing views we have of our body and what officialdom is allowed to do to it.

Torture of many forms was not uncommon in Britain until relatively recently, not only as a method for obtaining a confession and other information, but also as a form of punishment in its own right. The sentence of 'hard labour' that still obtains in many places is a recognition that the removal of a person's freedom is not enough, and that they should suffer physically as well. Indeed, the 'boot camps' and 'short sharp shocks' that recent British governments have introduced in the sentencing of young offenders is part of a long tradition of severe physical punishments. Many of those used in the past would today be regarded as torture. There are not only differences of degree but also probably of kind between currently acceptable punishments and the treadmill that was still in use in British prisons less than a century ago, and before that the 'cat' that was used to flog British soldiers for minor offences, or the various forms of rack of earlier centuries.

What has happened over the centuries that punishments that were once commonplace should no longer be acceptable? I would argue that it is the changing relationship between the person and the body. This relationship has been growing ever more complex over the centuries, as the clear distinction between the body and the spirit has eroded.

There are two different trends that these distinctions elucidate. One is the growing view that the person has to be changed by means that go beyond the modification of the body. Another is the growing reluctance to insult the person even when it is acknowledged that physical punishment is acceptable.

With the growth in the recognition of human identity and 'person-hood' has emerged a more psychological approach to torture. To change the nature of the person through fear and other devices is a method that has always been used; but mind-changing strategies have been lowered to new depths in the twentieth century. Indeed, if a person can be shown to have changed his allegiances, and thus, in effect, his identity, without any overt indication of physical coercion, that is now deemed more of an achievement than change effected through physical means. In the past the physical mark was seen as a prerequisite of an indication of change, often leading to the ultimate physical control of death.

The distance between Tara and her colleagues and the tortures of the Spanish Inquisition is very great indeed, but it is remarkable what people will inflict on themselves. From time to time suicide occurs accidentally in the pursuit of exquisite pain or extreme sensation. To attempt to grasp the huge variations there are between people in their reactions to violations of their bodies is something of a challenge. What is clear, though, from accounts of the suffering of martyrs, as much as from the sadistic and masochistic indulgences of fetishists, is that the role the person plays in the process is crucial to making sense of their reactions.

People who have been tortured comment on how they lose their sense of identity long before they lose consciousness. A possibly related process of feeling separated from their day-to-day existence seems to be what produces the heightened excitement characteristic in some people's experience of sado-masochism. It is the difference in the relationships people have to their bodies that, at its extremes, can make the difference between an act of violation being torture or a service for which people will pay. After all, it is the lack of reciprocal acceptance that makes sexual activity rape.

At first sight the key difference in circumstance appears to be volition; it is not a violation if you seek it out. But there is a rather subtler and potentially more important distinction – one that is the foundation for banning many forms of punishment and that is reflected in the American Constitution's Eighth Amendment forbidding 'cruel and unusual punishment' and Article Three of the European Convention on Human Rights banning punishment that is 'inhuman and degrading'. These laws capture the concern not to violate the *person* and the rights that person should have. It rests on the recognition that the *person* can be violated even if there is no physical damage. The clients of Tara and others claim the freedom to do to their *bodies* as they wish.

It is the significance of the actions on the body of a person, whether self-inflicted or not, that raises so many questions about what the bodies of others and ourselves mean. In many cases our transactions with people are mediated by transactions with their mortal flesh. The caresses and acts of love do of course reveal the significance of the relationship between the people concerned. A gentle touch from a lover can be a fearful act of gross violation from a stranger. But the offensive, destructive acts may offer as much of an insight, if not more, into the often confusing relationship between our bodies and our selves: the confusion that is at the very core of murder and rape.

A SCALE OF VIOLATION

The lover's touch, when unwanted, is at one end of a scale of bodily violations. Violent and abusive dismemberment of the body is at the other end. This scale seems to reflect an increasing desecration of the individual as more aspects of their personal, private selves are defiled through the actions on their bodies. For even the act of touching varies in its significance, depending on the body part touched as much as on the person doing the touching.[6] When two strangers have to squeeze past each other in a crowded public place there will be a tendency for them to pass back-to-back, or side-to-side. Great contortions will often be gone through to ensure that they do not touch face-to-face. This shows that it is our faces and the front parts of our bodies that carry so much social and related symbolic significance. These are the parts of our bodies that most capture our unique selves as individuals and which are therefore considered most vulnerable to violation.

One interesting consequence of this is that marks to the face have huge significance, as studies of even the smallest facial blemishes show. A number of psychological experiments, for example, have revealed that quite tiny facial scars can have a big impact on the judgements people will make of the scarred person. This is also illustrated in the big differences in the practice of tattooing that many young people accept. One current fashion is to have a tattoo on the upper rear shoulder so that it can be revealed or hidden as the person wishes. A tattoo on the face is part of a much more extreme expression of distinctiveness through group membership.

Beyond these forms of apparently minor violations are the wounding and mutilation that people in depressed and despairing states or ecstatic moods inflict on themselves. There are many forms of masochistic acts the world over, and the extent and nature of these acts are quite remarkable. But what is particularly notable is the range of facial modifications that are carried out for apparently cosmetic reasons. Another large group involves activities relating to sexual organs. Clearly both the face and the sexual organs play a significant role in all cultures in defining a person's identity. It is therefore perhaps not surprising that these are popular targets for both modification and violation.

The most obvious extreme form of violation is rape. It is important to ask why rape should be regarded as such a distinct crime from other forms of violent assault. A feminist interpretation could be that the value of a woman as a form of property is greatly reduced once she has been sexually violated, so special laws are required to protect this particular value. It can be seen that such an argument can readily be developed to recognise the special sensitivity of women and therefore the need for them to have special protection. This is particularly worth noting because the crime of male rape has only been recognised in many jurisdictions in very recent times. This is all probably part of the growing acceptance of the particular challenge of sexual violation to many people's identity. Certainly there is growing evidence that sexual assaults of all forms produce psychological confusion and often trauma that go far beyond the intensity of the physical insult itself. Yet again this reveals the very important symbolic qualities that our bodies carry for us.

STRATEGIES OF VIOLATION

When we turn to the extreme forms of violation that occur in murder we can see the way the meaning of the victim for the offender is enshrined in the actions committed on the body.

Two dominant strategies seem to capture most of the processes. One is the emphasis on the person with a limiting of the significance of the body, which can give rise to the mutilation of the body as a by-product of attempting to change the person. It is the person that is here the target of the actions. As I have mentioned, when considering, for example, Fred West's journal, this is the deadly drama that requires complete access to the victim and her total subjugation to the role the killer is inflicting on her.

This idea is open to empirical examination and test through the rather grisly consideration of what sorts of actions co-occur in crimes of violence, particularly those committed by serial killers. This is not an easy area in which to work. The data is hard to come by, partly because of the mercifully few cases available for study. The data that is available will invariably be crude and of low levels of reliability, having been collected by criminal investigators for legal reasons rather than the purposes of research. Often details of crucial psychological significance, such as at which stage during the murder sexual acts took place, will not be carefully determined or recorded because they have little legal significance. Yet in the Centre for Investigative Psychology at the University of Liverpool we have begun collecting appropriate data sets and some patterns are beginning to emerge that illustrate the processes being discussed here.[7]

Our hypothesis is that when the focus is on controlling and manipulating the person there are subsets of activities that share a common theme, or colour. This hypothesis is supported by our findings. So, for example, sexual activity and attacks to the upper torso, often with few immediately life-threatening implications, are likely to co-occur. Some of the victims may even be released, as happened in the cases of West, Dahmer and other focused serial killers.

This way of dealing with the victim can spill over into a distinct form, the second strategy, in which the person's body has become so much the focus that the individual is then ignored, giving primacy to the body. The victim becomes little more than an object to these offenders. Its use for their own ends is the driving force that leads them to kill. The finding supporting this is that these killings characteristically show the insertion of objects into the dead torso, necrophilia and ritual activities using the body. The killers may perhaps even indulge in cannibalism. This type of killer gets to a state in which the body is independent of any person.

When we have looked at other violent crimes like rape and the sexual abuse of children we find parallels. Some paedophiles, for example, are focused on using children's bodies for their own gratification.[8] These are the violent people, like Robert Black, who may kill to control or silence their victims. For others it is the childish person that draws their desires. They will spend a lot of time luring children into an apparently innocent relationship, possibly even believing there to be no harm in the acts of abuse they perpetrate.

THE PERSON AS INVENTION

In order to understand the further implications of these considerations of bodily violation it is necessary to realise that the 'person' is an invention of the human psyche. Being a 'person' cannot be a taken-for-granted 'given'. This is one of the most challenging implications of modern science. The recognition we each have of 'being me' is not merely a consequence of a corporeal existence, but requires that we each transcend our physical experiences and construct a notion of our selves that goes beyond our bodies.

The central message of many studies of child development, spurred on by the great contributions of Swiss psychologist Jean Piaget and the rich metaphors of Sigmund Freud, is that the crucial stages of early childhood concern the distinguishing of the self from others. This starts with the child becoming aware of the separateness of his or her body from those of others that succour it. It then evolves into an awareness of the unique qualities he or she has as a person. It is distortions in this process that undoubtedly lay the seeds for dysfunction in later life.

What our consideration of the violated body shows is that the notion of self is sometimes a difficult fiction to maintain. It is challenged every time the body is violated in any way. Therefore these violations and the reactions to them can help us to understand more fully the different ways we construct ourselves as people and the vulnerabilities inherent in those constructions.

Every one of us takes it for granted that we are a 'person': an identifiable, unique, sentient human being with a past and anticipated future. Furthermore, except in the most extreme states of mental disturbance, we see coherence in our 'self'. We know, more or less, who we are and what it means to be that person. We do not experience ourselves as animated organisms, as mechanico-physiological systems, or even animals struggling to survive. Even at our most atavistic we regard ourselves as *people* who have certain urges and desires, needs and aspirations.

Yet, evolutionary biology and the invasive insights of biochemistry and neuroscience are making it increasingly clear that this sense of self and the associated awareness of being a person are fictional constructions. Indeed, it is emerging as a by-product of the biological sciences of the past century that the belief we each have in our own identity as people is probably the greatest innovation in evolutionary history. It is a creative leap of the human imagination. We minimise any indications that we are merely conscious animals. We have to ignore all the biological and psychological changes that happen during our lives and turn us into very different entities from those we once were. We must construct a story about ourselves that encapsulates the central psychological continuity of our existence as the motif around which the variations in our life unfold. This story is fictional in the sense that it is a particular construction that presents a limited perspective on our selves, in which we are the main characters, carving our identities out of our transactions with the world. For the killers and rapists whose mental geography we have been studying the destructive constructions of themselves are revealed in the maps of their crimes.

This sense of self and 'person-hood' is a far more significant aspect of our experience than the much-studied area of consciousness. We may, after all, share aspects of consciousness with our close relatives in the animal kingdom. Conscious awareness of our surroundings and even our recognition that we have that awareness and share it with others, including other primates, may turn out to be a natural evolutionary product of a sophisticated cortex. But it requires much more inventive processes, utilising a combination of uniquely human talents such as language, social interaction and the creation of cultures, to produce the firm belief each of us has that we are people with a special identity as unique beings.

THE EMERGENCE OF THE PERSON

Perhaps the earliest recognition that the body had to be handled carefully because of the person it contained was indicated when early humans buried their dead and made provision for a non-corporeal hereafter. For early peoples the body was an inefficient container for the more important soul. But as science has dispelled the myths of religion, in parallel with giving us more control over our bodies, so the body and the person who inhabits it have become ever more closely equated. Even in these Godless times the care and respect with which the dead are disposed of is a continuing paean to the importance of our non-physical identity. That is why the worst atrocities to be pictured are those which involve unburied bodies. They challenge our fundamental faith in our own humanity.

There may appear, here, to be an equation of the person with other more religious notions like spirit or soul. But the very opposite is my intention. So long as the soul was considered a God-given force that vitalised the body it was feasible to carry out atrocities on the body in order to save the soul. Many of the tortures of previous centuries were supported because of the idea that the immortal spirit of a person was being hampered by the evils inherent in the body.

With the demise in the belief in the soul there is a temptation to believe that only the body matters. Its processes and products are seen as the answer to all human strengths and weaknesses. But this ignores the importance of the investment we each make in creating our selves. It ignores the existence of a person, which can never be totally reduced to biological and physical processes. It is this recognition of the need to respect a person and their identity that has led to the outlawing of extreme forms of torture. It is the confusion some individuals have regarding the nature of their identity and its relationship to their body that leads to self-mutilation and sado-masochism.

Attempts to modify the living are the obverse of the reflected sanctity of the dead body. Because we cannot shake off the body we must attempt to modify it, and in extreme cases violate it, in order for it better to reflect the person we want to be. This takes on an importance far beyond what may be achieved by the practical benefits of nips and tucks, marathon runs or other feats of endurance and prowess. This importance comes from the fact that the body is one of the basic metaphors for all human transactions. Any form of mutilation is thus essentially symbolic. This symbolism grows, in part, out of the very strong tradition that the flesh is profane and it is the spirit that is immortal and sacred.

COPING WITH THE PERSON/BODY PARADOX

The dualism of person and body is therefore not simply a product of rational thinking. It takes on a profound emotional significance. For many people there is a struggle between the things they do not like about themselves, as reflected in their body, and what they believe truly represents them, in the sort of person they are. Utilising the services of Severe Mistress may be one way of trying to cope with this. Other more extreme forms of self-mutilation may provide some temporary relief for more intense inner agitation.

The emotional release of inflicting wounds on the self is difficult for most people to understand. If a person has been abused by people close to them, especially in the early years when they are forming an image of themselves, then there are likely to be a variety of distortions in the way they see themselves and their bodies. This may emerge in many different forms, including anorexia or bulimia or, if the individual is in deep turmoil over their identity as a person, and the role their body plays in that, in self-injury. The distance self-injury places between body and person can be disturbingly soothing. One person who moved through these experiences into professional life has anonymously posted on the Internet a remarkably insightful and convincing account of her personal turmoil:

At the age of 13, I found that self-injury temporarily relieved the unbearable jumble of feelings. I cut myself in the bathroom, where razor blades were handy and I could lock the door. The slicing through flesh never hurt, although it never even occurred to me that it should . . . The blood brought an odd sense of well-being, of strength. It became all encompassing . . . With a safe sense of detachment, I watched myself play with my own flowing blood. The fireball of tension was gone and I was calm . . .

This can be contrasted with those beliefs, often based on religious fundamentalism, that emphasise the person so much that the body is totally its servant, and in some cases sacrosanct. The struggles that Jehovah's Witnesses have with the authorities because their beliefs allow no intervention into the body, or the dismay that many other fundamentalist religious believers have with post-mortem examinations, are founded on quite different views of the relationship between the person and the body than those dominant in Western society. Belief that the body is the person leads to the view that any modification of it is a violation, the reverse extreme from the earlier idea that any amount of drawing and quartering was permitted because it could drive out the devil. Apparently similar beliefs led the Inquisition to assume that the truly insane were so dissociated from their bodies that they would not really feel pain. It is also at the core of suicide bombings that use the body as an expendable tool in the quest for spiritual glory.

THE BATTLE FOR THE PERSON

There is a powerful belief system rooted in the knowledge that we are more than our bodies, but it is constantly challenged by our need to cope with our experiences as mediated by these bodies. The challenge that this paradox raises, of being both body and person, is resolved in many different ways by different people, but the most common strategy is to hold on to a firm dualism that distinguishes these two different realms.

On the one hand is the body with all its animal trappings, which shares all its major characteristics with every other human. In terms of scholarly debate this fosters studies in the natural sciences in which all humans are virtually the same because their bodies are essentially identical; indeed many of the properties of those bodies are so close to those of other animals that they can be studied interchangeably. Here is the root of the hoped-for magic of mapping out all the human genes and thereby solving the central conundrum of being human.

It is out of this perspective that there is the constant search for biological bases to phenomena such as criminal activity, aggression or other acts of violence and violation. Genetic make-up, brain damage or hormonal influences are held up as the primary causes of violence, aggression or criminality in general. But this has similarities to the perspective of the rapist seeing his victim as merely a body to be used, or the serial killer keeping body parts as souvenirs of his deeds. The body is taken as all that is significant.

Such a view ignores all those immaterial aspects of 'person-hood' that so enthral disciplines running the gamut from anthropology to psychology by way of linguistics and theology. Here the differences between people or the contexts they experience are a recurring source of debate. Those aspects of an individual that make them unique come to the fore when we consider them as people. Aspects such as their creativity, morality, passion, potential, or the particular point in the flux of cultures that they illustrate are recognised as transcending the bodily functions that support them.

Throughout history it seems to have been the case that the belief in 'person-hood' was protected by an elaboration of the distinction between the individual and the body. The soul, psyche, personality, mind, character and many other aspects of the person have always been regarded as quite distinct from the person's corporeal existence. Yet the fundamental paradox in being human is that the significance of any human body is in how it expresses its supra-corporeal capabilities. The spirit cannot throw off its mortal coil, but nor can the clay of which we are made be recognised as a being without evidence of its character as a person.

The struggle with this duality of mind and body is at the heart of most human endeavour. It is a struggle which aims constantly to re-create the fiction of 'person-hood' in defiance of the laws of nature; a fiction that casts its protagonists into opposing camps. Sin and evil are the products of the flesh that must be fought with the weapons of the inherently virtuous spirit. The profane is all that which relates us to our animal past, whether it be the subconscious urges of a Freudian id or the apparently more scientific, but no less pessimistic, claims of evolutionary bases for aggression and survival. The sacred is to be found in the purity of reason and the contemplative arts, as far from bodily functions as possible.

But when these protagonists – mind and body – share the same virtual reality (as they do for everyone who has some hold on actuality), then there is the constant need to attempt to modify one or the other, to make the person who houses them both more acceptable. The modification may come from upholding the significance of the mind and spirit, making them targets for manipulation and refinement in an attempt to distance them as far as possible from their degrading companion; or the body may be modified and in extreme conditions violated in order to make it more virtuous.

THE PERSON AS PRODUCT
The quest for the body beautiful is an interesting development of the 'corporo-centric' perspective. Some of this may result from a search for a better quality of internal life but a lot of it relates to the way a healthy body is seen as symbolising a good person. After all, there is still the temptation to blame people for their physical handicaps, as statements from such significant trendsetters as a former manager of the English national football team made clear. I think there are some gory parallels with serial killers like Jeffrey Dahmer, who clearly saw his victims as bodies to be modified and manipulated. He wanted to turn them into some sort of willing zombie for his own gratification.

For whose gratification is the consensual shaping of bodies by plastic surgery, or the other possibilities that genetic modification may allow? Often the determination to produce the perfect body seems to be a person's attempt to make themselves appear more spiritually pure. Yet this is always doomed by the paradox that the more we focus on the body the less able we are to allow those aspects of the person that capture their history and character to break free. It is in the transaction between self and non-self, the dialectical relationships between mind and body, that humanity emerges.

Voluntary as much as involuntary violations of the body are embedded in a psycho-social process that gives significance both to the body as object and to its reflection of the body as subject, the person. By ignoring the significance of the person and focusing on the body violent criminals teach us the civilising influence of recognising the importance of the person. This is a lesson that many scientists seeking to help humanity rather than destroy it would do well to master. Too great an emphasis on one or the other leads to barbarity and degradation, whether it is promulgated by genetic scientists or serial killers.

22. INVISIBLE CRIMINALS

A city from the air on an early evening in winter; the dark-grey sky gives just enough light to pick out the shapes of city blocks. The headlights of flowing traffic carve orange streams through the banks of buildings, out to parks and suburbs, revealing the patterns that people create en masse. No deep knowledge is needed to understand the shapes of people's lives captured in the shadowy outlines of city-centre offices crammed together, with little in the way of parks or other open spaces attached to any given building. Their very mass, concentration and location in the heart of the city tell us that this is where people come together to work. Here in the business district lives are as generic as the buildings. The urgent pressures of cars teeming away from the city tell us they must contain people on their way home. The density of the different streams of traffic points to dominant chosen routes, with the side trickles indicating less common activities and locations.

In a different city similar patterns are revealed in equally readable but distinct ways. I still remember the shock of recognition when I flew into Calcutta one morning. As the plane descended I first became aware of large numbers of white figures gathered in large groups along routes into the city. For a moment I thought they were flocks of pigeons until the plane got lower and the closer view made it clear that these were people dressed in their white dhotis, gathered in their hundreds at railway stations. Here the crowded, energetic journey to work was just as obvious, although I knew as little about the nature of that work as in any other strange city.

The myriad different private lives with all their diverse skills, hopes and personalities are of little consequence when those people are studied in huge aggregates as if viewed from the air. One person's hesitancy or confusion that may make his journey to or from work less direct will be lost in the mass of others' habitual flow. The person who has devoted himself to finding a quick route, or knows just where to wait on the station platform to get a seat, will not be distinguishable against the overall accumulation of human actions. By ignoring what makes people different from each other it is possible to map the trajectory of human habits as if they were soulless ball-bearings clattering down metal tubes, or to see the distribution of the places people create as similar to the growth rings of trees, or the gravitational coalescence of distant astronomical objects.

The early study of patterns of city use – and crimes within those patterns – took just such a bird's-eye view.[1] To develop our understanding further so that we can explain and predict the actions of individuals, especially individual offenders, we must highlight the subset of actions and particular locations that capture the life trajectory of those people. Those highlights can only be understood against the backdrop of what is going on around them, the rhythm of their pulse standing out as a counterpoint to the dominant themes and variations of ordinary lives.

As the anonymity of cities grows, and the mobility of even established rural communities is overlaid with the cosmopolitan values of the Internet and mass media, we all know each other less and less. Strangers who would once have stood out and been looked on with suspicion are now just unknown neighbours. People we would never have spoken to in the past, and had no call to greet, contact us in our homes by telephone and the Internet, generating a random bouncing interaction which, more often than not, quickly fades from memory.

All of this is making criminals invisible. They are becoming even more a part of the shadows of our society than ever before. A man can walk down a busy London street and shoot a television celebrity. No one sees him pull the trigger and, even though he is seen walking away, no one knows his name. A family living on the edge of a small city invites young women to stay with them and the women disappear without trace. There is no map on which the missing lives are marked. A massive police hunt across South Auckland does not find Joe Thompson because he has moved so often and there is no clear trace of where he has been.

A new sort of radar is being developed to find these invisible offenders: a search process that uses a different part of the information spectrum to make the few destructive criminal dots fluoresce against the backdrop of the city. This new radar looks at criminal actions in new ways. It remodels the data maps that are proving so productive to show more of what is beneath the surface of the dots. In some important senses maps are deceptive. They pretend to be accounts of the actual world as we see and feel it, but they do not record the really important locations. The point in the garden where I buried our dog, which I cannot pass without a feeling of sadness, is not on any maps. My old school, which has long been half-demolished and turned into bijou apartments, cannot be identified without special knowledge. The circuitous route I take to avoid the traffic snarl-up at the crossroads, which I only know because it meanders past places where I used to play as a child, would not be obvious to anyone who looked at the brown and red lines on a map. Maps are not reality but rather symbolic summaries: abstractions that draw out what is of value for the particular uses for which they were developed.

We saw with the Malaga rapist that a reflection of his mental map, in the sketch he drew of that confusing city, had some relationships to the map a tourist might buy. The tourist map would be of little value if it did not relate at all to how we experience a place. But the distortions in his map help us to understand how patterns of daily use alter the way we remember and perceive the world around us. Sketch maps show us that any representations of actions in a given place are abstractions that need to be interpreted.

MUTILATION BY PROXY

In 1992 a very strange series of crimes caused a number of women in Northamptonshire nasty injuries, although the malicious criminal involved was invisible to them.[2] He telephoned, claiming to have kidnapped their husbands.

These calls started in 1988, when 227 were reported to the police. The caller would state that he had kidnapped a member of the victim's family, usually a woman's husband or partner. He would say that the kidnap victim owed him money, and would demand an amount of money of between £1,000 and £3,000, saying a courier would be sent round with a photograph of the victim to prove that he was holding him.

From 1991, the calls became more malicious and obscene. He would insist to each woman that he had kidnapped their partner as retribution for a prison sentence of 7–15 years. He stated that the man would be harmed if the woman did not do as she was told. He demanded she undress, stick pins or needles through her nipples and set fire to her pubic hair. He said he had two colleagues who would come round to her house to check that she was performing these acts, and that she was being watched. At least nine women carried out such acts, injuring themselves, although many hung up the phone and did not hear any more from him.

Of course the caller was anonymous, or offered various aliases. Furthermore, the numbers called were not all in the telephone directory, although the police realised that many victims had appeared in the local press and could have been traced that way by the caller. Interestingly, the calls were made mostly between 9 a.m. and 5 p.m. during the week and mostly on Monday or Tuesday. They were also remarkably localised, covering little more than a ten-mile radius.

The regularity and almost workmanlike way in which the offender went about the calls suggested that there ought to be a pattern to them, perhaps not in the usual street level actions but in a virtual map of the people who had received the telephone calls. So when I was asked to help the police find this man I put the call recipients' locations on a map. I used the ideas that we have applied in many other cases and treated the recipients' locations like those of any other crime, putting them into our Dragnet software. This indicated to me that the caller was likely to live within a 2–3 mile radius of Sulgrave.

One victim managed to record a call. Armed with our analysis the police were confident that they were looking for a local man. They therefore brought together as many of the victims as they could, along with their husbands, to listen to the recording. One husband recognised the voice as that of local farmer Simon Wadland. He lived in the village of Woodford Halse, three miles from Sulgrave.

13. SIMON WADLAND'S TELEPHONE CALLS WITH DRAGNET ANALYSIS

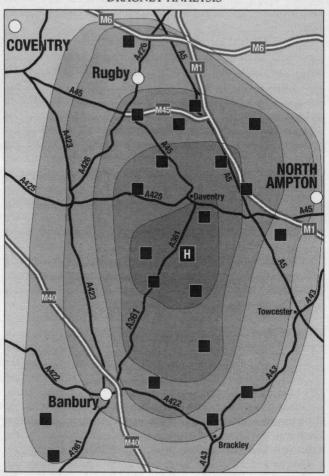

H = Great Ground Farm: Simon Wadland's place of work and home

Sentenced to five years in 1992 for making threats to kill and being a public nuisance, Simon Wadland was a kind of virtual offender in the telephone network. He was making phone calls from his home address, picking his victims from his wife's book while she was out working. He developed his network further by going to the local press and reading the forthcoming marriage announcements. The victim would be chosen as the result of those advertisements. It was very difficult actually to pin-point where the calls were coming from because the telephone system at that time was not digital. If it had been digital he could have been caught in the first few days, although computer and stolen mobile-telephone sources would be more difficult to track down.

Wadland's mental map was constrained and distorted by two processes. One was the cost of long-distance calls. A more important constraint, though, was the limits of his knowledge. He wanted to convince the women he called that he knew their husbands and had kidnapped them. The dots on the map of call recipients, like all crime locations, were a representation of the offender's knowledge; a reflection of the virtual reality through which he moved. It created an implicit world in which he could live out the role of kidnapper and controller of women, almost as if he had stepped inside a computer game. To find such offenders we need to join them in their video game, to travel in virtual reality through databases and other information sources.

CAUGHT BY HIS PIN

The evidence to support the abductions Robert Black had refused to comment on came from company records and petrol receipts. In large fraud investigations and money-laundering inquiries the detective work takes place almost entirely in databases and electronic information sources. In one case I worked on we were able to establish, from an office in an attic in London, that a man who had extorted $150,000 from a major international company based in Switzerland had just evaded imprisonment in Greece for traveller's-cheque fraud. This helped the company to brief its offices worldwide and avoid future losses.

So much of what we do, these days, leaves a trace; cashpoints record where a person is, when, and what transactions are done. The mobile-phone network records the locations and identities of who is communicating with whom and where. Closed-circuit television sees so much that the police can recreate where people went as if replaying a TV drama. As clients, customers, car drivers and citizens, we have a parallel existence in a virtual world, where our movement is monitored across notional maps, recording many aspects of our identity. Unseen cameras record our car number plates. The supermarket builds up an archive of what we each buy and when. Telephone companies serving our homes and offices know to whom we talk and how often. The records of us as tax-payers or voters now have an electronic presence that can be mapped and searched.

Most of the time, most of us are completely unaware of the electronic trail we leave in that invisible world. But detectives are beginning to recognise these footprints in the electronic snow and to follow them to find their culprit. One notable example was the detection and capture of a man who had been holding a bank and a supermarket chain to ransom.

For three and a half years home-made explosive devices with the label 'the Mardi Gra Experience'[3] on them had been left outside Barclays Bank and Sainsburys, and some had been sent to private individuals. There had been no loss of life from the Mardi Gra Experience but at times it had come close. It was fortunate that no one had been killed during his deadly spree but people had been injured, and the bombs were blamed for causing the premature death of the relative of a victim.

Anti-terrorist police came up with the idea of using the virtual networks that we now use every day to trap this dangerous man. In April 1998, the supermarket chain appeared to accede to the bomber's ransom demands and gave him a bank account, with its own cashpoint card and PIN.

The problem, though, was that to catch him they might have needed covert surveillance on every one of the thousands of possible cash machines across London. There was also the risk of him using machines in other cities, to cover which would have needed the deployment of huge numbers of police officers. However, they assumed that there were limits to the bomber's mobility, as for all other criminals. He would be constrained by what he knew and what he had ready access to.

14. MARDI GRA BOMB LOCATIONS WITH DRAGNET ANALYSIS

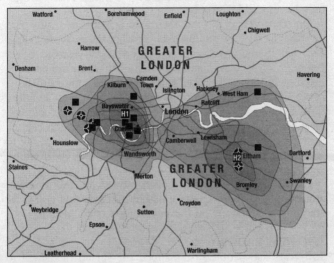

H1 = Edgar Pearce's home

H2 = Edgar Pearce's ex-wife's address

The map of where he had left his bombs gave some indication of the limits under which the offender was operating. Although he had posted bombs to various locations outside London, the pattern of the places he had left them in London spread out across a central zone from the west to the east. A geographical profile of this distribution, of the form calculated by Dragnet, emphasised to the police that there were two focal points to the pattern.

One centre was in the west of London, and seemed to have the highest number of offences around it, and there was a smaller one in the south-east. This indicated one or more offenders with two possible bases, but nonetheless emphasised a defined area in the west of London.

The gamble the police took was that these focal points would also cover the offender's preferred cash machines. Hundreds of cashpoints in the west of London were therefore put under close surveillance. It was a big but manageable job, relying on the bomber becoming visible to them when he showed up on the bank's computer, similar to a plane at night only being visible on radar.

On 28 April at 6.14 p.m., their fishing in virtual reality paid off. The secret PIN was used at a cashpoint in West Ealing. This led to the arrest and conviction of 61-year-old Edgar Pearce, a stroke victim and heavy drinker who claimed to be inspired by an earlier blackmailer, but had wanted to do it better. He lived in Cambridge Road North in west London, quite close to the centre of the west London cluster of bomb locations. His ex-wife lived in the south east of the capital, providing the second base from which he could move out to leave his bombs, again as revealed in the geographical analysis.

Pearce thought he could remain hidden, moving invisibly around the metropolis. But he underestimated how visible we are all now becoming on the radar of electronic databases.

THE NEW RADAR

150 years ago people first mapped the spread of disease to show its source. Now we can map the spread of criminal contagion across a district, a city or a country. It is even possible to map the spread of contagion from one criminal to another, helping to see who is at the centre of this map, with a leading role, and who is at the edge, and more vulnerable to police investigation. Providing an account of how that works is another book.[4] But what all these developments have in common is policing that interprets the virtual shapes and patterns to find criminals in the labyrinths of new information.

Geographical profiling software can allow us to turn our radar onto this sea of crime to see where offenders are most likely to be lurking. This can then be used to search through police databases for known offenders or to set up surveillance. These are early days for this new era of detective work, but if the results in practice are only a tenth of the results we have achieved in our researches,[5] they will still have a dramatic impact on the detection of crimes, running through the full alphabet of villainy from arson and burglary through extortion and kidnapping and on to murder, rape and even terrorism.

But as our methods become subtler, and the technology more widespread, there is a danger that we will be drowned by information. We need systems that sort through this sea of data, as has been seen by police forces around the world. Major inquiries, especially if they have been unsuccessful, become the motor for developing new systems. The Yorkshire Ripper inquiry gave rise to HOLMES and CATCHEM. The South Auckland rapist investigation led to the creation of a new unit with associated databases. John House was able to establish a suspect prioritisation system as a result of the detection and conviction of Garrett Young.[6]

In North America it took the death in the early '80s of at least fifty young women and girls to spur on the development of a new system. They disappeared and were found dead in and around the Green River, south of Seattle. The location of the crimes points clearly to the Green River Killer residing in the area at their centre, and a man from that location is now coming to trial twenty years on. In that time the need to be able to record and analyse murders in the north-west of the USA and to have a good record of possible criminals gave rise to the unique Homicide Investigation and Tracking System, HITS.[7] The great breakthrough in this system, which is being established slowly around the world, is that it links crimes with known criminals.

Most police information is stored in two very separate systems. One deals with the crimes that have occurred; these are often recorded purely for administrative purposes, to be able to produce the official statistics on numbers of different types of crime. This data is notoriously inaccurate because of the many problems of deciding exactly what type of crime has been committed, and also because of the more fundamental problem that few people join the police force to fill in forms: the data collection is often done under duress. This problem can be so bad that I have even seen notices in police stations listing the fines police officers will suffer if particular forms are not completed appropriately.

A quite distinct set of information, usually, is that held on suspects and convicted offenders. This is stored for legal reasons, typically in relation to court processes. It often has very limited information on the offender, and even that is not entirely correct all the time.

Yet, as we have seen over and over again, there is a distinct relationship between the crimes a person commits and other aspects of that person. The most important relationship is that between where the crimes are committed and where the offender has his base. Getting information about offenders' bases and their offence locations together into one integrated computer system remains one of the most elementary and significant challenges facing anyone doing research in this area. It is a challenge that many police investigation teams still do not even attempt.

The HITS team is some way along this road, although budgetary constraints and aging software limit how far they can travel. Their mission, though, is to collect all the homicide cases in the state of Washington and compare them with each other to see if there is any linkage between the cases. HITS not only houses the homicide cases but also the rape cases, especially those involving strangers. Part of the problem the system is set up to deal with is that police agencies often do not communicate with each other as well as they should. The HITS team therefore have a territory within the state of Washington over which they actively pursue information on cases. They contact the police agencies, talk to the detectives that do the work and develop a rapport with them; this enables them to put investigators in touch with each other.

In their database they also have information on offenders, including registered sex offenders, as required by state law, and details of many other people who have committed a wide variety of crimes, stored with information on residential locations. This allows multi-layered searches, which can start from the details of the crimes.

A search that was run for me to illustrate the process and show just how unusual the Green River killings were involved looking at homicides of females over the last five years. This search started by identifying 2,900 female homicides in the whole database. Of these 844 had happened since 1995. By looking for younger women, say those born after 1983, the system produced 112 names. Of these sixteen had taken place in open areas. Nine of those had been solved.

By looking through the file of the people convicted of these crimes it is possible to examine suspect information and characteristics – any scars, marks, or tattoos – as well as the addresses of any places where they may have lived. There is also information on whether any of these convicted killers were near the scenes of the unsolved crimes. This can be drawn from credit cards, or phone tolls if they were truckers, which a lot of them were. Any kind of a trucking log, bank statements or police reports are recorded. So in a serial murder investigation, a time line would typically be useful for finding other cases that could be associated with that suspect. In the US, where access to personal information is often easier than under British law, college records or even medical information can be integrated into these databases. In some cases the computer mapping information available is so detailed that investigators can even call up pictures of the insides of buildings.

All this information is helping to reduce the anonymity of offenders, enabling police forces around the world to search for criminals in this alternative, electronic reality. The availability of computerised information is also creating new challenges for police investigators and the crime analysts who support them. The task is no longer one of picking a good suspect from a pool of local knowledge, or even being aware of those subtle cues that police officers claim will enable them to recognise the culprit when they knock on his door. Many detectives now, and increasingly into the future, will not be pounding the beat keeping an eye out for dodgy characters; nor will they be cruising in patrol cars trying to find suspects on the street who match the photofit pictures they have been issued.

Detectives of the future will surely be cruising their beats in cyberspace looking for criminals, much as they do today on the streets of our cities. Many countries now have computer systems that can read number plates off CCTV pictures and search for the owner of the car or simply keep a record of the journeys the car makes. It is possible to take the electoral register and link it to maps and satellite photography.

The Japanese police have a system that allows the police to call up a map or satellite picture of a street with the names of every person who lives in every house superimposed. Links to car registrations, telephone numbers and other personal information are also possible. They have even mapped the areas of mobile-telephone transmitters to locate a building in which hostage-takers, using their cell phones, were hiding.

As our invisibility is lost to the radar that searches electronic databases there is the risk of eroding the privacy of law-abiding citizens and our liberties in a free society. Such searches are open to abuse or, even more likely, harmfully incompetent misuse; so careful control of access to private information about us is an essential protection of our democratic liberties. But this radar cannot be turned off. Never again can we hide in the anonymity of the city as we once could.

The importance of pulling back the veil of secrecy that makes criminals invisible was revealed most clearly on 11 September 2001. The first act in response to that outrage was to search the banking information systems for the accounts of those involved, freezing many millions of pounds that could have funded other terrorist acts.

Historically we treated strangers with suspicion, and crime was probably easier to detect. As society became more complex offenders became invisible strangers who were extremely difficult to pin-point. In our new electronic age we are all becoming visible again, but less in the reality of places on the surface of the earth than in that other parallel world of electronic records, databases, videotape and computer memories. Criminals who would have been hidden in the past are also becoming visible in this virtual world, provided we know how to look for them.

This parallel world is man-made, and is thus still infused with the foibles of humankind. It is still a landscape that can be mapped and searched; it will have busy areas that many people visit, like commuters. Many people will stay local to what and where they know, like marauding criminals who commit many assaults travelling out from their bases. There will be dominant routes through this world that we can keep track of and watch. The new technologies demand new ways of thinking about human actions.

Reading this radar involves more than just joining up the dots. It is a matter of understanding the drama they show that the criminal is living. Is he set on a path of personal destruction, forging a plight he sees as a heroic tragedy? Many of those criminals, like Fred West and Barry George, whose actions are focused on a particular person in a highly localised setting, seem to cast themselves in these catastrophic roles. For them the victims take on a particular significance that is absorbed into their personal world.

Other criminals, like Peter Sutcliffe or Joe Thompson, who more typically maraud out from a base to find vulnerable people, attacking them where they find them, have a less centred mission, although their home still usually acts as a hub for their activities. The world makes little sense to these people. They live in ironic relationship to its meaninglessness, taking what they want. Their victims become vehicles for expressing their rage or satisfying their lusts.

The most extreme group are those who travel far and wide. They seek out opportunities themselves as if they believe they are on a heroic adventure. Each potential victim is an episode in their quest. In the most extreme cases, like Robert Black, or Marc Dutroux and his associates, these men devote their lives to finding the opportunities for their crimes. They seek jobs that allow them the freedom to travel, or are involved in a network of criminal activity that supports the malicious core of abduction and murder. Or they may even, as in the case of the Washington snipers, create a vehicle specifically to allow them to carry out their murders and move on unseen.

The hunting styles of predatory offenders have been a topic for consideration by police forces, but there has not been any detailed consideration of the styles of police investigations used to find these violent men. 'Leaving no stone unturned' is a noble but inefficient way of searching for particular insects. Their haunts and feeding habits need to be understood in order to lift the appropriate rock carefully.

Police investigators have to build a picture in their minds of the killer and his actions. Mapping murder for them consists of creating both a mental map that attempts to reconstruct in the imagination the killer's psychological journey and an actual map of where a crime and related activities, or a series of crimes, have occurred. The real science of profiling consists of building up an understanding of how these two maps relate to each other. What sense can be made of the places in which a criminal gouges his marks in the lives of others? Can they help us to understand his own inner journey? It is at this interface between the detective's quest and the criminal's journey that profiling, especially geographical profiling, has its impact.

This means that the most effective police investigations match themselves to the style of the offender, although rather paradoxically they may be more effective when they counteract rather than mirror it. The military style of the Washington snipers gave rise to a military response, which did not appear to prevent a single killing. The snipers were caught by following the trail of particular clues that were mainly made available through contact with them. Sometimes a bloodhound will be more effective than an army.

There are many descriptions[8] of what makes a good detective. They read like the recipe for a superhero, or even a god. He is required to have 'an abundant store of energy . . . a high grade of real self-denying power . . . absolute accuracy . . .' and a knowledge of science, combined with the ability to read people and form cogent judgements quickly. All these qualities see the criminal investigator as a lone protagonist against the evil villain. Yet what is clear from the cases we have considered is that police work is always teamwork. To offer up the lone investigator, in the mould of some fictional thriller, is to ignore the humanity of investigators and the way they gain their results through co-operation with their colleagues, and indeed often lose their criminal through lack of co-operation.

An increasingly important part of that team is the analysis of the patterns of actions of known offenders, and their relation to what is known about a set of crimes. This is not a matter of handing over detection to the computers, which are then treated as gods, but rather a recognition that there is a crucial role for informed human beings in tackling crime. Those earthbound people will be greatly assisted, though, by having access to the virtual world in which our contemporary presence again finds some identity. Working together, the police and behavioural scientists are learning to uncover the secret world of criminals as it is revealed in the virtual reality in which no one is invisible forever.

Apollo thus: 'To combat for mankind ill suits the wisdom
of celestial mind:
For what is man? Calamitous by birth,
They owe their life and nourishment to earth;
Like yearly leaves, that now, with beauty crown'd
Smile on the sun; now, wither on the ground.
To their own hands commit the frantic scene,
Nor mix immortals in a cause so mean . . .'

The Iliad Book XXI, translated by Pope

POSTSCRIPT

I chose to finish the book with a slightly unexpected quote from the *Iliad* because I wanted to lead the thinking reader to appreciate that it is not possession by the devil or some other evil spirit that leads to human conflict. It is the very essence of being a person that means that from time to time aggression will flare up and, on occasion, lead to fatal violence. Paradoxically, it is this integral significance of violence within humanity that the creation of civilisation, the great achievement of *homo sapiens*, is shaped to manage. The examination and re-examination of acts of murderous violence, and the endless debate of how to control and manage it, is thus one of the most important ways in which society evolves.

It is this central significance to our lives that leads violent crimes, most especially murderous assaults against strangers, to create shock waves that echo for years, sometimes generations, after their initial impact. Many of the murders dealt with in this book still find their way into the news from time to time. Many of their consequences are still unfolding. Sometimes aspects of a murder that were hidden at the time of the killer's arrest are revealed in court proceedings, subsequent appeals and the inevitable book of the murder that key players go on to write. These may help us understand more of why a killer did what he or she did, but quite often they only deepen the mystery that so frequently shrouds this most human of crimes.

The 'beltway snipers' who traumatised America in October 2002, killing ten people, each with single rifle shots, showed how limited is the expertise on which the police draw to help them catch such maverick criminals. Experts were proved to have been wrong here from the start, as profilers pegged the sniper as a single white man, when in fact there were two, both of them black. People who claimed expertise insisted to anyone who would listen that the sniper would be a lone white male in his 20s and would live near the victims. Reports from the crime scenes drew police attention to a white van as the main clue. Malvo, seventeen years old, and Muhammad, 41, lived in Tacoma, and drove a blue Chevrolet Caprice sedan, in which they were more or less living at the time. The 'experts' had not tried to understand the message that was inherent in the *locations* of the crimes. They had assigned the simple-minded classification of 'serial killer' to the shootings and then taken off the shelf the even more naïve 'profile' of such killers. A 'profile' that does not even apply consistently to the sort of sex-crazed predator that Hollywood enjoys.

After their arrest it emerged that Malvo and Muhammad had been trying to extort $10 million as part of their rampage, but this did not really explain why they chose their own particular route as a source of income. It seems far more likely that this was an afterthought once they became aware of the huge impact their killings were having. What emerged after their arrest that gave more insight into their evolving personal narratives was the history of the crimes with which they were probably associated. As with so many criminals that attract public attention for what seems like a carefully planned series of crimes, in which little forensic evidence is left, their earlier criminal activities provided both the psychological breeding ground for their crimes and the forensic evidence that led to their capture. A number of robberies in Louisiana, Alabama, Georgia and Washington State involving shooting, that occurred months before the beltway murders, have been linked to Malvo and Muhammad. The police were even able to identify a tree stump that the snipers used for target practice and which provided forensic remains, hardly a clue that a thoughtful serial killer would leave.

In these earlier crimes a tragedy unfolds of two violent criminals aware of the power of their weaponry and their ability to avoid capture if they keep moving. Their narrative is shaped by the inability of law enforcement agencies to stop them immediately after their early crimes. The final acts of their drama were fuelled by the ignorance that blinded commentators and investigators to the psychological processes revealed by the patterns of beltway shootings on a map.

In the remarkable culture that is the present day United States, the impact of such devastating crimes reverberates for many years because of the legal processes the killings generate. The cost to the US judicial system of a series of violent crimes which cross state boundaries cannot be overestimated. The millions of dollars that Malvo and Muhammad demanded must already have been far exceeded by lawyers' fees and all the related legal paraphernalia. Both men have received a death sentence, but many more trials for related cases and many appeals against this ruling will continue to bring the men and their crimes to public attention, even when, sadly, the names of their victims and how their families' lives were destroyed are long forgotten.

In the case of Justin Porter the legal process continues to be drawn out, in part because he was seventeen years old at the time of his offences so there is debate about whether he should be tried as a juvenile or an adult. The latter could lead him to a death sentence; the former could, in an extreme decision, give rise to parole. So there is much for his lawyers to play for.

One matter they have been dwelling on is Porter's measured IQ. Five years after his campaign of crimes around Las Vegas he was assessed as having an IQ of 78. This is low enough to make him the class dunce in any normal school but still comfortably above the level that would have him identified as 'learning disabled' and thus in need of considerable special educational support. In the curiosities of the legal process the argument is not whether he had the intellectual ability to understand what he was doing when he committed his crimes. There is no doubt that he was all too aware of the implications of his acts. The courts are more concerned with whether he understands the legal process to which he is being subjected, including the initial caution the police gave him when he was arrested.

The emerging character of Justin Porter and the challenges to the legal system he poses have some interesting parallels to the conviction of Barry George for the murder of Jill Dando. The evidence is much stronger in the case of Porter but an understanding of why he did what he did is just as elusive. In the Las Vegas case the police were able to identify Porter very quickly because they got a clear fix on where he was based from their geographical analyses. That must have helped them to obtain a great deal of solid evidence as well as circumstantial support for his guilt. In George's case the delay in bringing him to justice has meant that doubts are still raised over his guilt.

The complexities of these cases pale into insignificance in comparison to the extended trial that unfolded around the conviction of Marc Dutroux. On 14 June 2004, at the age of 47, eight years after Dutroux's arrest, the jury were sent out to deliberate at the end of a three-month trial. The jurists were required to review approximately 400,000 pages of evidence, including the testimonies of over 500 witnesses. In addition the judge gave them 243 questions to evaluate. Three days later he was sentenced to life imprisonment. Should he ever receive parole, he will be sent back to prison by the Belgian government.

His wife, Michelle Martin, 44, a school teacher who had knowingly let two girls starve to death in the dungeon Dutroux had built, was sentenced to thirty years for kidnapping. Michel Nihoul, 62, whom many people thought was the money and brains behind Dutroux's kidnapping network, was acquitted of kidnapping, but convicted of smuggling drugs and people into Belgium and counts of fraud. He was sentenced to five years' imprisonment.

A fourth person had also emerged in the police investigations: Michel Lelievre, an accomplice who helped Dutroux to seize the hapless victims. At the age of 32 he was sentenced to 25 years for kidnapping and drug dealing.

The spread of abductions across Belgium spoke of an organised network. The details of the crimes themselves made it clear that more than one person was involved. Dutroux had buried one accomplice, Bernard Weinstein, in his garden. Three others were convicted in relation to the kidnappings and murders. The question therefore has to be asked, whether these five people were the only ones involved in these crimes that were so destabilising to Belgium, and so incompetently investigated. It seems remarkably unlikely that others were not aware of what this gang was doing. As I have reported in earlier pages, on more than one occasion informants indicated to the police that Dutroux and his associates were involved in serious crimes. Doubtless the extent to which the activities of this gang were known to the authorities, condoned or possibly supported, will eventually emerge. Crimes like these never totally disappear from the public imagination. Nor should they.

All of these cases return us to the pressing need, in present day, developed societies, for effective management of the vast amount of information that is now held on every citizen and the even greater amount of information held on anyone who has passed through the courts as an offender. Recently, from running training courses with senior police officers in India, I have been struck by how much this is a need of developed societies. For, although the principles I have discussed earlier still hold remarkably well in that very different context, the ways in which the police can make use of them are likely to be different. As was pointed out to me, the density of the Indian population and the existence of many people barely above subsistence level, whose mode of living keeps them out on the streets at all hours, means that for most crimes there is usually someone who has seen something of relevance to the investigation. They do not need closed-circuit television to watch their streets because there will nearly always be human eyes that have made sense of what happened. The task of the Indian police is to locate witnesses and to find a way of enabling them to help investigations. Once they have that information then the principles and processes I have been describing will help them to make sense of the material and to structure their investigation more intelligently.

On the much quieter streets of Europe and North America the challenge of obtaining information and using it effectively now relies increasingly, and much more than in developing countries, on the effective utilisation of electronically stored information. So it is exciting to note that since writing this book British police forces have started to fund major developments in computerised systems to help understand the patterns of crime. In one project in which I am closely involved, a system is being developed that I call iOPS (Interactive Offender Profiling System). The cost of developing this system runs into six figures and, as I write, about a dozen people are working on bringing it to life.

The central basis of iOPS is to allow the police to explore the information they have on crimes and criminals directly on a map. In the past it has been a remarkably laborious process, even with computer software like Dragnet available, to put crimes onto a map, then to carry out the sort of geographical analysis that would indicate where the offender might be based and, finally, to search for possible offenders within police systems. Now, in iOPS, there already exists a set of computer programmes that allows all these stages, as well as one or two intervening ones I have not mentioned, to be done at the click of a mouse button. The very existence of such software is changing the way police investigators think about recording crime and carrying out investigations. The emerging success stories that will eventually come out of the applications of systems like iOPS will change the whole nature of criminal investigations. I think that the decline in recent years in the number of reported serial murder cases in Britain, as well as the number of series of rapes of strangers, is a consequence of the great improvement in the way police use their computer-based systems to carry out investigations, as much as it is a consequence of the parallel improvements in how police conduct interviews or use forensic science.

Is it too much to expect that in the future people like Dutroux, Robert Black, and Fred West will find it much more difficult to perpetrate their crimes over many years without detection or apprehension? Will our ability to use our computerised mapping systems to follow in killers' footsteps help us to get to them before they kill and kill again? It is to be hoped so. But a further hope is that our understanding of how killers choose their targets and move around will give us further insights into the personal narratives they are building for themselves. They will assist our understanding of this most puzzling, yet most human, of frailties; the killing of one person by another.

NOTES

The following notes are intended as guidance for those who wish to study matters further.

I have assumed that with modern, Internet-based search engines, more obvious follow up can be made over the World Wide Web. Where the notes refer to books or papers listed in the Bibliography only the author and date are given.

CHAPTER 1: HUNTING KILLERS

1 There is extensive coverage of the Washington Sniper on the web, but I found the *Guardian* website especially helpful.
2 Canter (1995).
3 Canter and Gregory (1994).
4 A simple test of this idea is to relate the shortest distance offenders travel from their base with the largest. In a number of studies we have done the correlation between these two values is remarkably high (cf Canter and Larkin 1993, Lundrigan and Canter 2001).
5 Canter, 1995.
6 Hickey, 2001.
7 Canter and Larkin, 1993.

CHAPTER 2: DISTRACTIONS OF CELEBRITY

1 I am grateful to Chief Superintendent Hamish Campbell for the full, frank and honest way he has been prepared to discuss his investigation with me. Any errors of fact or interpretation in this chapter, though, are entirely my fault.
2 This examination of 'places' is drawn from Canter, 1977.
3 Perkins, DN, *The Mind's Best Work*, London, Harvard University Press, 1981.
4 Although I am reliably informed that there are plenty of female senior investigating officers, I have yet to meet one, to see one in a television appeal about a serious crime, or to read about one in an account of an investigation. I am therefore using the male pronoun to refer to SIOs in the

hope that any concern this causes will make female SIOs more obvious in the future.

5 Soothill, K, Peelo, M, Francis, B, Pearson, J and Ackerley, E, 'Homicide And The Media: Identifying The Top Cases', in *The Times Howard Journal of Criminal Justice* 2002.

6 Holden, R, *A Facet theory Approach to Homicide Crime Scene Analysis*, 1994. Unpublished Mphil dissertation, University of Surrey.

CHAPTER 3: THE SIGNIFICANCE OF PLACE

1 Wiener, RL, Richmond, TL, Seib, HM, Rauch, SM and Hackney, AA, 'The psychology of telling murder stories: Do we think in scripts, exemplars, or prototypes?' *Behavioral Sciences and the Law*, 20, pp. 119–139.

2 Burke, K, *A Rhetoric of Motives*, Berkeley, University of California Press, 1969.

3 Byford, L *The Yorkshire Ripper Case, review of the police investigation*, London, HMSO, 1981.

4 Macpherson, W, *The Stephen Lawrence Enquiry*, London, The Stationery Office, Cm 4262-I, 1999.

5 Snook, B, *Serial Crime and Distance: An Analysis of Serial Offender Spatial Behaviour*, unpublished PhD Thesis, The University of Liverpool, 2003.

CHAPTER 4: CRIME IN ITS PLACE

1 John McVicar's book *Dead on Time*, Blake, London, 2002, was a useful if rather idiosyncratic source of background information on the investigation into Jill Dando's death and the trial of Barry George.

CHAPTER 5: MEMOIR OF A KILLER

1 I am grateful to Freya Newman and Kate Moser for their help in preparing the text of West's journal and their insightful comments on it.

2 The following books have been by my elbow throughout writing this chapter: Howard Sounes – *Fred And Rose: The full story of Fred and Rose West and the Gloucester House of Horrors*, Warner Books, 1995; Geoffrey Wansell – *An Evil Love: The Life of Frederick West*, Headline, 1996.

3 The Confessions of St Augustine are available online at www.ccel.org/a/augustine/confessions/confessions.html.
4 Keppel, RD, *The Riverman: Ted Bundy and I Hunt for the Green River Killer*, Pocket Books, 1995.
5 Ian Brady, *The Gates Of Janus: An Analysis of Serial Murder by England's Most Hated Criminal*, US, Feral House, 2001.
6 Gordon Burn, *Happy Like Murderers*, London, Faber and Faber, 1998, p. 144.

CHAPTER 6: THE SUSTAINING WEB

1 Williams, JMG, *Cry Of Pain: Understanding Suicide and Self Harm*, London, Penguin, 1997.

CHAPTER 7: DARKNESS VISIBLE

1 Brantingham and Brantingham, 1981.
2 Norris, J, *Jeffrey Dahmer*, London, Constable, 1992.
3 Masters, B, *The Shrine of Jeffrey Dahmer*, London, Hodder and Stoughton, 1993.

CHAPTER 8: A FRAUGHT INVESTIGATION

1 A significant portion of this chapter started life as a foreword for the second edition of Shirley Harrison's book. Her generosity in sharing with me her knowledge and experience of the diary is greatly appreciated. Her book *The Diary of Jack the Ripper*, Blake, 1993, was my main source of reference. Bernard Ryan's *The Poisoned Life of Mrs Maybrick*, Penguin, 1977, was another valuable resource.
2 Cornwell, P, *Portrait of a Killer: Jack the Ripper Case Closed*, The Putnam Publishing Group, 2002.
3 Charles Hamilton's 1991 book *The Hitler Diaries: Fakes that Fooled the World*, The University Press of Kentucky, is a delightfully thorough account of this whole débâcle.
4 Graham, AE and Emmas, C, *The Last Victim: The extraordinary life of Florence Maybrick, the wife of Jack the Ripper*, London, Headline, 1999.
5 Aked et al. (1999).
6 Harrison, S, *The Diary of Jack the Ripper: The American Connection*, London, Blake, 2003.

7 Wason, PC, 1960, 'On the failure to eliminate hypotheses in a conceptual task', *Quarterly Journal of Experimental Psychology*, 12, pp. 129–140.

8 Feldman, PH, *Jack the Ripper: The Final Chapter*, London, Virgin Books, 2002.

9 The general explanation of how horoscopes, astrologists, psychics, graphologists and the like are apparently so effective whilst being completely invalid is known in social psychology as 'The Barnum Effect'. An early overview of studies of this phenomenon is given in Dickson, JE and Kelly, IE, 1985, 'The Barnum Effect in Personality Assessment: A Review of the Literature', *Psychological Reports*, 57, pp. 367–382.

10 Morris, R, *Forensic Handwriting Identification: Fundamental Concepts and Principles*, London, Academic Press, 2000.

CHAPTER 9: PROFILING THE DIARIST

1 Gaskins, D, *Final Truth: The Autobiography of a Serial Killer*, Titan Books, 1993.

2 Tulley, B, 'Statement Validation', in Canter, D and Alison, L (eds.) *Interviewing and Deception*, Aldershot, Dartmouth 1999, pp. 83–104.

CHAPTER 10: MAPPING THE MURDERS

1 Rumbelow, D, *The Complete Jack the Ripper*, London, Penguin, 1988.

2 Ryan, B, *The Poisoned Life of Mrs Maybrick*, London, Penguin 1977.

3 Lundrigan, S and Canter, D, 2001.

4 Canter, D and Larkin, P, 1993.

5 Canter, D and Gregory, A, 1994.

6 James Tyler Kent, 1921, *Lectures on Homeopathic Materia Medica*, B Jain Publishers, New Delhi.

CHAPTER 11: LAS VEGAS SURVIVORS

1 Dan Helms's lively and informed contribution to this chapter is obvious. I am deeply grateful to him for all he has shared with me. He has now left the LVMPD for more academic pursuits.

2 www.jdi.ucl.ac.uk.

3 Canter, D, Coffey, T, Huntley, M, and Missen C (2000) – also see www.i-psy.com.

CHAPTER 12: CRIMINAL GRAVITY

1 Obituaries appeared on April 30 2003 in the main UK national broadsheets.

2 Kind, S, *The Sceptical Witness*, Hodology Ltd., for the Forensic Science Society, 1999, quotations taken from Chapter 6 – The Yorkshire Ripper, p. 71 onwards.

3 Canter, 1995.

4 Kind, S, 1987, 'Navigational ideas and the Yorkshire Ripper investigation', *Journal of Navigation*, 40, pp. 385–393.

5 Kind, S, 1987, *The Scientific Investigation of Crime, Forensic Science Services Ltd.*

6 Kind, S, *The Sceptical Witness*, Hodology Ltd. for the Forensic Science Society, 1999.

7 Canter, 1977.

8 Snow, J, *On the Mode of Communication of Cholera*, London, 1855.

9 Mizutani, F, 'Home range of leopards and their impact on livestock on Kenyan ranches', *Zoological Symposium*, 1993, 65, pp. 425–439.

10 Bromley, RJ, 'Trader Mobility in Systems of Periodic and Daily Markets', in DT Herbert and RJ Johnston (eds.) *Geography and the Urban Environment, Volume III*, 1988, pp. 132–174.

CHAPTER 13: MENTAL MAPS OF CRIME

1 Byford L, 1981, *The Yorkshire Ripper Case, review of the police investigation*, HMSO.

2 Canter, D, 1995.

3 Carrothers, GAP, 'An historical review of the gravity and potential concepts of human interaction', in PJ Ambrose (ed.) *Concepts in Geography*, 1969, London, Longmans, pp. 226–241.

4 Canter, D, Coffey, T, Huntley, M, and Missen C, 2000.

5 Rossmo, DK, 1993, 'Geographic Profiling: locating serial killers' in D Zahm and PF Cromwell (eds.) *Proceedings of the International Seminar on Environmental Criminology and Crime Analysis*, Florida Criminal Justice Executive Institute.

6 Canter, D and Gregory, A, 1994.

7 Canter, 1977.

8 I am extremely grateful to Per Stangeland for his willingness to share his important work on the Malaga rapist with me, to give me access to the maps he has prepared and to other material prior to publication. The map is published here with his permission, but any errors in their interpretation are mine.

CHAPTER 14: STEALING SEX

1 I am grateful to Detective Sergeant DB ('Chook') Henwood and Detective Inspector John Manning for the extremely thorough, full and frank accounts they have given me of all aspects of the investigations covered in this chapter. Any errors of fact or interpretation in this chapter, though, are entirely due to me. Although I got hold of Jan Corbett's book, *Caught by his Past*, after completing the chapter, I recommend it as a serious and thorough account of the investigation and of Jo Thompson's background. It is now out of print but was published by Tandem Press in 1996.

2 This is a composite of a number of rape statements in order to hide the distinct identity and experience of particular victims.

3 Some of this material is based on information at www.crime.co.nz as well as reports made available to me by the police.

4 Canter, D and Kirby, S, 1995.

5 Masters, W H, and Johnson, V E, and Kolodny, R C, *Human Sexuality* (5th edn.) 1995, HarperCollins.

6 Groth, AN, *Men who Rape*, New York, Plenum Press, 1979.

CHAPTER 15: 'I'VE BEEN WAITING FOR YOU GUYS'

1 Sherpherd, M, *Sherlock Holmes and the Case of Dr Freud*, London Tavistock Publications, 1985.

2 Klein, M, 'Offence specialisation and versatility among juveniles', *British Journal of Criminology*, 1984, 24, pp. 185–194.

CHAPTER 16: A PATH OF VIOLENCE AND TERROR

1 I am deeply indebted to Sergeant John House for all the help he has given me in preparing this chapter. Detective

Constable Rupert Heritage was working with me at the time we did the report to John House. For simplicity I have kept to the first person singular in describing our work at that time, but here, as so often with my work with the police in the late 1980s, it is impossible to separate Rupert's contribution from my own.

2 Barnard, M, Benson, C, Church, S, and Hart, G, 'Client Violence Against Prostitutes Working from Street and Off-Street Locations: A Three City Comparison', 2002, www.1.rhbnc.ac.uk.

3 The quotations are drawn from the transcripts from the Newfoundland Supreme Court.

CHAPTER 17: TRAVELLING OFFENDER
1 Lundrigan, P, and Canter, D, 2001.
2 Gebhard, PH, et al., 1965, p. 204.

CHAPTER 18: *VICTIMES DE PEDOPHILIE*
1 I am especially grateful to Donna Youngs for her assistance in preparing this chapter; Annemie Bulté at *Humo* Magazine, and Jo Boageart have been very helpful in providing in-depth background and commentary.

2 Canter, D, and Kirby, S, 1995.

3 Gebhard, PH et al., 1965, p. 54.

4 The Belgian police force has had some re-organisation since these weaknesses have been so openly revealed.

5 Rubin, Z and Peplau, LA, 'Who believes in a just world?', *Journal of Social Issues*, 1975, 31, pp. 65–89.

CHAPTER 19: A DESTRUCTIVE GEOGRAPHY
1 Lundrigan, P and Canter, D, 2001.
2 Blackburn, R, *The Psychology of Criminal Conduct*, Chichester, Wiley 1993 p. 83.
3 Drawn from the website material of investigative *Guardian* journalist, Olenka Frenkiel.

CHAPTER 20: FINDING A TRAVELLING KILLER
1 Anna Gekoski, www.crimelibaray.com/serial9/robert-black, Chapter 10.

2 Brian Marriner, 1999, *A New Century of Sex Killers* London, New Crime Library, p.259.

3 Bennell, C and Canter, D, 2002.

4 Canter, D, Missen, C, and Hodge, S, 'Are Serial Killers Special?' *Policing Today*, 1996, December, pp. 62–69.

5 Hickey, E, 2001.

6 I am grateful to Chuck Burton for this summary of his findings.

7 Chenery, S, Henshaw, C, and Pease, K, 'Illegal Parking in Disabled Bays: A Means of Offender Targetting', *Policing and Reducing Crime Briefing Note*, 1/99, London, Home Office, 1999.

8 Wyre, R and Tate, A, *The Murder of Childhood*, London, Penguin, 1996.

CHAPTER 21: BODILY VIOLATIONS

1 This chapter started life as an invited lecture to the Darwin lecture series on The Body at Darwin College, Cambridge. An earlier version of it was first published as Canter, 2002.

2 Chandler, R, *The Long Goodbye*, Harmondsworth, Penguin, 1951.

3 Jones, S, *Understanding Violent Crime*, Milton Keynes, Open University, 2000.

4 Katz, J, *The Seductions of Crime: Moral and sensual attractions in doing evil*, New York, Basic Books, 1988.

5 Bolitho, W, *Murder for Profit*, New York, Garden City.

6 Thayer, S, 'The Psychology of Touch', *Journal of non-verbal behavior – special issue*, 1986.

7 Canter, D, 2000.

8 Canter, D and Kirby, S, 1995.

CHAPTER 22: INVISIBLE CRIMINALS

1 White, RC, 'The relation of felonies to environmental factors in Indianapolis', *Social Forces*, 1932, 10, p. 459.

2 I am grateful to Detective Sergeant Bob Stapleton, now retired, for his guidance on the Wadland case.

3 Cooper S, *Welcome to the Mardi Gra Experience*, 1999, London, Blake.

4 Canter, D and Alison, L, *The Social Psychology of Crime*, Aldershot, Dartmouth, 2000.

5 Canter, D, Coffey, T, Huntley, M and Missen C, 2000.

6 House, J C, 'Towards a practical application of Offender Profiling: The RNC's Criminal Suspect Prioritisation System', in JL Jackson and DA Bekerian (eds.) *Offender Profiling: Theory, Research and Practice*, Chichester, Wiley 1997, pp. 177–190.

7 I am grateful to the HITS team for their assistance and to Robert Keppel for his guidance and support.

8 Gros, H, 'Certain qualities essential to an investigator', *Criminal Investigation: A Practical Textbook for Magistrates, Police Officers and Lawyers*, London, Sweet and Maxwell, 1962, pp. 15–19.

SELECTED BIBLIOGRAPHY

The following books provide further background reading to the more academic issues raised in *Mapping Murder*. Where there are specific citations to these works in a particular chapter this is given in the notes, the book being referenced simply by author and date.

Ainsworth, Peter, *Offender Profiling and Crime Analysis*, Devon, Willan, 2001.

Brantingham, PJ and Brantingham, P, *Environmental Criminology*, Beverley Hills, Sage, 1981.

Burke, Roger Hopkins, *An Introduction to Criminological Theory*, Devon, Willan, 2001.

Canter, David, *The Psychology of Place*, London, Architectural Press, 1977.

Canter, David, *Criminal Shadows*, London, HarperCollins, 1995.

Downs, RM, and Stea, D, *Maps in Minds: Reflections on Cognitive Mapping*, New York, Harper and Row, 1977.

Gebhard, PH, Gagnon, JH, Pomeroy, WB and Christenson, CV, *Sex Offenders: An Analysis of Types*, New York, Harper and Row, 1965.

Frye, Northrop, *Anatomy of Criticism*, New Jersey, Princeton University Press, 1957.

Hickey, E, *Serial Murderers and Their Victims*, California, Wadsworth, 2001.

Kind, Stuart, *The Sceptical Witness: Concerning the Scientific Investigation of Crime against a Human Background*, Harrogate, The Forensic Science Society for Hodology Ltd., 1999.

Lee, Raymond M, *Unobtrusive Measures in Social Research*, Buckingham, Open University Press, 2000.

A collection of 37 academic papers of general relevance is given in:

Canter, DV and Alison, LJ (eds.) *Criminal Detection and the Psychology of Crime*, Aldershot, Dartmouth, 1997.

The main technical/academic papers I have published of relevance to the present volume are listed below. In the notes that follow, they are referenced by author(s) and date.

Aked, JP, Canter, D, Sanford, AJ and Smith, N, 1999, 'Approaches to the Scientific Attribution of Authorship', *Offender Profiling Series Vol II, Profiling in Policy and Practice*, Aldershot, Ashgate, pp. 157–187.

Bennell, C, and Canter, D, 2002, 'Linking commercial burglaries by Modus Operandi: Tests using regression and ROC analysis', *Science and Justice*, 42, pp. 153–164.

Canter, D, 1983, 'Way-finding and Signposting: Penance or Prothesis?' In Easterby, R (ed.), *Information Design: The Design and Evaluation of Signs and Printed Material*, pp 245–264 Wiley, Chichester.

Canter, D, 1988, 'Action and Place: An Existential Dialectic', in Canter, D et al. (eds.) *Ethnoscapes: Current Challenges in the Environmental Social Sciences Volume 1 – Environmental Perspectives*, pp. 1–17 Aldershot, Avebury.

Canter, D, 1988a, 'To catch a rapist', *New Society*, 4 March, pp. 14–15.

Canter, D, 1989, 'Offender Profiling', *The Psychologist*, 2, pp. 12–16.

Canter, D, 1990, 'In Search of Objectives: An Intellectual Autobiography' in Altman I and Christensen, K (eds.) *Intellectual Histories in the Environment and Behavior Field (Human Behavior and Environment*, Volume 11, New York, Plenum.

Canter, D, 1990a, 'Understanding, Assessing and Acting in Places: Is an integrative framework possible?' in Garling, T and Evans, G (eds.) *Environmental Cognition and Action: An Integrated Approach*, New York, Oxford University Press, pp. 191–209.

Canter, D, 2000, 'Offender Profiling and Psychological Differentiation', *Journal of Criminal and Legal Psychology*, 5, pp. 23–46.

Canter, D, 2000a, 'Seven Assumptions for an Investigative Environmental Psychology' in S Wapner, J Dmick, T Yamamoto and H Minami (eds.) *Theoretical Perspectives in Environmental Behaviour Research: Underlying assumptions, research problems and methodologies*, New York, Plenum, pp. 191–206.

Canter, D, 2002, 'The Violated Body in Sweeney, S and Hodder, I, (eds.) *The Body*, Cambridge, Cambridge University Press, pp. 57–74.

Canter, D, Alison, LJ, Alison, E and Wentink, N, 2003, 'The Organized / Disorganized Typology of Serial Murder: Myth or Model?' *Psychology – Public Policy and Law*.

Canter, D and Alison, LJ, 2003, 'Converting Evidence Into Data: The use of Law Enforcement Archives as Unobtrusive Measurement', *The Qualitative Report*, June, 8, (2).

Canter, D, Bennell, C, Alison, LJ and Reddy, S, 2003, 'Differentiating Sex Offences: A Behaviourally Based Thematic Classification of Stranger Rapes', *Behavioral Sciences and Law*.

Canter, D, Coffey, T, Huntley, M and Missen C, 2000, 'Predicting Serial Killers' Home Base Using a Decision Support System', *Journal of Quantitative Criminology*, Vol 16, No 4.

Canter, D and Fritzon, K, 1998, 'Differentiating Arsonists: A model of fire setting actions and characteristics', *Legal and Criminal Psychology*, 3, pp. 73–96.

Canter, D and Gregory, A, 1994, 'Identifying the residential location of rapists', *Journal of the Forensic Science Society*, 34, pp. 169–175.

Canter, D and Heritage, R, 1990, 'A multivariate model of sexual offence Behaviour', *The Journal of Forensic Psychiatry* 1, (2) London, Routledge, pp. 185–212.

Canter, D and Hodge, S, 2000, 'Criminals' Mental Maps', in L S Turnball, E H Hendrix and B D Dent (eds.) *Atlas of Crime: Mapping the Criminal Landscape*, pp. 186–191, Oryz Press, Phoenix, Arizona.

Canter, D and Hodge, S, 1998, 'Victims of Male Sexual Assault', *Journal of Interpersonal Violence* 13, (2), Sage publications, pp. 222–239.

Canter, D Hughes, D, and Kirby, S, 1998, 'Paedophilia: Pathology, criminality, or both? The development of a multivariate model of offence behaviour in child sexual abuse', *The Journal of Forensic Psychiatry*, 9 (3), Routledge, pp. 532–555.

Canter, D and Kirby, S, 1995, 'Prior convictions of child molesters', *Journal of Science and Justice*, 35 (1), pp. 73–78.

Canter, D and Larkin, P, 1993, 'The environmental range of serial rapists', *Journal of environmental psychology*, 13, pp. 63–69.

Canter, D, Missen, C and Hodge, S, 1996, 'Are serial killers special? A case for special agents', *Policing Today* (1).

Canter, D, and Youngs, D, 2002, 'Beyond Offender Profiling: The need for an Investigative Psychology', in R Bull and D Carson (eds.) *Handbook of Psychology and Legal Contexts*, pp. 171–205.

Lundrigan, S, and Canter, D, 2001, 'A multivariate analysis of serial murderers' disposal site location choice' in *Journal of Environmental Psychology*, 21, Academic Press, pp. 423–432.

Snook, B, Canter, D, and Bennell, C, 2002, 'Predicting the home location of serial offenders: A preliminary profiling system of the accuracy of human judges with a geographic profiling system', in *Journal of Behavioral Sciences and the Law*, 20, pp. 109–118.

ACKNOWLEDGEMENTS

Mapping Murder started life because Chris Shaw and Channel Five saw fit to commission it as a six-part documentary series for me to present. Jennifer Wilson took up this baton and set in motion the production of the programmes. Together they provided the support, guidance and encouragement to get that show on the road. Nigel Swettenham developed my outlines into shooting scripts and then directed the programmes. He showed me how to tell stories on television and educated me, in lengthy late-night discussions whilst we were on location, about the value of reaching out to a wider audience. Much of what he put into those scripts has doubtless found its way into this book, as the roles of writer, presenter and director did, on occasion, run into each other.

At the University of Liverpool a number of people helped behind the scenes. Marion Lloyd was the main researcher for the television series and has maintained the task of helping me trace sources and check facts for this book. She has been unstinting and determined in pulling together and preparing the maps used in this book, in which she was assisted by Brenda Colbourne-Snook. Susan Giles has been very helpful in reviewing drafts of chapters, as has Maria Ioannou. Dr Donna Youngs provided an especially valuable running advice centre for me on all aspects of the book, always being ready to provide supportive and insightful comment at length on any aspects I was struggling with. Craig Bennell, Brent Snook and Karen Shaler have also been helpful with various aspects of this work. They will all recognise references to their studies and findings, sometimes without as thorough a citation as is probably deserved. My daughter Lily also draws on her considerable journalistic skills to advise me on many aspects of the text. I would also like to record my gratitude for the continuing support and encouragement from the people at Virgin Books, notably Kerri Sharp, and my agent Doreen Montgomery at Rupert Crew Ltd.

Various police officers, and others with special knowledge of the cases I have reviewed, have been especially helpful in commenting on cases and my accounts of them. Their details and my gratitude are recorded in the notes for each chapter.

All quotations from Chapter 7 are from the original manuscript purported to be by James Maybrick, and first published in *The Diary of Jack the Ripper: The Chilling Confessions of James Maybrick* by Shirley Harrison, published by Blake, 1998.

As ever, my wife has tolerated my preoccupation as the book became more and more of an obsession, managing somehow to keep me on the acceptable side of sanity.

INDEX

A55 Murders 237–41
American Constitution 288
Anatomy of Criticism (Northrop Frye) 19, 95, 157, 243
Atkinson, Patricia 166
autobiographies, criminal 64–6, 87–8

Bandara, Upadhya 167
Banks, John 212
Barrett, Anne 100–1, 120
Barrett, Michael 100–1
Behavioural Science Unit, St John's 237
Belgium, paedophilia in 244–54, 255–64, 319–20
Bianchi, Kenneth 64
Black, Robert 265–81, 313
'black holes' 83–93
Blank, Larry 1
Bolitho, William 284, 286
Brady, Ian 65
Bridges, Kenneth 5
Buchanan, James 'Sonny' 4
Bundy, Ted 65
Burton, Detective Inspector Chuck 271
Byford report 37, 161–2, 174

Campbell, Hamish 21, 23, 27, 31–2, 33, 34, 36, 37–42, 47–9
Canada 217–27
Carthy, Edward 238–40
CATCHEM system 271–2, 273–5
CBCA (Criteria Based Content Analysis) 111–12
CCTV 32, 34, 46, 311
celebrity, distractions of 20–33

Centre for Investigative Psychology, University of Liverpool 291
Chandler, Raymond 282–3
Chapman, Annie 125, 126, 127
Chapman, Jessica 27
Charles, Prince 51
Charlot, Pascal 5
cholera 158, 169–71
Clark, Deputy Chief Constable Hector 266, 267–8, 269, 272
Claxton, Marcella 166
coincidences, the plague of 38–40, 103
Columbine (1999) 3
'commuters' 180–2
computerized mapping 144, 150–2, 178–80, 320–1
Confessions of Augustine 19, 61
'confirmation bias' 103–5
Cooper, Carol Ann 90, 91
corrupt networks, Belgium 261–3
Cosey, Joseph 98
crime mapping 145–6
Crimewatch 21, 28, 35, 47
criminal autobiographies 64–6, 87–8
criminal journeys 10–13
Criminal Profiling Squad, New Zealand 215
Criminal Shadows (David Canter) 185, 195
Criteria Based Content Analysis (CBCA) 111–12

Dahmer, Jeffrey 84–5, 298
Daily Mail 20
Dando, Jill 20–43
Dardenne, Sabine 248–9, 257, 258, 260

Das Kapital (Karl Marx) 88
Delhez, Laetitia 248–9, 258, 262
Diana, Princess 46, 49
diaries *see* journals,
Diary of Jack the Ripper, The 97–108,
    109–21, 134–9
Dirty Harry 240
DNA evidence 48
    Garrett Young 227
    Joseph Thompson 192, 196, 203
    Justin Porter 149, 151, 154
'doorpushers' 141–4
Dragnet system 151, 178–80, 240,
    303, 304, 307
Duffy, John 12, 161, 174–8, 215
Dutroux, Marc 12, 244–54,
    255–64, 313, 319–20

Eddowes, Catherine 125, 126, 128,
    130
electronic information sources
    305–8
European Convention on Human
    Rights 288
expert testimony 234–7

Feldman, Paul 105
Fianda, Ms 237
Flemming, Dr 235
forensic science 25, 31–2, 151, 158,
    192, 269
Franklin, Linda 5
Freud, Sigmund 292
Frye, Northrop 19, 95, 157, 243

Gacy, John Wayne 83
'gang-Dutroux' 262
Gaskins, Pee-Wee 111
geographical profiles
    Fred West 92
    Joseph Thompson 213–15
    Mardi Gra bomber 307–8
    Railway Rapist 176
    Washington Snipers 8–10

Yorkshire Ripper 160–9
George, Barry 40–54, 313
Gough, Lynda 91
graphology 105–6
Green River Killings 65, 309, 310

Hamlet (William Shakespeare) 157
handwriting experts 105–6
Harper, Sarah 268–9, 274
Harrison, Shirley 98, 102, 104–7,
    116, 135
Helms, Dan 141–4, 147–55, 180
Henry IV part I (William
    Shakespeare) 243
Henwood, Detective Sergeant 188,
    191–2, 194–5, 199, 203, 205,
    206, 215
Heritage, Detective Constable
    Rupert 174–5
Herkes, David 265
Hill, Jacqueline 167
'Hillside Strangler' 64
'Hitler Diaries' 98, 109
HITS (Homicide Investigation and
    Tracking System) 309–10
Hogg, Caroline 265–81
HOLMES system 269–70
'home,' comforts of 83–93, 279
Home Office Central Research
    Establishment 158
Homeopathic Materia Medica (Dr
    James Tyler Kent) 136
Homicide 6
Homicide Investigation and
    Tracking System (HITS)
    309–10
House, John 217–18, 220, 222–7,
    237
Hubbard, Shirley 90
Hughes, Richard 34
Huntley, Malcolm 179

Iliad, The 315, 316
incest 206, 207–8

information overload 29–31
Institute of Sex Research, Indiana 236
iOPS (Interactive Offender Profiling System) 320–1
Ireland, Henry 70, 98

Jack the Ripper 11–12, 96–108, 109–21, 122–39, 256
Jackson, Emily 166
Jamelske, John 85–6
Japanese police force 311–12
Jill Dando Institute for Crime Science 146
Johnson, Conrad 5
Jordan, Jean 167
Journal of Environmental Psychology 19, 95, 157, 243
Journal of Navigation 163
journals
    Fred West 54–81, 87–8, 110–11
    'Hitler Diaries' 98, 109
    Jack the Ripper 97–108, 109–21, 134–9
'just world-belief' 251

Katz, Jack 283
Keller, Jerry 147
Kelly, Mary Jane 125, 126, 129
Kent, Dr James Tyler 136
Keppel, Bob 41
Kind, Dr Stuart 129, 158–69, 174, 178, 180, 185
Koren, Anna 105–6
Kujau, Konrad 98

Ladha, Dr 235
Lambreks, Eefje 247–8, 250, 258
Lantz, Ronald 1
Las Vegas 141–55, 318–19
Lawrence enquiry 38
Leach, Barbara 167
Lejeune, Julie 246–54, 258, 263
Lelievre, Michel 319

Letts, Bill 70–1, 72, 73–5
Letts, Glenys 52, 70
Levin, Brian 6
Lewis-Rivera, Ann 5
libraries, the value of 185
Lindhal, Mary 6
Lizin, Anne-Marie 261–2
Long, Maureen 166
Long Goodbye, The (Raymond Chandler) 282–3
Louf, Regina 263
Love, Debbie 147–8, 152–4

Malaga Rapist 183–5, 275, 302
Malvo, John Lee 1–17, 316–17
Manning, Detective Inspector John 187, 194, 199
Mansfield, Michael 49–50
Manson, Charles 111
maps
    Barry George's area of activity 44
    cholera in Soho, 1853 170
    Fred West's victims 90
    Jack the Ripper's victims 126
    Las Vegas crimes 151
    Malaga Rapist 184
    Marc Dutroux's abductions 258
    Mardi Gra bomb locations 307
    Railway Rapist 177
    Robert Black's abductions and murders 274
    Simon Wadland's telephone calls 304
    South Auckland rapes 200
    Washington Snipers 4
    Yorkshire Ripper's Crimes 166
'marauders' 180–2
Marchal, An 247–8, 250, 258
Mardi Gra bomber 22, 305–8
Martin, James D. 4
Martin, Michelle 250, 319
Marx, Karl 88
Maxwell, Susan 265–81

Maybrick, Florence 96–7, 100, 104–5, 118, 135–6
Maybrick, James 96–108, 109–21, 122, 134–9
McCann, Wilma 166
McCrary, Gregg 6
McDonald, Jayne 166
McFall, Anna 54, 55, 63, 66–8, 76–7, 78
media pressure 26–9, 194
memoirs, Fred West 54–81, 87–8, 110–11
mental maps 23–4, 151, 182–5, 257, 302, 303–5, 313–14
Meyers, Dean Harold 5
'Midland Triangle' 268
Millward, Vera 167
Milwaukee murders 84–5
MO (modus operandi) 189–91
Moore, Marilyn 167
Moore, Peter 237–41
Moors Murderer 65
Moose, Chief 2
Mott, Juanita 90
Muhammad, John 1–17, 316–17
Mulcahy, David 176, 178
Murder for Profit (William Bolitho) 284, 286
mutilation, symbolism of 295–6

National Institute of Justice (US) 141, 145
New Zealand rapes 187–98, 199–216
Nichols, Mary Anne 125, 126, 127
Nickell, Rachell 21
Nihoul, Jean Michel 262, 263, 319
Nilsen, Dennis 83–4

Ogden, Howard 60–1
Operation Park 194–5, 199–216
Owens, Caroline 90

paedophilia, Belgium 244–54, 255–64, 319–20
Partington, Lucy 90, 91–2
Pearce, Edgar 22, 305–8
Pearson, Yvonne 167
phone calls, hoax 302–5
physical punishment 287–9
Piaget, Jean 292
Porter, Justin 14, 148–55, 158, 318–19
Poster Despatch and Storage (PDS) 275
'power-reassurance' rapists 197
psychological profiling
    Jill Dando murder 33, 42–3, 48–9
    Joseph Thompson 195–8
    Washington Snipers 7–8
psychopaths 259–61

racism, Stockholm (1992) 3
Radio Times 49
Railway Rapist 12, 163, 174–8, 215
Ramos, Sarah 4
Rayson, John 278
Richardson, Irene 166
Ring, Sergeant Bob 162–3
Robinson, Shirley 63, 66, 68, 76, 77
Rogulskyj, Anna 166
Roper, Sir Hugh Trevor 98
Rossmo, Kim 180
Russo, Melissa 246–54, 258, 263
Rytka, Helen 167

Sade, Marquis de 65
San Ysidro McDonald's (1984), shootings in 3
Savage, Hazel 92
school shootings, Columbine (1999) 3
self-injury 295–6
September 11th attacks 312
sexual deviance 70–2

Shakespeare, William 95, 157, 243
Shipping News, The 221
Sickert, Walter 97
Simpson, Detective Sergeant 203, 206
Smelt, Olive 166
snipers
  Charles Whitman 10
  Stockholm (1992) 3
  Washington Snipers 1–17, 22, 40, 314, 316–17
Snow, Dr John 169, 171, 180
St John's, Newfoundland 217–27
Stern 98, 109
Stockholm (1992) 3
Stride, Elizabeth 125, 126, 127, 130
suicide, Fred West 59, 80–1
Sutcliffe, Peter 12, 37, 129, 158–73, 174, 215, 266, 313
Sykes, Theresa 167

Tagliaferro, Bruno 263
Tamboezer, Maartje 174
telephone calls, hoax 302–5
Thompson, Joseph 22, 187–98, 199–216, 313
TIE procedure 41
Titus Andronicus (William Shakespeare) 95
torture 287–9
'tubsnatchers' 143–4
Turvey, Brent 7

Van Espen, Judge 263
violations, the psychology behind 282–99

Wadland, Simon 302–5
Walekar, Prem Kumar 4
Walls, Marguerite 167
Washington Post 6
Washington Snipers 1–17, 22, 40, 314, 316–17
Washington Times 57
Wathelet, Justice Minister Melchoir 246, 254
Weinstein, Bernard 250, 319
Wells, Holly 27
Welner, Dr Michael 7
West, Anna Marie 73–5
West, Dr Adrian 33, 48–9
West, Fred 11, 13, 55–81, 82, 87–93, 110–11, 251, 264, 313
West, Heather 92
West, Rena 63, 66, 70
West, Rosemary 63, 66, 69, 70, 71, 76, 77, 87
West, Stephen 62, 69
Whitaker, Josephine 167
Whitechapel murderer *see* Jack the Ripper
Whitman, Charles 10, 284–5
Wyre, Ray 279–80

Yorkshire Ripper 12, 37, 129, 158–73, 174, 215, 266, 313
Young, Garrett 13, 21, 217–37

'Zorel' 6, 9